Richard A. McCabe

THE PILLARS OF ETERNITY

DUBLIN STUDIES IN MEDIEVAL AND RENAISSANCE LITERATURE

Series Editor
JOHN SCATTERGOOD
Professor of Medieval and Renaissance English
Trinity College Dublin

This new series is concerned with significant aspects of medieval and renaissance literature up to the end of the seventeenth century. It will include studies of important single works, of major authors and of broad movements. It is intended to publish both monographs and collections of essays on particular topics. The research of established academics will be made available as will studies by the new generation of younger scholars. The series will include reviews and revaluations of major aspects of the literature of the period as well as original studies which break new ground or offer fresh approaches to familiar areas; but however detailed the research, it will be presented in such a way as to be accessible both to specialists and non-specialists alike.

Richard A. McCabe

The Pillars of Eternity

Time and Providence in *The Faerie Queene*

IRISH ACADEMIC PRESS

The typesetting of this book was produced by
Gilbert Gough Typesetting, Dublin for
Irish Academic Press, Kill Lane, Blackrock, County Dublin.

BRITISH LIBRARY CATALOGUING IN PUBLICATION DATA
McCabe, Richard A. (Richard Anthony), *1954-*
The pillars of eternity: time and providence
in 'The Faerie Queene'
1. Poetry in English. Spenser, Edmund.
Faerie queene. Study outlines
I. Title
821'.3

ISBN 0-7165-2428-7

Printed and bound in Great Britain at
The Camelot Press plc, Southampton

To the Master and Fellows
of Pembroke College, Cambridge

Then gin I thinke on that which Nature sayd,
Of that same time when no more *Change* shall be,
But stedfast rest of all things firmely stayd
Vpon the pillours of Eternity,
That is contrayr to *Mutabilitie*:
For, all that moueth, doth in *Change* delight:
But thence-forth all shall rest eternally
With Him that is the God of Sabbaoth hight:
O that great Sabbaoth God, graunt me that Sabaoths sight.

Contents

Preface

The purpose of this study is to examine the themes of time and providence as they effect the romance narrative of *The Faerie Queene*, and the vision of human history which emerges through it. The intricacies of the story-line seem designed as fictional analogues to those of recorded history, but the relationship between the two is highly complex since the narrative itself constitutes an 'historical fiction' and the Muse frequently invoked is Clio rather than Calliope. The 'historicall' element lends the work an immediate relevance to Spenser's contemporaries while the element of 'fiction' releases it from the tyranny of the historian's 'bare was', opening up vast possibilities for imaginative exploration. Of central importance here is the concept of the fairy race with its remarkable vision of civic progress reflecting the Renaissance dream of fulfilled potential while at the same time revealing several unresolved dichotomies in the thinking of the age.

From the point of view of the individual, time is destructive or benign as it effects his own interests or those of his immediate party, but as the outlook widens to that of the race, the concept of perpetuity puts such judgements in a new perspective. It is not that the pain or joy experienced are in any sense diminished, but that what had previously appeared to be isolated events fully explicable in and for themselves now emerge as vital links in a chain of moral and historical causality. As the perspective widens even further, history itself becomes merely one small component in a cosmic pattern of birth, decay, and renewal. Indeed the cycles of activity become so vast and daunting that man stands in danger of losing all sense of his own significance, and this is particularly true when the circular patterns are imagined as continuing indefinitely. Only a belief in providence can alleviate such anxieties, but Spenser's outlook is in no sense naïve and he recognises the problem of maintaining a providential outlook while subject to contingency.

The Faerie Queene allows of no easy solution to the problem of pain; it is all the more appropriate, therefore, that it should end not in assertion but in prayer. Spenser's insight into the emotional complexity of human nature exposes the limitations of all the philosophies upon which he draws whether classical or Christian. However potent the spiritual armour his knights may don, the flesh beneath is doomed to bleed: a major motif of the epic tradition, and one to which Spenser does full justice, is the description of horrendous wounds. Time is the proverbial healer, and doctrines of providence invest scars with significance, but the agony remains acute for all that. As Spenser presents it, the essence of the heroic quest is the struggle for self-knowledge in a world where experience constantly frustrates theory.

The relationship between time and providence is one of the central issues of Western philosophy. Attempting to explain the nature of time in his *Confessions*, for example, Augustine turns almost inevitably to the concept of providence. Working in the opposite direction, Boethius resolves the riddle of the relationship between providence and free-will in the light of God's transcendence of time. In effect, the two are inextricable. Used correctly, the doctrine of grace reconciles man to the vicissitudes of fortune not by ignoring the problem of pain, but by recognising the problematic nature of providence itself. As a result, typological modes of thought become as relevant to contemporary historiography as to biblical exegesis. The 'acts and monuments' of the chosen race extend from the Fall to the reign of Elizabeth I.

Spenser explores the creative and destructive aspects of time from the conflicting viewpoints of the individual and the race, at some moments leading his readers to identify closely with the joy or sorrow of individual characters while at others supplying a distancing perspective. Again, the further one reads the more one becomes aware of a pattern underlying the apparent confusion, as the 'providence' or foresight of the artist begins to mirror the divine providence which is his theme. The Renaissance mind was ill at ease with intimations of the absurd. Rather, its quest was for meaning, stability, and endurance. Its interest in the problems of time and eternity was primarily motivated by a desire to understand the value of human life. The emphasis was on man, but as a creature of dual nature. The proper study of mankind was its exact spiritual destiny. Once the concept of eternity is allowed, however, the final goal becomes an escape from time, and moments of vision take on an importance entirely disproportionate to their temporal duration. The effect is often to diminish the value of civic and cultural achievements. It was, therefore, necessary to find some *modus vivendi* between the demands of an active life and the call of the eternal.

In organising the following study I have chosen to abandon the prevalent procedure of progressing book by book in order the better to examine the operations of time, providence and polity within the total world-view of the poem. In any case, the apparent autonomy of individual 'legends' proves on closer inspection to be largely illusory; the famous alteration to the final stanzas of book three seems designed to encourage the reader to regard the poem as a unity by emphasising romantic continuity over epic closure. Furthermore, as 'revision' is literally 're-seeing' the text proves as mutable as the phenomena it 'mirrors'. My chapters are, therefore, arranged by theme moving through various aspects of time and experience to providence and eternity. Yet the structure of the commentary must not be imposed upon that of the poem. In Spenser, eternity is immanent in the products of time, and providence acts through contingency. Despite the popular critical paradox alleging that *The Faerie Queene* is essentially 'complete', Spenser reaches no 'conclusion' either narrative or thematic. Rather, he adheres to a coherence of questioning in preference to a simplistic coherence of assertion, to a coherence of quest over attainment. Providence remains the supreme interpreter of time but to the extent that human prudence partakes of the same nature the task of exegesis is, of necessity, obligatory and self-perpetuating. As for Lord Herbert of Cherbury the basic premise is that 'Truth exists', but in *The Faerie Queene* this is no matter of doctrinal complacency. Though frequently recognised, and even entertained, the potential consolation of moral or intellectual relativity is invariably diagnosed as the malaise of lazy souls. Such desperate faith in the existence of truth aggravates its elusiveness until the pursuit becomes obsessive, frustrating, and, in terms of narrative structure, tortuously repetitive and complex. Little by little author, reader, and knight errant are drawn into the maze. An essential premise of my approach is that allegory provides Spenser with the means for exploring experience but not necessarily for explaining it.

This study was substantially completed early in 1986. Since then I have attempted shorter studies of the historical allegory — not a primary concern of the present work though related to it — and the role of Prince Arthur (*ELR* 17 and forthcoming). While every effort has been made to incorporate the results of these analyses and to take note of recent criticism this has not always proved possible. I have tried to acknowledge all specific debts in the footnotes but I also wish to express my gratitude to the many colleagues and students whose opinions, arguments and suggestions have contributed to the development of my ideas. Particular mention should be made of Dr Howard Erskine-Hill who read the first draft of the typescript and offered valuable criticisms of method and content. I am also grateful for the immense stimulation provided by the contributors to the Spenser Conference at University College, Cork in November 1985: Pàt Coughlan, Nicholas Canny, Ciaran Brady, John Mann and Anne Fogarty. The Master and Fellows of Pembroke College, Cambridge provided a quiet haven for research and reflection while I was working on the project in the University Library during the summers of 1983, 1984 and 1985. As a result, much of my book was written in Spenser's College where the quest for truth continues unabated.

Abbreviations

Bacon, *Works*	*The Works of Francis Bacon*, edited by J. Spedding, R.L. Ellis, and D.D. Heath, 14 vols (London, 1857-74)
Minor Poems	*The Works of Edmund Spenser*, Variorum Edition Volumes VII and VIII, *The Minor Poems*, edited by Charles Grosvenor Osgood, Henry Gibbons Lotspeich, and Dorothy E. Mason, 2 Pts (Baltimore, 1943-7)
Prose	*The Works of Edmund Spenser*, Variorum Edition Volume IX, *The Prose Works* edited by Rudolf Gottfried (Baltimore, 1949)
CL	*Comparative Literature*
EHR	*English Historical Review*
ELH	*English Literary History*
ELN	*English Language Notes*
HLQ	*Huntington Library Quarterly*
JEGP	*Journal of English and Germanic Philology*
JWCI	*Journal of the Warburg and Courtauld Institutes*
MLN	*Modern Language Notes*
MLR	*Modern Language Review*
NQ	*Notes and Queries*
PMLA	*Publications of the Modern Language Association of America*
PQ	*Philosophical Quarterly*
RES	*Review of English Studies*
SP	*Studies in Philology*
SR	*Studies in the Renaissance*
TSLL	*Texas Studies in Literature and Language*
UTQ	*University of Toronto Quarterly*

CHAPTER ONE

Perspectives

> The first of them could things to come foresee:
> The next could of things present best aduize;
> The third things past could keepe in memoree,
> So that no time, nor reason could arize,
> But that the same could one of these comprize.
> (II. 9. 49)

I *The Heroic Continuum*

The first tense of *The Faerie Queene* introduces the complexity of its time scale: 'A gentle Knight was pricking on the plaine'. We are fixed in the past but a past that is active and continuous. We are not informed who the knight is, nor when he lived. We know neither his point of origin nor his destination. 'The plaine' implies a certain familiarity yet the place remains forever unidentified. The hasty progress combined with the 'gentle' nature of the traveller engross our attention. It is an extreme example of the technique of plunging the reader *in medias res*, and in his 'Letter to Raleigh' Spenser duly acknowledges that were his story to be 'told by an Historiographer' the beginning would be 'the twelfth booke, which is the last': 'the beginning of the whole worke seemeth abrupte and as depending upon other antecedents'. 'The Methode of a Poet historical', he continues,

> is not such, as of an Historiographer. For an Historiographer discourseth of affayres orderly as they were donne, accounting as well the times as the actions, but a Poet thrusteth into the middest, euen where it most concerneth him, and there recoursing to the thinges forepaste, and diuining of thinges to come, maketh a pleasing Analysis of all.[1]

The poet's conception of history is highly dynamic. He appreciates the unity of diverse incidents and times. Grasping the crucial significance of a fleeting moment by isolating the point in time 'where it most concerneth him', he takes upon him the labours of both historian and prophet, interpreting the past in relation to the present, 'divining' the future, and demonstrating an

1 *The Faerie Queene*, edited by A.C. Hamilton (London, 1977), pp. 737-8.

unsuspected but gratifying unity of design informing the entire experience. Past, present, and future coalesce, as providence replaces contingency. The 'poet historical' is committed to the view that life has a meaning, that the events of human history however perplexing or even calamitous lead mankind to a preordained end in the light of which all preceding phenomena become explicable.[2] Chronology is not the best guide to the significance of any event since the historian's 'bare *was*' lacks the dimension of ultimate truth.[3] The beginning of *The Faerie Queene* is also its end. As we shall see, the poem is designed as a great paradigm of the pattern of providential history.

'Y cladd' introduces a note of conscious archaism. Out of context we might place the line two centuries earlier in the age of Chaucer. The first sense of period is therefore conveyed by language. Both Sidney and Jonson objected to this, but the employment of a special diction — often an antiquated one — appears to form part of the decorum of romance.[4] Spenser wants not merely to write about the past but to recreate its flavour. Yet one would hardly mistake the whole of *The Faerie Queene* as one might a single line. In a sense it is true, as Jonson said, that Spenser 'writ no Language', following neither the accepted norm of his own day nor that of Chaucer. There is a timeless quality to the language of *The Faerie Queene* which enhances the timeless quality of its allegory. 'The plaine' defies identification as much in chronological as in geographical terms. The normal rules of sequential development seem not to apply there — or what is more perplexing still seem sometimes to apply and sometimes not. An example of this occurs in the very first stanza. Our 'gentle Knight' is,

> Y cladd in mightie armes and siluer shielde,
> Wherein old dints of deepe wounds did remaine,
> The cruell markes of many' a bloudy fielde;
> Yet armes till that time did he neuer wield:
> His angry steede did chide his foming bitt,
> As much disdayning to the curbe to yield:
> Full iolly knight he seemd, and faire did sitt,
> As one for knightly giusts and fierce encounters fitt.

2 S.K. Heninger argues that Spenser uses the term 'history' in the Latin sense of story or fable, but this is unlikely in the light of the letter's obvious concern with the historical element of the narrative (a question much disputed by the leading sixteenth-century critics) and its discussion of the role of the 'historiographer'. 'The Aesthetic Experience of Reading Spenser' in *Contemporary Thought on Edmund Spenser*, edited by Richard C. Frushell and Bernard J. Vondersmith (Carbondale, 1975), pp. 85-92.

3 Sir Philip Sidney, *An Apology for Poetry*, in *Elizabethan Critical Essays*, edited by G. Gregory Smith, 2 vols (Oxford, 1904), I, 168. See below pp. 80-1.

4 *Elizabethan Critical Essays*, I, 196; Jonson, *Works*, edited by C.H. Herford, Percy and Evelyn M. Simpson, 11 vols (Oxford, 1925-53), VIII (1947), 618; Northrop Frye, *The Secular Scripture* (Cambridge, Mass., 1976), p. 110.

The mystery deepens. At first sight the ravages of battle detected on the armour suggest the personal history of the man who wears it: an experienced warrior victorious in many combats. This is what we are intended to surmise when suddenly the initial 'yet' of line six dashes such interpretations. The arms have a history of their own in which the knight does not share. Until 'that time' — and we are still unsure what time it is — he had never worn arms. This, then, is a critical period in the life of the protagonist, the period upon which his entire history depends, 'euen where it most concerneth him'. He is not at the end of his career but at the beginning. What seemed time-honoured is actually new. And 'seemed' is the operative word. The prowess of the 'gentle Knight' has never been tested: 'full iolly knight *he seemed*, and faire did sitt,/ As one for knightly giusts and fierce encounters fitt'. As the narrative unfolds he must prove himself worthy of his appearance.

The 'Letter to Raleigh' identifies the armour as the 'whole armour of God' spoken of by St Paul (Ephesians 6:11-17), the armour which enables the Christian to 'stand against the wiles of the devil'. St Paul regards this conflict as an eternal struggle, 'for we wrestle not against flesh and blood, but against principalities, against powers, against the rulers of the darkness of this world, against spiritual wickedness in high places'. The armour is, therefore, composed of the timeless and invulnerable qualities of truth, righteousness, peace, faith, salvation, and the Word of the Lord. Yet so far as man is concerned, the struggle is embodied in flesh and blood since he himself is doomed to exist and act within time. The paradox of his situation is that his temporal deeds take on a spiritual and therefore eternal significance. Allegory provides the perfect medium for simultaneously suggesting these two dimensions of design and intent.

In Fairyland where life is seen *sub specie aeternitatis* the eternal significance of finite time becomes clear, at least to the poet and his readers. In that they represent the 'whole armour of God', the arms of St George are outside time and his own ultimate goal is the eternal state of sainthood. However, in so far as God's plan for mankind must be worked out within the temporal sphere of human existence, the armour may also be said to reflect the history of the Church Militant another chapter of which George is about to write. The history of the specific armour described in stanza three has been traced from Joseph of Arimathea who gave it to King Averagus, through King Lucius and Constantine the Great, to Sir Galahad.[5] Not merely is George placed in the universal tradition of Christian knighthood but in the more

5 John Erskine Hankins, *Source and Meaning in Spenser's Allegory* (Oxford, 1971), pp. 218-9; James Nohrnberg, *The Analogy of 'The Faerie Queene'* (Princeton, 1976), p. 170; Roland M. Smith, 'Origines Arthurianae: The Two Crosses of Spenser's Red Cross Knight', *JEGP*, 54 (1955), 670-83 (pp. 670-2); Michael Leslie, *Spenser's 'Fierce Warres and Faithfull Loves'* (Cambridge, 1983), pp. 101-31.

The trauailed Pilgrime

¶ The childe signifieth good Infancie : the rod, Correction : the auncient or aged man, Reason : the booke, Truth : the armed Knyght, youthfull Courage : the speare, good Gouernment : the shielde, Hope : the sword, Courage : standing in the fielde called Time.

Here the Author beginnes his voyage, being ready armed, bidding Infancie farewell, and now growing by Reason to further possibilitie and strength.

Stephen Batman, *The Travayled Pilgrime* (1569), Sig. Blv.

narrow and precise tradition of unmistakably British Christianity. The latter tradition ushers in one of the work's most important themes.

Only gradually does the reader begin to realise that the 'gentle Knight' of the opening line is in fact the patron saint of England. The self-evidently iconographic grouping of knight, lady, ass, and lamb recalls the tableaux of medieval pageantry in which the figures were enshrined in characteristic pose for all time.[6] But George himself has no such knowledge. Breaking with the traditional accounts of such authorities as *The Golden Legend* or Mantuan's *Life of St George*, Spenser has chosen to represent the discovery of personal identity as an important stage in the spiritual quest. An emblem from Stephen Batman's *Travayled Pylgrime* (1569) conveniently illustrates his method: A group of iconographical figures representing the three ages of man pose in an almost existentialist landscape. 'The childe', explains the motto, 'signifieth good Infancie: the rod, Correction: the ancient or aged man, Reason: the booke, Truth: the armed Knyght, youthfull Courage: the speare, good Government: the shielde, Hope: the sword, Courage: standing in the fielde called Time'. Spenser's 'plaine' is closely akin to Batman's heraldic 'fielde'. Within the allegorical compass of both lie instruction, conflict, and maturity. As the 'old man' subsumes the experience of 'childe' and 'knyght', his book is partly autobiographical. Indeed, Batman applies the emblem to his own literary development: 'here the Author beginnes his voyage, being ready armed, bidding Infancie farewell, and now growing by Reason to further possibilitie and strength' (sig. Blv). Similarly Spenser develops his own aesthetic identity as he traces the moral development of his characters. Omnipresent as detached moral commentator, he finally enters the narrative itself in book six in an attempt to identify the source of his own artistic life.

Inseparable from this question of identity, both for poet and characters, is that of nationality. Throughout *The Faerie Queene* character is closely related to environment. Long held to be a 'fairy's son', the Redcross Knight discovers himself to be 'St George of mery England'. Ironically, the vision which roots him firmly in time and space also serves to lift him beyond both. The immediate result is his desire to abandon Cleopolis for the New Jerusalem, but Spenser's Protestant insistence upon the active life combines with his historical outlook to oppose such a course. Instead the saint must undertake the completion of the quest within the linear time-scale of book one. His final union with Una is similarly deferred as he re-enters the sphere of mortal combat for a fixed period of six years. That one of the poem's earliest readers should have interpreted this span of time as an allusion to the reign of Mary

6 C.S. Lewis, *Spenser's Images of Life*, edited by Alastair Fowler (Cambridge, 1967), p. 3.

Tudor attests to the contemporary significance of the old legend.[7] The period of most 'concern' is that of the poem's composition.

Of all previous epochs of British history that of Arthur had become the most closely related, for a variety of political reasons, to that of Spenser's own time.[8] The past he chose to evoke was dynamically active in the present: Arthur's lance may still be seen in Fairyland (I. 7. 36). The point is well made in one of the legends associated with Merlin, the figure who stands as a link between Arthurian and Elizabethan times. Lured to his end by the Lady of the Lake, he leaves behind his sprights and familiars working upon the brazen wall with which Britain is to be protected:

> Nath'lesse those feends may not their worke forbeare,
> So greatly his commaundement they feare,
> But there doe toyle and trauell day and night,
> Vntill that brasen wall they vp doe reare. (III. 3. 11)

'To this day' we are told the 'feends' continue their work 'for terror of his fame'. The ethos of the passage is undeniably comic, but it constitutes an amusing emblem of the poem's time-structure. The powerful forces set in motion during the reign of King Arthur for the defence and security of the realm continue with daemonic energy in the age and person of the Virgin Queen whose coming the seer foretold. Not surprisingly, the location of the great forge is in Wales whence the ancient Briton line has returned.

II. *Renaissance Theories of Time*

From the time of Petrarch onwards the Renaissance mind was obsessed by problems of time, mutability and providence. Many of its anxieties were, of course, inherited from the late Middle Ages, but its unique emphasis on human potential deepened the need for a sense of permanence. Throughout Spenser's work, from the boyhood sonnets translated from Petrarch's *Rime Sparse* to the magnificent *Mutabilitie Cantos*, time enforces itself upon the reader as a major theme. *The Shepheardes Calender* introduces us to a poet preoccupied by the passing of the years, morbidly conscious of how life and happiness are slipping away.[9] The sequence begins and ends in winter. The

7 *The First Commentary on 'The Faerie Queene'* [1597], edited by Graham Hough (Privately published 1964), pp. 9-10; Carol V. Kaske, 'Spenser's Pluralistic Universe', in Frushell and Vondersmith, pp. 121-49 (p. 138).

8 Dryden read the poem as a roman à clef. *Essays of John Dryden*, edited by W.P. Ker, 2 vols (Oxford, 1900), II, 28. See also Alastair Fowler, 'Oxford and London Marginalia to *The Faerie Queene*', *NQ*, 206 (1961), 416-9.

9 Robert Allen Durr, 'Spenser's Calendar of Christian Time', *ELH*, 24 (1957), 269-95. See also Haruhiko Fujii, *Time, Landscape and the Ideal Life: Studies in the Pastoral Poetry of Spenser and Milton* (Kyoto, 1974), pp. 32-65.

January eclogue closes as the passage of time, in this case the transition from day to night, forces Colin ('vnder which name this Poete secretly shadoweth himself') to end his complaints and drive off his flock. The manner of night's coming suggests weariness and despondency, as if time itself were a party to the poet's disappointment:

> By that, the welked *Phoebus* gan availe
> His weary waine, and nowe the frosty *Night*
> Her mantle black through heauen gan ouerhaile.
> Which seene, the pensife boy halfe in despight
> Arose, and homeward droue his sonned sheepe,
> Whose hanging heads did seeme his carefull case to weepe.

The emblem, 'anchora speme', is suggestive of hope, but by the time we reach December even such muted optimism is qualified. Since the structure of the work is uncompromisingly circular the speaker once again is Colin: 'this Aeglogue (euen as the first beganne) is ended with a complaynte of Colin to God Pan'. Colin now considers not merely the annual revolution of planets and seasons, but the corresponding cycle of human life: 'weary of his former wayes, he proportioneth his life to the foure seasons of the yeare, comparing hys youthe to the spring time . . . His manhoode to the sommer . . . His riper yeares . . . to an vnseasonable harueste . . . His latter age to winters chyll and frostie season'. This act of 'proportioning' establishes an important relationship between the rhythms of Colin's life and those of nature. Even the most unseasonable harvest must be reaped: the death he awaits is described as 'timely death'.[10] This adjective develops the message of the November eclogue, the emblem to which argues that 'although by course of nature we be borne to dye, and being ripened with age, as with a timely haruest, we must be gathered in time, or els of our selues we fall like rotted ripe fruite fro the tree'. Of primary importance is the word-play latent in the phrase 'gathered in time'. In keeping with the pervasive imagery of fruit and crops, not to be 'gathered' is to rot. As a result, 'death is not to be counted for euil, nor . . . as doome of ill desert'. As the image of rotting upon a tree recalls the biblical account of the Fall, a spiritual dimension is added to the argument which now returns upon itself:

> For though the trespasse of the first man brought death into the world, as the guerdon of sinne, yet being ouercome by the death of one, that dyed for al, it is now made (as Chaucer sayth) the grene path way to lyfe.

10 S.K. Heninger, *The Cosmographical Glass* (San Marino, 1977), pp. 110-5.

Since the conclusion is a Medieval platitude Chaucer is well invoked, but the Renaissance poet demands a more personal form of immortality. Chaucer might have allowed the sequence to end with the emblem Spenser assigns to November. As it is, December's emblem alters the emphasis: 'Vivitur ingenio: caetera mortis erunt'. The gloss explains that whereas 'all thinges perish and come to theyr last end . . . workes of learned wits and monuments of Poetry abide for euer'. The work ends on a note of enduring accomplishment:

> Loe I have made a Calender for euery yeare,
> That steele in strength, and time in durance, shall outweare.

The poetic artifact takes the place which November attributed to Christ, just as the gloss transfers its poetic allegiance from Chaucer to the classical authorities Horace and Ovid. Yet there is something incongruous about the notion that a calendar can 'outweare' the force which alone gives it meaning. The boast continues,

> And if I marked well the starres reuolution,
> It shall continewe till the worlds dissolution.
> To teach the ruder shepheard how to feede his sheepe,
> And from the falsers fraud his folded flocke to keepe.

There is at least a suggestion here of the Stoic Great Year, although without the Stoic doctrine of renewal. The first two lines promise immortality but the qualification implied by the word 'till' reintroduces the victory of time. No doubt deliberately, December ends with less conviction than November, and the finality of 'the world's dissolution' qualifies the poem's cyclical pattern. Consolation, however, is drawn from the enduring impact of the work's moral force within time. In this sense, by lasting until the world's decay, it fulfills its limited potential. Thereafter neither time nor didacticism has any function.

Spenser's 'calendar' is designed 'for every year' thereby implying cyclical recurrence through the signs of the Zodiac. The structure supports this idea. The Tudor year normally began not in January but in March, as Mutability's pageant of months begins with March and ends with February.[11] Spenser may have been influenced by the arrangement in Guy Marchant's *Le Compost et Kalendrier des Bergiers* (1493) translated into English as *The Kalendar of*

11 When the Tudor year should properly begin was a matter of controversy. In the 'Description of England' incorporated into Holinshed's *Chronicles*, William Harrison reviews the problem and argues for 1 January. See Raphael Holinshed, *Chronicles of England, Scotland and Ireland*, 6 vols (London, 1806-8), I, 410. See also Sherman Hawkins, 'Mutabilitie and the Cycle of the Months', in *Form and Convention in the Poetry of Edmund Spenser*, edited by William Nelson (New York, 1961), pp. 89-91.

Shepherds (1503). Nevertheless, despite his decision to begin with January, he retains the older form of computation. Within *The Shepheardes Calender* itself February is still the last month ('the year now drooping, as it were drawing to his last age') and March the first. Spenser's arrangement allows first and last to be juxtaposed within a different cycle. Within the modern calendar year the seasonal year ends and begins anew. Within the seasonal year the opposite occurs. That the two shall always be out of phase adds to the elusive quality of time and mutability. Properly speaking, there are no endings or beginnings, except, of course, for the individual. Such concepts are confounded in the endless revolution of planets and seasons 'till the world's dissolution'.

'Time' is a key-word in E.K.'s gloss to *The Shepheardes Calender* but we may well ask whether Renaissance thinkers developed or inherited any conceptual notion of its meaning distinct from the annual cycle of birth, maturity, and death? According to Plato's *Timaeus* — one of the best known of the dialogues, thanks to the commentary of Calcidius — time is the moving image of eternity, the motion in question being that of the heavenly bodies.[12] Their mysterious, turbulent relationship is hauntingly evoked by Henry Vaughan:

I saw Eternity the other night
Like a great *Ring* of pure and endless light,
    All calm, as it was bright,
And round beneath it, Time in hours, days, years
    Driven by the spheres
Like a vast shadow moved, in which the world
    And all her train were hurled.[13]

Whereas earthly time is guided by the rotation of the sun and the moon, the real time of the universe depends upon the revolution of all the planets and fixed stars. Such theories are discussed in the *Mutabilitie Cantos* when Jupiter asserts that the motion of the planetary bodies occasions temporal succession:

        But, who is it (to me tell)
  That *Time* himselfe doth moue and still compell
  To keepe his course? Is not that namely wee
  Which poure that vertue from our heauenly cell,
  That moues them all, and makes them changed be?
So them we gods doe rule, and in them also thee. (VII. 7. 48).

12 *Timaeus* (39d), translated by Benjamin Jowett, in *Plato: The Collected Dialogues*, edited by Edith Hamilton and Huntington Cairns (Princeton, 1963), p. 1168.

13 *Works*, edited by L.C. Martin, second edition (Oxford, 1957), p. 466.

The exact duration of the resulting 'great year' was a matter of dispute, but the idea of a simultaneous return of all heavenly bodies to their original alignments remained one of the most potent factors in the development of the philosophy of time.[14] However, to speak in terms of such a return while at the same time denying the existence of a former great year is to imply an act of creation, and more perplexing still, creation in time before time existed. In the *Timaeus* Plato has recourse to an explanatory myth which Aristotle interpreted as implying that time and the heavens began at the one moment, an implication strongly denied by later Platonists.[15] By way of refutation he postulated a world-order without beginning or end thereby creating enormous difficulties for his medieval admirers. Even Aquinas had to admit that the Christian doctrine of creation depended primarily upon revelation since creation from eternity could not be faulted on logical grounds. That God 'began time' was an article of faith not a philosophical deduction and the Averroists were correct in asserting that such a belief was contrary to the Aristotelian viewpoint. Nevertheless, by postulating the simultaneous creation — and simultaneous demise — of time and matter, it remained possible to claim without any sense of blasphemy that the world had always existed and always would.[16] Spenser exploits this notion in his treatment of primeval matter in the Gardens of Adonis.

Fundamental to most classical and medieval conceptions of time is the notion of change. Plato's time is the moving, and therefore changing, image of something which neither alters nor moves. As a result the immobility of the eternal is as strongly maintained as its perpetual duration. By contrast to this supreme state, Aristotle postulated for the present world cycles of temporal flux, defining time as 'the calculable measure or dimension of motion with respect to before-and-afterwardness'.[17] A disconcerting element of circularity is thus infused into the discussion since 'we measure the length of uniform movement by time, but also the length of time by uniform movement, since they mutually determine each other'. Time is continuous by virtue of an endless succession of 'now' moments linking past to future.[18]

Reacting against the various paradoxes arising from the Aristotelian system (including the implication that time has no substantive existence), Plotinus attempted to develop the Platonic theory. He rejected the identification of time and motion, which he wrongly ascribed to Aristotle, on the

14 Heninger, *Cosmographical Glass*, p. 141.

15 Richard Sorabji, *Time, Creation and the Continuum* (London, 1983), p. 269.

16 Ibid., pp. 193-4.

17 *Physics* (IV. 219b), translated by Philip H. Wicksteed and Francis M. Cornford, Loeb Classical Library, 2 vols (London, 1929-34), I, 387.

18 *Physics* (IV. 219b-220b); Loeb, I, 391-3, 399.

grounds that time is also the measure of rest.[19] Disagreeing with Spenser's Jupiter, he regards time as the medium in which all movement, including that of the heavens, occurs. Indeed this phase of the great debate on Arlo Hill may well have its origin here since Plotinus begins by attacking 'false' notions of time before moving on to more positive formulations. According to his final view, movement is merely the measure of time, otherwise there arises the insupportable paradox that 'time is the distance of movement in time'.[20] Nevertheless, time had its origin in the *first* motion of the All-Soul in which it inheres as an image of eternity. It may, therefore, be defined as the life of the soul in movement whereas eternity is life in repose.[21] At this stage, however, Plotinus makes the important qualification (already implicit in his definition) that human understanding cannot measure the passage of time except with reference to some form of motion. In a certain sense, therefore, it is permissible to say 'that the movement and the heavenly circuit in a way measure time . . . in that the circuit shows by its extent the extent of time, which it would not be possible to grasp or understand otherwise'.[22] Aristotle's 'measure of motion' is hereby complemented by the 'motion of measure'.

By locating time not merely within the All-Soul but also within the human soul, Plotinus opened the way for the most profound of all ancient interpretations, that undertaken by St Augustine in his *Confessions*. The intensely personal context of this discussion is significant since Augustine is primarily interested in the problem of time in relation to the working of the human mind and it is there he finds his solution. Beginning from the premise that 'if time never changed it would not be time', he focusses upon the theoretical difficulty in describing any time as present:

> In fact the only time that can be called present is an instant, if we can conceive of such, that cannot be divided into the most minute fractions, and a point of time as small as this passes so rapidly from the future to the past that its duration is without length.[23]

To his way of thinking the conclusion is inevitable: 'we can be aware of time and measure it only while it is passing. Once it has passed it no longer is, and therefore cannot be measured'. Aristotle had made much the same point, but Augustine develops it on a deeper psychological level arguing that

19 *Enneads* (III. 7. 8), translated by A.H. Armstrong, Loeb Classical Library, 6 vols (London, 1965-), III (1967), 321-7.
20 *Enneads*, III. 7. 8; Loeb, III, 327.
21 *Enneads*, III. 7. 11; Loeb, III, 339-41.
22 *Enneads*, III. 7. 12; Loeb, III, 347.
23 *Confessions* (XI. 14-16), translated by R.S. Pine-Coffin (Harmondsworth, 1961), pp. 263, 266.

if time be 'an extension of some sort' it may well be 'an extension of the mind itself'. Thus time is mental space and the 'measure of time' becomes an operation of thought:

> It is in my own mind then that I measure time... It is the impression that I measure, since it is still present, not the thing itself, which makes the impression as it passes and then moves into the past. When I measure time it is the impression that I measure. Either, then, this is what time is, or else I do not measure time at all.[24]

Modern man is apt to find here a denial of time's objective reality but, writing in the context of similar ancient paradoxes, Augustine is anxious to defend its existence by internalizing its measurement. The past exists as memory, the present as attention, the future as anticipation.[25] The resulting association of time and mental state is of further interest in that it provided philosophical justification for the common literary topos (fully exploited in the fifth act of Marlowe's *Doctor Faustus*) of hours passing like minutes and minutes like hours. A long past is merely a long memory, a long future a long expectation.[26] The speed or quality of time owes its character to the motion of the mind. Thus in *The Faerie Queene*, for example, time is variously 'long', 'short', 'happy', 'sad', 'just', 'wicked', 'idle', 'full', 'present', or 'ancient' depending on the perspectives of individual characters. References to time are commonly qualified by adjectives of mood. Yet even when the mood is the product of illusion, enchantment, or ignorance an objective criterion may still be applied. However 'fantastic' Amoret's tortured experience, for instance, she spends 'seven moneths' (in effect, seven 'moons' as the etymology suggests) in the House of Busirane (IV. 1. 4).

Augustine recognises the traditional connection between time and the motion of the heavenly bodies, but rejects the implication that they are therefore to be identified. If the sun were to stand still, as the Book of Joshua asserts it once did, time would continue regardless.[27] Writing in the fifteen-nineties Richard Hooker upheld this distinction but with the important qualification that time cannot be defined at all without some reference to motion through space. This would appear to have been Spenser's view also since he refers in *An Hymne of Heavenly Love* to the primeval state,

> Ere flitting Time could wag his eyas wings
> About that mightie bound, which doth embrace
> The rolling Spheres, and parts their houres by space. (24-6).

24 *Confessions* (XI. 23-27), pp. 272, 274, 276.
25 Sorabji, pp. 29-32.
26 *Confessions* (XI. 28), pp. 277-8.
27 *Confessions* (XI. 23), p. 272.

At the moment of creation time began its fledgeling flight along the periphery of the universe and the distance it travels, traditionally divided by twenty-four, marks the stations of the sidereal hours. The cosmic clock, like its humbler mechanical counterparts, denotes the passage of time by spatial motion. This is why the concept of motion figures so prominently in Mutability's reply to Jove. 'Time', Hooker writes, 'considered in itself is but the flux of that very instant wherein the motion of the heaven began, being coupled with other things it is the quantity of their continuance measured by the distance of two instants. As the time of a man is a man's continuance from the instant of his first breath till the instant of his last gasp.'[28] For all practical purposes, the universal clock, though theoretically fallible, provided a convenient standard of objective measurement. Hours which pass like minutes are hours still.

Doubtless the most influential of Augustine's theories was that of a timeless God existing in the eternal present of the *nunc-stans*. Since such a being has neither past nor future it is absurd to wonder what he did prior to creation. Words such as 'before' and 'after' apply only to man.[29] Augustine's outlook laid the foundation for Boethius's resolution of the problems of fate, foreknowledge, and free will, and was further developed by Thomas Aquinas for whom time was largely determined by chronological succession.[30] It would be quite misleading, however, to suggest a direct development from the classical to the Christian period. It is not merely that the Church Fathers endorsed a creation myth similar to that which Plato used only for illustrative effect, but that the coming of Christianity altered the whole concept of the relationship between time and eternity. The nature of this change is well brought out in George Herbert's poem 'Time'. Meeting man's old opponent the poet adopts the odd course of encouraging his operations but explains that,

> Christs coming hath made man thy debter,
> Since by thy cutting he grows better.
>
> And in his blessing thou art blest:
> For where thou onely wert before
> An executioner at best;
> Thou art a gard'ner now, and more,

28 *Works*, edited by John Keble, seventh edition, 3 vols (Oxford, 1888), II, 382.

29 *Confessions* (XI. 30), p. 279. See also David Scott Kastan, *Shakespeare and the Shapes of Time* (London, 1982), pp. 5-12.

30 *De Consolatione Philosophiae*, V; F.C. Copleston, *Aquinas* (Harmondsworth, 1955), p. 79.

An usher to convey our souls
Beyond the utmost starres and poles.[31]

The moment of the incarnation signalled the meeting of time and eternity thereby altering the course of human destiny: the practice of dating events *anno domini* began as early as the sixth century.[32] As in Spenser's November eclogue, the destructive scythe becomes an instrument of God's harvest and time merely an antechamber to eternal joy or eternal agony. Furthermore, Christianity's adoption of the Hebrew creation myth, together with the various Apocalyptic expectations generated both by the Gospels themselves and by the Book of Revelation, worked to ensure that henceforth time would be regarded as finite. Attempts to establish the exact chronology of this finite time date back to Julius Africanus and Eusebius.[33] Augustine's notion that human history falls into a cosmic 'week' of seven millennia was repeated *ad nauseam* throughout the Middle Ages, and finally enshrined during the Reformation in the annotations to the Geneva Bible.[34] There were, of course, many variations on the basic pattern such as the tripartite scheme of Joachim de Fiore, but all had one end in view: the culmination of human history in a final millennium under the personal rule of Christ himself. [35] The more fanatical responses to this doctrine were vigorously suppressed by Church and State and the nature of the seventh millennium was hotly disputed.[36] By contrast, almost unanimous assent was gained for the subordinate theory that the common course of human history would extend for no more than a mere six thousand years.[37] By the sixteenth century the allotted time was rapidly running out. Millenarian expectations fired by the Reformation were supported by radical interpretations of the Book of Revelation designed to identify the Church of Rome with the Whore of Babylon.[38]

Such thinking underlies the plentiful use of Revelation imagery in the first book of *The Faerie Queene*, but George's abandonment of Una for a further

31 *Works*, edited by F.E. Hutchinson (Oxford, 1941), pp. 122-3.

32 C.A. Patrides, *The Grand Design of God* (London, 1972), p. 21.

33 Patrides, pp. 15-16; Stephen Toulmin and June Goodfield, *The Discovery of Time* (London 1965), pp. 59-61; S.G.F. Brandon, *History, Time and Deity* (New York, 1965), pp. 191-7.

34 *The City of God*, XXII. 30; *De Genesi contra Manichaeos*, I. 23; Toulmin and Goodfield, p. 61.

35 Marjorie Reeves, *Joachim of Fiore and the Prophetic Future* (London, 1976), pp. 83-115.

36 Norman Cohn, *The Pursuit of the Millennium* (London 1970 — first pub. 1957), chapters 11-13.

37 Don Cameron Allen, 'The Degeneration of Man and Renaissance Pessimism', *Studies in Philology*, 35 (1938), 202-227 (pp. 213-4).

38 John Bale was particularly influential. See Leslie P. Fairfield *John Bale, Mythmaker for the English Reformation* (West Lafayette, Indiana, 1976), pp. 50-85.

period of Christian militancy underlines Spenser's reluctance to commit himself to any fixed timetable. His choice of six years was no doubt influenced by the fact that George has not yet attained the sabbath of rest which the seventh presumably represents. As Richard Hooker complains, expectations of Apocalypse were particularly strong during the fifteen-nineties; contemporary mystics such as Tomasso Campanella emphasised the supposedly magical qualities of the date 1600.[39] But with the extremes of the Millenarian movement Spenser would have nothing to do. While he suggests, he refuses to dogmatize. Influenced by the great Neoplatonists of the fifteenth century, he remains on the speculative side of the debate. According to Marsilio Ficino, for example, 'the reasonable soul is set on a horizon, that is the line dividing the eternal and temporal, because it has a nature midway between the two. Being in the middle, this nature is not only capable of rational power and action, which lead up to the eternal, but also of energies and activities which descend to the temporal'. Such, too, is Spenser's man, a creature of the borderline, 'in confinio aeternitatis et temporis'.[40] Consequently, always supposing that existence is not meaningless, life becomes a quest for eternity:

> In this present state of life only man cannot rest, only he is discontented here. Accordingly only man wanders through these terrestrial regions unable to find repose along the way in his pursuit of the celestial homeland sought by all of us, although such is the diversity of opinions and counsels we scurry towards it along very different paths. Yet if inferior things find rest once they have attained their natural habitat and proper home we too must be able to attain these things sometime and take our rest. In the present life this is not granted to us. (My translation).[41]

39 Hooker, *Works*, II, 4-5; Frank E. Manuel and Fritzie P. Manuel, *Utopian Thought in the Western World* (Oxford, 1979), p. 270.

40 *The Letters of Marsilio Ficino*, translated by Members of the Language Department of the School of Economic Science, London (London 1975-), I, 160-1. For the Latin text see *Opera Omnia* 2 vols (Basle, 1576), I, 657-8: 'Anima rationalis quemadmodum omnes ibi convenimus in orizonte, id est, in confinio aeternitatis et temporis posita est, quoniam inter aeterna et temporalia naturam mediam possidet, et tanquam media rationales vires actionesque habet ad aeterna surgentes, habet quoque vires operationesque declinantes ad temporalia.'

41 'Quamobrem homo solus in praesenti hoc vivendi habitu, quiescit numquam, solus hoc loco non est contentus. Solus igitur homo in regionibus his peregrinat, et in ipso itinere non potest quiescere, dum ad patriam aspirat coelestem, quam petimus omnes, quamvis propter varietatem opinionis atque consilij diverso calle proficiscamur. Si ergo quae nobis inferiora sunt, quandoque naturalem habitum patriamque sedem adepta quiescunt, nos quoque necesse est . . . haec assequi posse quandoque, atque quiescere. In vita praesenti non datur.' *De Immortalitate Animorum*, XIV. 7 in *Opera*, I, 315-6.

This outlook provides the essential rationale for the ceaseless wanderings of Spenser's knights. Quite appropriately, its inner meaning is revealed to St George by Heavenly Contemplation since, in Ficino's view, only the practice of contemplation can elevate man to a perception of the *nunc-stans* while still enmeshed in the coils of time. The belief that Plato and St Paul concurred in such a view was a central tenet of his 'Platonic theology'.[42]

In *The Faerie Queene* Spenser generally employs spatial images to represent duration or extent of time while employing personifications of various sorts to represent its effects. In the Gardens of Adonis, for instance, time is personified, scythe in hand, in the traditional manner but functions nonetheless within a finite spatial environment: even the naked babes pursue a predetermined journey into life and back. Similarly the chivalric quest has spatial and temporal dimensions which defy extrication, just as in the *Amoretti* (86) grief 'maketh every *minute* seem a *mile*'. Time, like distance, determines and alters perspectives. The extent of any given quest, for example, is generally measured in terms of its duration in time — Arthur's 'nine monethes' search for Gloriana (I. 9. 15) — while time itself is measured in terms of the distance traversed by the heavenly bodies (I. 2. 1). Fusing both ideas Arthur attempts to express his frustration to Guyon by drawing a comparison between himself and the sun: 'Now hath the Sunne with his lamp-burning light,/Walkt round about the world, and I no lesse' (II. 9. 7). The image is particularly effective thematically since Arthur is visually and symbolically associated with the sun from his first entrance into the poem (I. 7. 29). Arthur is a child of light and a year's light has been wasted.

At the moment we meet them, the present identity of any knight is virtually determined by the space he has travelled and the places he has stopped. This is partly, but not exclusively, a consequence of the allegorical nature of the landscape. Particular emphasis is also laid on the moral influence of environment in the 'Briton Chronicles' where not merely the race but the land evolves, and the 'Chronicles' themselves unfold the history of Britain through the spatial sequence of Spenser's stanzas while the reader is reminded of the time he must spend moving through them by Alma's unexpected reference to the lateness of the hour as Arthur reads the same material (II. 10. 77). Similarly, in *A View of the Present State of Ireland*, as time erodes laws and manners so the geographical sphere of English influence contracts with the obvious political implication that the 'value' of Irish time is directly proportional to the spatial extent of English rule. By contrast, in the 'Fairy Chronicles', as time progresses so does the spatial extent of the Fairy empire.

In terms of the romance narrative, the history of the poem's first 'gentle knight' is equivalent to the spatial and temporal duration of the quest from

42 *De Immortalitate Animorum*, XII. 2 in *Opera*, I, 269.

the Wood of Error to the Slaughter of the Dragon. Surprisingly he ends in Eden as if the past where a place to which one could return — a notion inspired by the doctrine of Redemption whereby man, like Fraudubio and Fraelissa, is doomed to suffer until, 'Time and suffised fates to former kynd/ Shall vs restore, none else from hence may vs vnbynd' (I. 2. 43). In this sense time is circular just as George's quest, seen in proper perspective, proceeds from the Court of Gloriana back to its point of origin. In the world of *The Faerie Queene* to cross paths is to cross histories. When knights meet they engage as the sum total of their respective pasts. Guyon and the Palmer recognise in George's person the full effects of his recent quest (II. 1. 32). Indeed Guyon's desire to emulate George enforces the similarity of structure which informs the first two books.

All of the poem's great allegorical centres have important temporal dimensions. The House of Pride, for instance, 'ruinous and old, but painted cunningly' (I. 4. 5) is locked in an ultimately futile battle with decay since its dungeons contain the very image of its own future in the shape of the corrupt and rotting splendour of all former history (I. 5. 51). By contrast, the House of Holiness affords glimpses of eternity with the prospect of escape from a world where even the sturdy bastions of the Castle of Alma are doomed to dissolution (II. 9. 21). The physical attributes of the Bower of Bliss convey the deceptive impression of an atemporal paradise while the 'Song of the Rose' paradoxically warns its inmates of the brevity of their stay. The Gardens of Adonis represent the renewing and envigorating force of sexual reproduction while the Temple of Venus sets this force in the social perspective of the perpetual rites of courtship and marriage. The Temple of Isis, pervaded by solar and lunar imagery, symbolises the eternally enduring aspect of social justice whereby civilizations continue to subsist while the fleeting Dance of the Graces projects, like Prospero's masque, a peculiarly fragile vision of cosmic harmony. Arlo Hill is pervaded by images of time, change and endurance.

Throughout the poem caves, prisons and dungeons are frequently represented as places of wearyingly repetitive or 'solipsistic' time, offering repetition without renewal. The larger and more pervasive images of sea and forest, populated by Protean gods, visionary hermits, and assorted primitives, are similarly significant. Through the iconography of its various trees, for example, the Wood of Error becomes a gigantic emblem of the vanity of human wishes — 'The Laurell, meed of mightie Conquerours . . . the Maple seeldom inward sound' — in which the travellers 'beguile' both their time and their 'way'. The 'beaten' path of the labyrinth, itself a testimony to aeons of previous travel, leads them 'at length' (in both senses of the term) to the Cave of Error, centre of all confusion. The forests of books two to six display similar qualities while the increasingly prevalent imagery of 'the deuouring sea' is persistently associated with 'tract of time, that all things doth decay' and the vicissitudes of 'fortune' (V. 4. 8-14).

Not surprisingly, adventures undertaken in such a landscape are all to a greater or lesser extent concerned with the use or abuse of time usually in relation to timeless moral and spiritual values. This is, perhaps, most obvious in book one where Una (Truth, and therefore 'Daughter of Time') leads George from despair to a vision of the New Jerusalem, but it is central to all the later books also. Book two, pervaded as it is by images of 'fraile mortalitie's' failures of endurance — the suicide of Amavia, the collapse of Guyon, the erosion of Alma's castle, Arthur's fall during his combat with Malegar — relates self-knowledge and self-discipline to an awareness of one's personal and national history. If holiness sees beyond time, temperance finds the strength and inspiration to work within it by contemplating the lessons of the past. Mammon, 'greatest god below the skye', is the evil genius of fallen time (II. 7. 8) but the Castle of Alma corrects his cynical perspective on human history supplying visions of hope in the fairy chronicles. While Verdant merely wastes 'his dayes' in 'horrible enchantment', the temperate man keeps on the move 'whilest wether serves and wind'. The very word 'temperance' is cognate with 'tempus' implying a need to discriminate between 'occasions' variously appropriate for action or restraint. Both the Cave of Mammon and Alma's castle are timebound, but whereas Mammon's porter is 'self-consuming', in his paranoiac vigilance, Alma's is 'neuer out of time' in raising necessary moral alarms. In *Mother Hubberds Tale* we learn that 'no temperance, nor no regard of season' can restrain the ape (1132), but Guyon must 'apply' his life to temperance 'framing' each seasonable 'action' accordingly (II. 5. 1).

In book three Britomart emerges from the painful years of adolescence, recalled in vivid flashback, to the dynamic time of sexual generation represented in the Gardens of Adonis and travestied in the recurrent horrors of the House of Busyrane. In personal terms she passes from a time of childhood protected by Glauce, her nurse, to a time of maturity as protectress of Amoret, or 'womanhed'. In public terms she learns to relate her private desires to national destiny by accepting the political role foretold for her by Merlin. Book four introduces the Fates themselves and in Agape's bargaining with them attempts to establish a permanent value for friendship and love in a world of bewildering flux. The book is particularly notable for the reconciliation of the repellently self-centred Marinell to the necessity of natural emotion, 'so fertile be the flouds in generation' (IV. 12. 1). Excluded from the banquet of the gods, he finally comes to terms with his own humanity. His abandonment of Proteus's prophecy, emphasised by the rescuing of Florimell from Proteus himself, represents a victory for the human spirit over its fears of temporal vicissitude. In *The Faerie Queene* characters are expected to take the risk of love thereby promoting the work of 'generation'.

Book five is much concerned with the 'ruins of time' as civilization degenerates from the manners of the Golden Age to those of the modern world. This is represented at the outset by the spatial disorientation of the constellations: as they violently displace one another the 'times' grow 'worse and worse'. So it must be since the motions of the heavenly bodies 'make time'. Erratic violent motion produces erratic violent time. Even Mercilla, whose court emerges as an oasis of peace in a desert of dissension, appears embattled. Indeed the execution of Duessa moves the violence of the outside world within the court itself. Such is the central problem of Spenser's concept of justice. Working within fallen time, the patrons of justice differ from their opponents in motivation *but not in method.* Too often ends justify means and timeless ideals wither into expedient policies.

Book six brings the work closest to Augustine's internalized theory of time, time as 'an extension of the mind'. Here Spenser's 'tedious trauell' through the land of Faery is sustained by the 'secret comfort' of poetry itself. For his characters it is a book of retreats — Timias's and Matilda's retreat with the hermit, Calidore's pastoral retreat with Meliboe, Colin Clout's solitary retreat to Mt Acidale. Yet there is as much action as anywhere else. It is merely that the emphasis falls on personal as against public time in recognition of the twin assurances that 'vertues seat is deepe within the mynd' (Proem, 5) and that 'it is the mynd, that maketh good or ill' (VI. 9. 30). Long before its capture, personal 'discipline' cures wounds inflicted by the Blatant Beast (VI. 6. 5). Calidore's 'weariness' is dispelled by his concern for Pastorella, yet the quest and the enemy remain the same. Everything, including man's perception of the passage of time, appears to depend on mental attitude as Meliboe himself suggests (VI. 9. 29). Through the complexity of the narrative there begins to emerge the realization that those who speak of 'fortune' and those who speak of 'providence' describe the same phenomena from different levels of perception. It is the lack of inner discipline that releases the Blatant Beast which 'rends without regard of person or of time' (VI. 12. 40). The two are intimately related.

Into the spatial structure of the quests, as indeed the spatial structure of the various books, Spenser builds elaborate patterns of recurrence designed to explore topical notions regarding the 'shape' of time. Images of circularity pervade the poem.[43] St George ends his quest where all human history began and returns to Gloriana in a book where even the punishment of Duessa recurs annually (I. 2. 40). Book two largely reproduces the pattern of book one, ending in a false Eden where men are perpetually turned to animals. At the

43 Joanne Field Holland, 'The Cantos of Mutabilitie and the Form of *The Faerie Queene*', *ELH*, 35 (1968), 21-31. See below pp. 214-7.

heart of book three lie the recurrent and inescapable cycles of the Gardens of Adonis; at the heart of book four the inexorable spinning, carding, and snipping of the Fates and the relentless generative cycles of the sea. Central to book five is the symbolism of Isis and Osiris, sun and moon, with all their implications of periodicity while book six presents the revolving concentric circles of the cosmic dance in the vision of the Graces. All such vibrant images of circularity culminate in the pageants of years, seasons, days, and hours summoned up by Order on Arlo Hill.[44] These in turn recall the great plan for the poem expounded in the 'Letter to Raleigh' according to which all of the quests were destined to return to their point of origin, the court of Gloriana. Spenser appears to have preserved this goal as late as book six:

> Then pardon me, most dreaded Soueraine,
> That from your selfe I doe this vertue bring,
> And to your selfe doe it returne againe:
> So from the Ocean all riuers spring,
> And tribute backe repay as to their King.
> Right so from you all goodly vertues well
> Into the rest, which round about you ring,
> Faire Lords and Ladies, which about you dwell,
> And doe adorne your Court, where courtesies excell.
> (Proem, 7)

In general, the more polished the circle the clearer its reflection of eternity, and the repeated use of the word 'eternal' throughout the poem ensures that the symbolism cannot easily be forgotten. In theory *The Faerie Queene* should constitute a great 'year' of twelve heroic 'months' charting Arthur's progress through an allegorical Zodiac of achievement. As in *The Shepheardes Calender*, however, fluctuations in the organic shape of time distort aesthetic form and the poem hovers indecisively between Virgilian epic and Ariostan romance. In seeking to accommodate Renaissance notions of cyclical renewal to Reformation ideals of spiritual regeneration, involving various types of 'return' to the ill-assorted values of Rome and Jerusalem, Spenser has created one of the most complex and asymmetrical structures in literature. 'Straight lines' curve imperceptibly, 'parallels' mysteriously intersect, circles collide or collapse into a point until distortion grows integral to design. Eternity, reflected in the mirror of art, produces strange effects of narrative anamorphism which only the oblique perspective of allegory can reduce to meaning.

44 For close parallels see Cecil C. Seronsy, 'The Doctrine of Cyclical Recurrence and some related ideas in the *Works* of Samuel Daniel', *SP*, 54 (1957), 387-407.

Augustine's fascination with the concept of eternity reinforced by his Christian Platonism had the effect of greatly lessening the value of all but the most spiritual human events. His *City of God* established a perspective on secular affairs which could be regarded as diminishing the significance of history although its determined rejection of the Stoic doctrine of perpetual recurrence enforces the uniqueness of all human experience, a uniqueness Spenser much prized.[45] Nevertheless, for Augustine the Christian became first and foremost a citizen of the heavenly city and only secondarily a member of the civic community. The great object in the pilgrimage of life is the pilgrim's destination.[46] Despite this, by adopting the Hebrew scriptures as part of its sacred literature, the Church was forced to recognise the importance of a sequence of secular events directed by a shaping spiritual power. As Calvin was later to point out, Psalm 107 could be regarded as demonstrating that 'what in common estimation are thought whims of fortune, are in fact so far from being imposed by blind chance, that they clearly mirror the goodness or the wrath or the justice of God'.[47]

The Church's insistence upon the three cardinal points of Fall, Redemption and Second Coming established a linear structure for Christian historiography opposed to the random power of classical *Fortuna.* The 'meaning' of history now lay in the recognition of divine intention beneath the flux of daily events. It was obvious, however, that the material and physical circumstances of human life had not been altered by the Incarnation. The vicissitudes of war and politics contined as before and fortune continued to allot its benefits in apparent indifference to the moral qualities of the recipients. Nevertheless, inspired by the techniques of biblical exegesis, commentators were now disposed to interpret whole epochs of history as part of a universal plan for the eternal salvation of mankind. In Calvin's words, 'scripture builds for us a higher watch-tower from which to observe God overruling all the works of men so as to direct them to the end appointed by Him'.[48] As the mind of God remained beyond the reach of the human intellect, rational interpretation often gives way to faith: 'Only God from the *nunc-stans* perceived the full meaning of the sequence of particular events, and it was easier to conceive of him as willing it. Providence was the name of his will as directing this sequence, at least as that will was perceived by men from

45 J.G.A. Pocock, *The Machiavellian Moment* (Princeton, 1975), pp. 34-6; Roy W. Battenhouse, *A Companion to the Study of St. Augustine* (New York, 1955), pp. 325-6; See *City of God*, XI. 4.

46 Samuel C. Chew, *The Pilgrimage of Life* (Port Washington, New York, 1973 — first published 1962), pp. 144-252.

47 *Concerning the Eternal Predestination of God*, translated by J.K.S. Reid (Cambridge, 1961), pp. 163-4.

48 *Ibid.*, p. 172.

inside time; and to them, who had no *nunc-stans*, it was inscrutable and mysterious'.[49] History, therefore, retains a meaning but this can be assessed only in terms of a spiritual perspective established not by rational enquiry but by belief. All subsequent interpretations posited the existence of a benevolent deity controlling and directing human affairs. Acts of direct intervention in the course of history were regarded as miracles. The result was a distinction between Providence and Fate (the classical *Fatum*) which sought to explain the relationship between order and change, unity and multiplicity, eternity and time. Boethius's account of these matters is perhaps the most succinct and influential the Medieval mind was able to formulate. 'It is easy', he tells us,

> to see that Providence and Fate are different if we consider the power of each . . . For Providence embraces all things equally, however diverse they are, however infinite. Fate, on the other hand, sets particular things in motion once they have been given their own forms, places, and times. . . . Although the two are different things, one depends upon the other, for the process of Fate derives from the simplicity of Providence . . . whatever strays farthest from the divine mind is most entangled in the nets of Fate.[50]

This was the view that sustained Medieval historiography and set the church at the centre of human affairs. But the Middle Ages were never as static as Renaissance man supposed. All sorts of tensions put such dogma under severe strain, and not least the growing hostility of secular authorities to the papacy's interference in temporal government. Furthermore, with the re-emergence of Aristotelian philosophy from the eleventh century onwards it became clear that some measure of reinterpretation was required. Aristotle's views on the nature of time conflicted, as we have seen, with those of Plato and consequently with those of Medieval Christianity. Whereas Aquinas attempted to resolve this disagreement, the influence of Averroes contributed to the condemnation of several of his illustrious contemporaries including Siger of Brabant.[51] Perhaps the most positive result of this controversy was the development of the concept of *aevum*, midway between that of time and eternity. This was prompted by the difficult position of the angels in regard to established theory since they seemed at once free of time and incapable of eternity. The solution envisaged 'a state of existence in which all progress, growth and change are excluded', a perpetuity in which suc-

49 Pocock, pp. 29-30.

50 *The Consolation of Philosophy* (Book 4, Prose 6), translated by Richard Green (Indianapolis, 1962), pp. 91-2. See below p. 159.

51 Gordon Leff, *Medieval Thought: Saint Augustine to Ockham* (Harmondsworth, 1958), pp. 226-31.

cession (*prius et posterius*) may be experienced but not transitoriness.[52] Angelic moments were from now on regarded as discontinuous. The angels did not enjoy the stillness of the *nunc-stans* — except through angelic contemplation — but neither were they subject to the vicissitudes of earthly time. Aquinas regarded them as instruments of motion, allowing them to occasion terrestrial time by moving the spheres.[53]

The concept of *aevum* is undeniably difficult and the perplexities of angelic nature render it even more so, but for our purpose the crucial aspect of the issue is the extension of the idea of perpetuity from the angelic to the human world.[54] It was soon discovered that, properly applied, the theory of *aevum* made possible the much-needed rapprochement between Platonic and Aristotelian philosophy. One could distinguish, for example, between the perpetuity of a political or religious office and the transience of the individual who happened to occupy it at any given time. Such a distinction gave rise to the legal theory of the 'king's two bodies', the idea that the monarch 'never dies' since his office is made perpetual by succession.[55] One could therefore discriminate between the official actions of a ruling monarch and his activities as a private individual.[56]

The concept of *aevum* particularly recommended itself to Renaissance lawyers, but it also harmonised with new developments in the interpretation of secular history. Aristotle had postulated an unending cycle of recurrent events which at first seems difficult to reconcile with the linear view of history adopted by the early Church fathers. The rediscovery of classical civilization which gave rise to Italian Humanism led of necessity to a denigration of the supposedly 'dark' ages intervening and to the replacement of the linear historical outlook with a cyclical one — the development of the mechanical clock in the thirteenth and fourteenth centuries lent visual support to the cyclical view, albeit cyclical within finite time.[57] This new combination of outlooks made possible the Christianization of the Aristotelian viewpoint while at the same time satisfying the Renaissance interest in the enduring value of human works.[58] It represented less a complete break with the past

52 Frank Herbert Brabant, *Time and Eternity in Christian Thought* (London, 1937), p. 79.

53 Brabant, pp. 76-82; 'God's own eternity is the hand which leadeth Angels in the course of their perpetuity; their perpetuity the hand that draweth out celestial motion, the line of which motion and the thread of time are spun together'. Hooker, *Works*, II, 381.

54 Ernst H. Kantorowicz, *The King's Two Bodies: A Study in Medieval Political Theology* (Princeton, 1957), p. 274. See below p. 135.

55 *Ibid.*, pp. 291-302.

56 Kantorowicz, pp. 7-23; Marie Axton, *The Queen's Two Bodies* (London, 1977), pp. 35-9.

57 Quentin Skinner, *The Foundations of Modern Political Thought*, 2 vols (Cambridge, 1978), I, 109-110.

58 Herschel Baker, *The Race of Time* (Toronto, 1967), pp. 60-2.

than a reinterpretation of old ideas. One notices, for example, that the word 'clock' is never used in *The Faerie Queene* as Spenser prefers to measure time traditionally according to the movements of the heavenly bodies. His time is organic not mechanical and to its cyclical rhythms the 'humours' of the human constitution are intimately attuned.[59] Regarded optimistically, as healer, preserver, and generator, time is 'treasure' (IV. 10. 14).

The hazards of contingency ensured that much of the old distrust remained. According to Ficino, optimistic as he was, to set one's expectations upon the often delusive promises of time was the mark of the sensual mind. 'Time', he wrote, 'is a pernicious doctor and daily misleads the sick by their hope of the future, and before he heals old sores he adds new sorrows. Thus day by day time accumulates evil and leads man to death in a fallacious hope for life'.[60] Such is the lesson learned the hard way by Shakespeare's Macbeth, and Ficino proceeds to expound his philosophy in what might well be used as a prose gloss upon the great 'tomorrow and tomorrow' speech. His source is Martial (I. 15):

> Believe me, it is not wise to say I shall live; tomorrow is too late for living; live today. . . . As you know, you should often live for others if you wish to live for yourself. But do both for the sake of God. It was first of all for His sake that you were born, then for the sake of yourself and others. . . But make me no more promises for the morrow; promising what you neither have nor know that you will have. If it is only tomorrow that you eat or drink, my friend, will you not be dead in three days? Let this tomorrow die today, let it die at once, lest you yourself should die; nothing is more false than this tomorrow, which has deceived all men that the earth has brought forth.[61]

59 For an account of time and the humours see William Harrison's 'Description of England' in Holinshed, I, 405-6. Harrison also reminds us that the 'smallest part of time knowne vnto the people' was the minute. It is also the smallest known to Spenser's Mutability, VII. 7. 23.

60 *Letters of Ficino*, I, 93-4; For the Latin text see *Opera*, I, 632.

61 *Letters of Ficino*, I, 131; *Opera*, I, 646-7: Redime te, quaeso, ab hac misera captivitate dum potes, solum autem potes hodie, hodie primum tui iuris esto. Non est, crede mihi, sapientis dicere, Vivam. Sera nimis vita est crastina, vive hodie . . . Reliquum, si libet, vive alijs: nam et alij, ut scis, saepe vivas oportet, si vis tibi vivere. Sed utrumque Dei gratia facito. Nempe adeo Dei gratia primum, deinde tui aliorumque gratia es procreatus . . . Sed noli mihi cras ulterius polliceri, polliceris quod neque habes, neque te scis habiturum. Si cras tantum comederis, biberisve, nonne triduo peribis amice? Pereat cras istud hodie, pereat, atque primum, ne tu pereas, nihil crastino isthoc fallacius, fefellit omnes, quos terra protulit homines . . . Omnes hoc morbo gravissime laboramus. Cras istud fiet. Vix praesens tempus habemus: nam ita leviter habemus, ut parumper retinere non valeamus. Futurum autem nihil est, futurum igitur nullus habet. O dementes, o miseri, spes nostras in nihilum iacimus.

For Ficino, as for Spenser, man fulfils himself in time but is not fulfilled by it. It is through his contribution to history that the Redcross Knight becomes St George, but he can only *be* St George in another life. Contemplation's assurances are couched in the future tense. Such an emphasis could easily return us to a world-view very like that of St Augustine, particularly were one to regard George's actions solely as repetitions of those of Christ, or even as remote prefigurations of Apocalypse. Both of these approaches have an important validity, as one might expect in so consciously allegorical a poem. Nevertheless, what Spenser emphasises in his refusal to allow George to linger on the Mount of Contemplation, and even more pointedly in his refusal to allow him to remain with Una, is that individual contributors to the historical process retain an independent significance however past events or future expectations may influence their assessment.

The existence of a pattern or type — of which the hero himself is usually unaware — does not detract from the individual achievement. The story of St George loses none of its distinctiveness through its structural similarities with that of Christ or other Christian knights. Rather, such coincidences tend to enforce its own peculiar identity, just as George himself labours towards self-knowledge on the quest. The more Christlike he becomes, the more he becomes St George. The same applies to Foxe's *Acts and Monuments* where the marked similarity of the stories recorded enhances their significance. Essentially all martyrs repeat the sacrifice of their prototype St Stephen, but Foxe's respect for the historical process, for the enduring dignity of the individual human act, renders every aspect of their tribulations worth recording in detail. His providential theory of history does not, as is sometimes supposed, render the new Renaissance historiography inappropriate to his narrative. His accounts of the machinations of Rome imply not a little familiarity with the outlook of Guicciardini and Machiavelli. Similarly the providential attitudes underlying Spenser's 'chronicles' of British history merely serve to enhance the value of their detail.

III *Ireland: History and Politics*

Spenser's *View of the Present State of Ireland* is notable for the way in which it combines a fundamentally providential view of human history with acute practical analyses of contemporary politics.[62] At one stage it can regard the fall of Rome not as a cultural disaster but as part of God's plan for spreading Christianity amongst the barbarians (p. 92), while at another it can echo Machiavelli's *Discourses* (p. 229). These attitudes are reconciled by the repeated assertion that in the long run the just cause invariably wins. Success

62 All quotations in the text are from the Variorum Edition, *Prose*. Occasionally punctuation has been supplied to clarify the sense.

in warfare, for example, 'vsethe Comonlie to be accordinge to the Iustnes of the Cause for which it is made' (p. 169). Spenser, therefore, strikes much the same balance as John Foxe, minutely analysing the details of human policy but ultimately deferring to a supernatural agency working through man.

This being the case, he is at considerable pains to preface his suggestions for the reorganisation of the country with an elaborate defence of the justness of the English cause, tracing the claim to sovereignty far beyond the time of Henry II and Strongbow to that of King Arthur who 'had all that Ilande in his Allegiance and Subieccion' (p. 95). The 'good recorde yeat extante' used as authority for this conquest is presumably Geoffrey of Monmouth who chronicles a swift campaign resulting in the capitulation of the whole island.[63] It seems clear from this reference that Spenser entertained no serious doubts as to Arthur's historicity, despite the attacks of Polydore Vergil.[64] The major rebuttal, John Leland's indignant *Assertio Inclytissimi Arturii* (1544), was translated into English by Richard Robinson in 1582 and dedicated to Lord Arthur Grey 'Lord Deputie and Leifetenant Generall for the Queenes Maiestie in Ireland'.[65] Spenser uses the coincidence of Christian names to good effect in the 'Legend of Ivstice' where Artegall-Arthur Grey acts with absolute propriety in his treatment of Irena. It is her captor Grantorto who seeks to 'iustifie his wrong' through force (V. 12. 14). In his conquest of Ireland Arthur Grey is 'equal to Arthur' as the etymology of the hero's name suggests.

It is not merely that the cause is historically justified, however, but that direct intervention is necessary from a Christian and humanitarian point of view. The island in which Grey operates is 'saluage' — as Artegall describes it in *The Faerie Queene* (VI. 1. 9) — and it falls to his lot to endow it with the blessings of civility and peace. From the outset to the conclusion of the treatise the term applied to the government's activities is 'reformation'. At the time of Grey's recall, for example, the country was 'made readie for reformacion' (p. 159) but the chance was subsequently lost through mismanagement. That the civil 'reformation' was intended as a prelude to the introduction of the Protestant faith there can be no doubt since Irenius stresses the need to create the appropriate circumstances in which to preach the true Gospel (p. 139). As far as is possible, the repeated use of the term here and in *The Faerie Queene* is intended to set the Irish wars in the context of the great European battle against Rome. The cause is God's, and the Elizabethan

63 *History of the Kings of Britain*, IX. 10.

64 Edwin Greenlaw, *Studies in Spenser's Historical Allegory* (Baltimore, 1932), pp. 2-22.

65 Leland's text is published in Christopher Middleton, *The Famous Historie of Chinon of England . . . The Assertion of King Arthure translated by Richard Robinson from Leland's Assertio Inclytissimi Arturii together with the Latin Original*, edited by William Edward Mead, Early English Text Society, Original Series, 165 (London, 1925).

administration is doubly justified by virtue of its ultimate spiritual aim. Accordingly, both parties to the dialogue 'pity' the condition of the state and lament the probable loss of so many souls — although Irenius does hold out the possibility of salvation for some few through the special grace of God (pp. 137-8). The difficulty is that Roman Catholicism is (allegedly) upheld more through opposition to the English than from any sense of spiritual conviction and is consequently unable to exercise an influence over the moral standards of its adherents (p. 221). For the most part, the population is 'so blindelye and brutishly enformed . . . as that ye would rather thinke them *Atheists* or infidles' (p. 136).

At the beginning of the dialogue Irenius refers to the increasingly popular opinion that the failure to reform Ireland is attributable to the 'fatall destinie' of the country, 'which wheather it proceed from the *very Genius* of the soile, or influence of the starres, or that Almighty god hathe not yeat Appointed the tyme of her reformacion or that he reserueth her in this vnquiet state still, for some secrete skourge, which shall by her Come vnto Englande it is harde to be knowen but yeat muche to be feared' (p. 43). The explanation moves from natural circumstances to the mysterious will of God entirely excluding human policy from any share in the failure. While the implications of such an outlook are, perhaps, acceptable from a naïvely providential point of view, they tend to minimise the value of human effort and promote a crippling mood of determinism. It is noteworthy, however, that Irenius reports rather than endorses the popular outlook, and throughout the rest of the work he argues in quite a different vein. Furthermore, Eudoxus raises the obvious objection that the concept of providence is commonly misused to excuse the 'follies and imperfeccions' of misguided policy by attributing the resulting 'absurditye' to 'the heavens' (p. 44). The true explanation resides either in 'the vnsoundnes of the Counsells and Plottes' adopted, or in the degree of 'faintnes in followinge and effectinge the same'. In the very first exchange, therefore, particular emphasis is laid upon man's responsibility for his own fate and facile, defeatist attitudes towards providence and 'fatall appointment' are relegated to the realm of 'vaine Conceipt'. The 'tyme of . . . reformation' has come and gone, but the authorities have failed to take advantage of the proffered opportunities.

By contrast, in dealing with the Irish problem, Grey has acted in accordance with necessity, fitting both his policy and his character to the circumstances. Overcoming the tendencies of a 'gentle, affable Lovinge and temperate' nature he has 'forced' himself to the 'violence' of which his opponents complain and 'allmoste Changed his verye naturall disposicion' in order to meet 'the necesitye of that presente state of thinges' (p. 160). Hence the part played by Talus in book five labouring the political fiction that the ruthlessness of Grey's policy is alien to, and even detachable from, his own nature. It is literally another character. What the Elizabethan court lacks is precisely this realistic attitude to the inevitability of justified violence in the pursuit of lasting reformation. As in the Bible, even famine and disease must become tools of correction:

> Therefore by all meanes it muste be forsene and assured that after once entringe into this Course of reformacion, theare be afterwardes no remorse or drawinge backe, for the sighte of anie suche rufull obiectes as muste thearevppon followe, nor for Compassion of theire Callamityes, seinge that by no other meanes it is possible to recure them, and that these are not of will but of verye vrgente necessitye' (p. 163)

Thus is the 'tyrant's plea' reconciled to the imperial ideal of Christian government. One recalls how 'heauenly Contemplation' reconciles St George to the necessity of the quest while admitting that 'bloud can nought but sin, and wars but sorrowes yield' (I. 10. 60). As Spenser sees it, Grey's enemies have taken unscrupulous advantage of the resulting dilemma to 'blot' him with 'the name of a bloddye man' (p. 160). The shedding of blood is a moral necessity in a fallen world. What Spenser envisages, therefore, is a limited war strategy, of admitted ruthlessness, leading to conditions of 'eternall peace' and 'profit', a war to end all wars (p. 197).

The 'necessitye' of any given situation may be determined correctly only in the light of historical understanding. Accordingly, the *View* takes as its starting point the history of the Celtic nations from ancient times, explaining contemporary customs and attitudes by examining their cultural evolution. This understanding is seldom, if ever, sympathetic. For example, the manner in which the first Norman settlers have come to identify with the 'mere Irish' is very accurately analysed, but the subject is regarded as a study in moral degeneracy rather than cultural assimilation (p. 117). In effect, the two are made synonymous. Similarly, the scholarly disquisition on Irish antiquities is intended primarily as a guide to present policy. Not merely does the ancestry of the Celts demonstrate 'a wonderfull providence and purpose of Allmightye God' in mingling so many distant nations (pp. 95-6), but what appears to be a digression in the course of the dialogue becomes 'trulye verye materiall' in forming the basis for the eventual conclusion. At the close of this section of the work Eudoxus remarks, 'ye bringe your selfe *Irenius* verye well into the waye againe notwithstandinge that it semethe ye weare never out of the waye' (p. 97). The technique is identical to that encountered in *The Faerie Queene* where apparent digressions or flashbacks prove thematically essential to the concerns of the book in which they occur. Towards the close of book six, surely one of the most digressive of all, Spenser himself draws the reader's attention to the subtle appropriateness of his narrative method

(VI. 12. 1). The value of understanding the past is to a large extent pragmatic.

Spenser goes into some detail as to how such an understanding is to be gained. While written sources, such as ancient poems and chronicles, are not to be trusted 'absolutelye', 'yeat theare remaynethe amongest them some relickes of the trewe Antiquitye thoughe disguised, which a well eyde man maye happelye discouer and finde out' (p. 86). Such evidence must be evaluated in the light of contemporary scholarship — Buchanan is particularly favoured — and 'the experience of the presente time'. Through 'comparison of times, likenes of manners and Customes, Affinytie of wordes and names, properties of natures and vses, resemblaunces of rightes and Ceremonies, monimentes of Churches and Tombes' the historian gathers a 'likelyhode of truethe . . . a probabilitye of thinges' upon which the reader must pass judgement (pp. 84-5). Mere tradition is to be discounted 'since all men be lyars and many lye when they will' (p. 87). More important still, whereas tradition lends a spurious justification to native customs, scholarly research exposes their barbaric origins ('verie strange and allmoste heathenishe') and consequently discredits them (p. 97). Antiquarian lore is a valuable weapon of propaganda. There is a clear distinction in Spenser's mind between the aesthetic use of romance materials and the establishment of historical fact. In one manuscript he even casts doubt upon the ancient legend, recounted afresh in *The Faerie Queene*, that Britain was originally colonized by Brutus.[66] Similarly, despite their plentiful use throughout the poem, the closely related legends of the Giants are dismissed in the *View* as self-indulgent 'ymaginacions' (p. 131). The 'Letter to Raleigh' describes the epic very accurately as an 'historicall fiction'.

Particularly revealing are Spenser's attitudes towards time and social development. Society is regarded as establishing itself slowly and painfully through centuries of turmoil. Irenius reminds Eudoxus 'by how manye

66 The reasons Spenser gives for discounting the Brutan legends are interesting. The reference occurs in the course of a discussion upon the alleged colonization of Ireland by the mythical Spanish hero Gathelus or Gaedhal. This, Spenser argues, is merely the Irish equivalent of the 'Tale of *Brutus*' put abroad by 'vaine *Englishmen*', 'it being as impossible to proove, that there was ever any such *Brutus* of *England*, as it is, that there was any such *Gathelus* of *Spaine*' (p. 82). This passage, however, was not included in the manuscript entered for publication in the Stationers' Register in 1598, where the Gathelus story is dismissed, without any reference to Brutus, as a grotesque example of 'forged histories' delivered to, and accepted by, 'fooles' (p. 89). Whereas Spenser accepted the basic veracity of the Arthurian legends — probably under the influence of antiquarians such as Bale and Leland — his attitude towards Geoffrey of Monmouth cannot have been entirely uncritical. Even though an explicit denunciation of Brutus was deleted from the 1598 manuscript, perhaps for patriotic reasons or even to avoid a direct clash with the poem, few perceptive readers would miss the obvious similarity between the two legends.

thornye and harde waies . . . by how manye Civill broiles, by howe manye tumvltuous rebellions, that even hazarded often times the whole saftye of the kingedome' the 'civilytie' of Tudor England has emerged (pp. 54-5). Indeed 'it is but even the other daye since Englande grewe Civill' (p. 118). The state of Ireland bears direct comparison with the England of Alfred when, as is 'manifest by reporte of the Chronicles and other ancient writers', the whole country was 'greatlie infested with Robbers and outlawes' (p. 201).[67] Ironically, while the early Norman settlers have degenerated since the time of the first invasion, 'the rude Irishe whiche beinge verie wilde at the firste are now become somwhat more Civill' (p. 209).

Ireland's troubles are not the result of a divine curse, as we read in the fiction of the *Mutabilitie Cantos*, but of the absence of any strong figure, comparable to Alfred, prepared to impose order despite the cost.[68] Societies do not simply evolve of their own nature, but develop in accordance with the judicious exercising of firm discipline and royal vigilance. In England's case it was 'the Continvall presence of theire Kinge whose onelye persone is often times in steade of an Armye to Contayne the vnrvlye people from a thowsande evill occasions' that proved the deciding factor (p. 55). One must not suppose, therefore, that the central position assigned to the monarch in the 'Briton Moniments' or Merlin's prophecy is to be regarded merely as evidence of Spenser's addiction to '*res gestae*'.[69] Rather, the role of the monarch is central to his concept of civil development.[70] In Ireland, owing to the lack of such a figure, the flaws in the original 'ordinaunce and institucion' of government have through 'ouersighte' run 'more out of square to that disorder which it is now Come vnto, like as to indirecte lynes the further they are drawen out, the further they goe asunder' (p. 146). For Spenser, savagery is not merely a phase of the historical process but a condition endemic in the nature of the human 'beast'. Were it not continually restrained, 'history' itself could not exist. Not surprisingly the *View* ends with a request for the appointment of a strong 'Lorde Liuetennante' permanently resident in the country to regulate the course of government (p. 228).[71] The alternative is perpetual disorder. As

67 For contemporary attitudes to the primitive state of Ireland see Arthur B. Ferguson, *Clio Unbound: Perception of the Social and Cultural Past in Renaissance England* (Durham, Nt. Carolina, 1979), p. 381.

68 In the *View* the 'curse' is occasioned not by Diana but by a series of inconsistent policies foolishly or selfishly pursued (p. 145).

69 Ferguson, pp. 3-27.

70 The 'Briton Moniments' tell the story of Britain from ancient times 'till it reduced was to one mans gouernments' (II. 9. 59). The establishment of monarchy is presented as the natural goal of civil progress.

71 The person 'vppon whom the ey of all Englande is fixed and our laste hopes now rest' is generally thought to be Essex. See *Prose*, pp. 428-9; Rudolf Gottfried, 'Spenser's *View* and Essex', *PMLA*, 52 (1937), 645-51.

time passes and circumstances change, 'good vse' turns to 'abuse' (p. 129). Ordinances originally intended for the common good become so 'prevaricated thoroughe Change and Allteracion of tymes' that they effect the opposite (p. 46). 'So muche time dothe alter the manners of men' that the original settlers, freed of the royal authority which guided them at home, have become 'muche more Lawles and Licentious' than the people they were intended to 'reforme' (p. 113). Left to itself, time breeds decay:

> Neither is it the nature of the Countrye to alter mens manners, but the bad mindes of the man, whoe havinge bene broughte vp at home vnder a streighte rule of dutie and obedience beinge allwaies restrained by sharpe penalties from lewde behauiour, so sone as they Come thither wheare they see lawes more slacklye tended and the harde Constrainte which they weare vsed vnto now slacked, they growe more lose and Careles of theire duetie and as it is the nature of all men to loue libertye So they become Libertines (p. 211).

The present condition of Ireland is a sad testimony to the government's failure 'to goe on in anie one Course' in administering the country's affairs (p. 228). Official policy has become as changeable as fortune (p. 145). Sussessful government results from an ability to formulate and execute a policy meticulously adapted to the needs of the time. The ideal governor 'shalbe forced oftentimes to followe the necessitye of present occasions and to take the sodaine advantage of time which beinge once loste will not be recouered' (p. 229). In formulating military strategy and directing the course of future plantations, the Privy Council should consider 'the Course which the Romaines observed in the Conquest of Englande' making practical use of former experience (p. 180). In this view of affairs, the progress of civilization centres upon the fostering of 'husbandrie' (p. 216) and the establishment of 'market Townes' (p. 225). The former accustoms warlike populations to peaceful modes of life while the latter strengthens the economy, fortifies the administration, and generally furthers social progress 'by reasone that people repairinge often thither for theire nedes will dailye see and learne Civill manners of the better sorte' (p. 225). Reading such passages, one begins to appreciate more fully the political implications of the desire 'to fashion a gentleman or noble person in vertuous and gentle discipline'. Civility no less than justice is an instrument of government. Calidore is the appropriate successor to Artegall and the movement of *The Faerie Queene* from justice to courtesy reflects the ideal movement of Irish politics. As for the ancient Romans, civilization is both imposed through military strength and insinuated through example. While it was wrong for the early Normans to become assimilated to their Irish neighbours, the opposite process is both desirable and necessary, particularly in relation to religious attitudes since the 'time' is not yet 'convenient' for a full Protestant reformation. While the good of the soul is admitted to take precedence over that of the body, in cases of dangerous illness when both are 'recouerable', one sends for the 'phisicion' before the 'preacher' (pp. 138-9). In the natural order of things settling the 'course of gouerment' paves the way for social and ecclesiastical reform.

Throughout the dialogue, even at its most historical, Spenser's emphasis falls on the 'present state' of the country. Everything else is subordinated to that. Naïve providential opinions give way to the complexities of practical politics, yet a more subtle providential outlook determines that polity. There is no question, for instance, as to the justification of what is going on. The work of 'reformacion' is obviously the work favoured by God, the difficulties lie in the irresolution of his human agents. In the final analysis, the nature of 'time' is determined by the nature of the men who operate within it. 'Time alters manners' but only when 'licentiousness' facilitates the change or when government either abnegates or becomes unable to fulfil its moral role. We are left in no doubt that, given the right moral and social attitudes, the creation of a better, if not perfect, society is both possible and practical. Indeed the whole purpose of the treatise is to let us see both what the country is currently like, 'and allsoe what it maie be by good Care and amendement' (p. 230)

The present state of Ireland is the result of gross mismanagement, its future state, for better or worse, may be decided by the Elizabethan administration. If its decisions are to be beneficial, they must be made in the light of the ancient and recent history supplied in the *View* as interpreted by practical experience. Under the guidance of providence, to which both speakers respectfully refer, time affords plentiful opportunities for 'reformacion', but it is left to man to recognise them for what they are and act accordingly in the light of an informed faith. Bloodshed is accepted as a necessary evil, the price that must be paid for the establishment of order in a 'saluage' environment. Lord Grey, no less than Artegall, is regarded as an 'heroicke spirite' committed to such an ideal (p. 162). In official dispatches to England, Sir Nicholas Malbey had compared him to Hercules, Artegall's mythical prototype, as early as the autumn of 1580. Spenser's defence of Grey constitutes the apotheosis of that conceit.[72]

Perhaps what emerges most strongly from the *View* is a sense of the value of human endeavour when morally directed — 'morally', that is, from Spenser's viewpoint. One could hardly expect the Celtic poets, whose artistry he praises even as he deplores their lack of principle, to agree (pp. 125-6). In them, he sees the mirror image of himself — Catholic writers who

72 *Calendar of State Papers (Irish), 1574-85*, p. 247.

countenance violent opposition to the Elizabethan regime on political and religious grounds — and finds the spectacle repellent. It is hard to resist the suspicion that the virulence of his response is partly born of an uneasy sense of kinship. Whenever Spenser speaks of Ireland, assertion is qualified by self-justification. It is as though he were conducting an inner dialogue: both Irenius *and* Eudoxus voice his thoughts, the former his public policies, the latter his private doubts. The very urgency of the passages defending Grey — years after their subject's death — bespeak an exercise in self-defence. Spenser, too, would put off the name of a 'bloudie man', if he could. But Grey's failure in Ireland disrupts the ideal movement from war to civilization. Even though we have supposedly left the 'saluage' island behind, savages of various sorts pervade the 'Legend of Covrtesie' and Calidore responds violently. As Grey suffers the ignominy of slander at the close of book five, his loyal poet suffers the same at the close of book six. Thus the ideal coincidences of victory demanded by the epic form are degraded into coincidences of defeat.

IV. *Foresight*

The attribution of 'providence' to man was as common during the Renaissance as its attribution to God. The claim involved no blasphemous presumption except when it operated to the exclusion of higher concerns. In *The Atheist's Tragedy*, for example, D'Amville initially restricts the term to political cunning, to the ability to shape future events to one's personal benefit. Only as the play progresses do the wider implications of the concept make themselves felt.[73] Similarly, while Claudius laments the failure of human 'providence' (IV. 1. 17), Hamlet takes comfort in the unfailing providence of God (V. 2. 231). The crucial distinction is that, when applied to the deity, providence involves the notion of absolute power, whereas applied to man it denotes only a limited capacity to guard against probable eventualities. But this renders it central to the arts of personal and political government and the subject is discussed at some length by a host of popular authorities such as Elyot in *The Book Named the Governor*, Cinthio in *De Vita Civile* and Bacon in *The Wisdom of the Ancients*.[74] Regarded in this light, *A View of the Present State of Ireland* is an expression of human providence intended to pre-empt possible rebellions.

The future orientation of the human mind was regarded as one of its most distinctive and valuable features. Spenser accurately reflects such attitudes

73 *The Atheist's Tragedy*, edited by Brian Morris and Roma Gill (London, 1976), p. 7.

74 Elyot, *The Book Named the Governor*, edited by S.E. Lehmberg (London, 1962), pp. 81-3; Cinthio, *Hecatommithi*, Parte Secunda, 'Della Vita Civile' (Venice, 1608), p. 79; Bacon, *Works*, VI, 746-7.

by ascribing to the true 'genius' inherent in each individual an innate foresight regarding 'things concerning our welfare'. Since genius frequently functions through the medium of 'straunge phantomes' (including dreams and visions), this power inextricably links the imaginative to the rational faculties (II. 12. 47). According to Natalis Comes, Spenser's source, the Genii govern our whole lives, secretly persuading or dissuading us from various courses of action and moderating our wills. They operate through spectral images apprehended by the soul but of little avail unless weighed in the reason ('ratione perpendantur') to produce a proper determination of the conscious mind ('recta . . . animi deliberatio'). Neglect of this rational process ('posthabita ratione') leads of necessity to delusion and error ('in multos errores incurrat necesse est').[75] Providence and prudence are closely allied. Famine must be 'forsene' in Ireland as God 'foresees' natural disasters (*Prose*, p. 163).

Entering the chambers of the mind in the House of Alma, Arthur and Guyon encounter Phantastes ('a man of yeares yet fresh'), Reason ('a man of ripe and perfect age'), and Eumnestes ('an old oldman, halfe blind'). These figures represent not merely the three faculties of the mind — fantasy, reason, and memory — but more specifically the three facets of prudence as defined by Cicero: 'memoria, intelligentia, providentia. Memoria est per quam animus repetit illa quae fuerunt; intelligentia, per quam ea perspicit quae sunt; providentia per quam futurum aliquid videtur ante quam factum est'.[76] Thus 'providence' emerges as an essential constituent of prudence, an acquaintance with the workings of which is of obvious benefit to the patron of temperance:

> The first of them could things to come foresee;
> The next could of things present best aduize;
> The third things past could keepe in memoree;
> So that no time, nor reason could arize,
> But that the same could one of these comprize.
> (II. 9. 49)

Of the three, however, only one, reason, gains unqualified praise. Phantastes is prone to illusion, and Eumnestes to debility and decay. Reason's central position between the other two suggests the superiority of his controlling power, and in his chamber are represented all the civic and social achievements Spenser normally associates with order and progress:

75 *Mythologiae*, 2 vols (Frankfurt, 1584), I, 296.
76 *De Inventione*, II. liii. 160.

Of Magistrates, of courts, of tribunals,
Of commen wealthes, of states, of pollicy,
Of lawes, of iudgements, and of decretals;
All artes, all science, all Philosophy,
And all that in the world was aye thought wittily. (53)

Surprisingly, it is in this chamber too, and not in that of Phantastes, that 'famous Wisards' are depicted. The 'foresight' of seers such as Merlin is being distinguished from,

Deuices, dreames, opinions vnsound,
Shewes, visions, sooth-sayes, and prophesies;
And all that fained is, as leasings, tales, and lies. (51)

Phantastes enjoys 'sharpe foresight' but remains a textbook melancholic with 'sharpe staring eyes,/That mad or foolish seemd' (52). The repetition of 'sharpe' suggests how closely his strengths are allied to his weaknesses. His 'idle thoughts' rush about his chamber like a swarm of restless bees and the overall impression is one of frantic bewilderment. Generally speaking, throughout *The Faerie Queene*, the connotations of fantasy are bad. Phaedria, for example, has a 'fantasticke wit' (II. 6. 7), and the masque of Cupid is a pageant of disturbing 'phantasies' (III. 12. 26). By contrast, in displaying his 'spirite' to Britomart and Glauce, Merlin seems a model of rationality (III. 3. 21), yet 'of their comming well he wist afore' (15). He shares the 'sharpe foresight' of Phantastes, but not his confusion. Only at the end of his prophecy, as he looks beyond the Tudor dynasty, in an 'halfe extatick stoure' does he display the sort of behaviour Phantastes exhibits. This is directly in keeping with Plato's concept of the role of reason in prophetic insight:

> No man, when in his wits, attains prophetic truth and inspiration, but when he receives the inspired word, either his intelligence is enthralled in sleep or he is demented by some distemper or possession. And he who would understand what he remembers to have been said, whether in a dream or when he was awake, by the prophetic and inspired nature, or would determine by reason the meaning of the apparitions which he has seen, and what indications they afford to this man or that, of past, present, or future good and evil, must first recover his wits[77]

As he peers beyond Elizabeth, Merlin reaches the limits of rational interpretation and may go no further. He begins to experience visions his mind cannot yet encompass. Like the dream vision of Isis Church, the workings of

77 *Timaeus* (7le-72a), translated by Jowett in Hamilton and Cairns, pp. 1194-5.

the fantasy, considered solely in themselves, are perplexing and confused. Britomart's dream requires rational interpretation and becomes meaningful only in the light of its subsequent explanation. As Plato put it, 'it is customary to appoint interpreters to be judges of . . . true inspiration. Some persons call them prophets being blind to the fact that they are only the expositors of dark sayings and visions, and are not to be called prophets at all, but only interpreters of prophecy'.[78] Merlin is a true 'prophet' since he both sees and interprets visions, but in Isis Church the true prophet is Britomart herself. Similarly in book one Contemplation serves to interpret George's vision of the New Jerusalem and explain its significance to his present state. Without such informed exposition 'foresight' takes on the perplexing, and even malign, characteristics of the prophecies in *Macbeth*, 'that palter with us in a double sense' (V. 8. 20). A good example of this in Spenser's poem is the wholly misleading prediction delivered — significantly by Proteus — to Marinell's mother:

> So tickle be the termes of mortall state,
> And full of subtile sophismes, which do play
> With double senses, and with false debate,
> T'approue the vnknowen purpose of eternall fate. (III. 4. 28).

In its early stages the Marinell episode seems more closely related to the ethos of Greek tragedy than Christian providence, but the final outcome re-establishes the proper perspective.

The first chamber of the mind is of positive value only in relation to the contemplative cast of the second. Phantastes is beset by a chaos of illusory or conflicting visions but Reason sits meditating in tranquil composure 'right wise, and wondrous sage'. Properly speaking his temporal sphere is that of 'things present' but in practice he utilizes the insights of memory and foresight. Whereas the other two seem limited to a single dimension of time he appears to harmonise all three. In fact, as Spenser depicts him, he resembles the Aristotelian virtue of Eubolia or Good Counsel, a virtue associated with, but technically distinct from, prudence.[79] He can 'best aduize' of present affairs and has 'growne right wise' through the 'continuall practise and vsage' of meditation. No less than prudence itself, Good Counsel was regarded as spanning all three dimensions of time. Richard Hooker described the position very well when he asserted that 'in matter of consultation, we account them wisest, to whom through experience, the most approved principles of action

78 *Ibid.*, p. 1195. For the importance of reason see also Paul Oskar Kristeller, *The Philosophy of Marsilio Ficino*, translated by Virginia Conant (Gloucester, Mass., 1964), p. 313.

79 *Ethics*, 1142a-b.

are so familiarly known, and by particular notice the matter whereof they deliberate so thoroughly seen into, that having considered both the one and the other, they are able to forecast the surest effects that causes subject to so great variety will in likelihood of reason bring forth'.[80] One must distinguish, of course, as Plato did, between the special foresight of prophetic inspiration and the mind's innate power of planning for the future.[81] In Spenser's presentation, however, they are closely related and reason is central to both alike. For Britomart, Merlin is both 'prophet' and counsellor, and in accordance with his prophetic visions, rationally explained, she affirms her resolve to pursue the quest, leaving his cave, 'well instructed . . . of all, that needed . . . to be inquird' (51). The positive value of both types of foresight lies in the rational direction of 'things present'. Perhaps nowhere is the moral function of man's use of time so strongly insisted upon, and for good reason: the three dimensions of prudence were often held to reflect the influence of the Trinity.[82] According to Sir Walter Raleigh, 'Prouidence is . . . deuided into Memorie, Knowledge, and Care: Memorie of the past, Knowledge of the present, and Care of the future; and wee our selues account such a man for prouident, as, remembering things past, and obseruing things present, can by iudgement, and comparing the one with the other, prouide for the future, and times succeeding'.[83] The prudent man is 'provident' resembling his God since every truly moral action partakes of the three aspects of time. During his encounter with Malegar, for example, Arthur pauses to evaluate his present condition, recalls what he has learned of his opponent's nature, and deduces that only the waters of the standing lake will destroy him.

In the world of art, the 'poet historical' sits like Reason between Phantastes and Eumnestes 'recoursing to the thinges forepaste, and diuining of thinges to come'. Dealing with the distant past in the light of Tudor politics, *The Faerie Queene* is future-orientated in the sense that Arthurian heroism is as much an ideal towards which Britain must strive as an image of past glory. While making no specious claim to prophetic foresight, Spenser assumes the role of good counsellor both here and in his treatise on Ireland. According to Philip Sidney, heroic poetry is 'the best and most accomplished kinde' because the 'loftie image of such Worthies most inflameth the mind with desire to be worthy, and informes with counsel how to be worthy'.[84] *The Faerie Queene* is designed to inspire commitment to the sort of imperial

80 *Works*, edited by John Keble, seventh edition, 3 vols (Oxford, 1888), II. 560.

81 *Timaeus*, 72a.

82 Edgar Wind, *Pagan Mysteries in the Renaissance*, second edition (London, 1967), pp. 261-2. See below p. 100.

83 *The History of the World* (London, 1614), p. 15.

84 *Elizabethan Critical Essays*, I, 179. For Spenser's very similar views see *Prose*, pp. 124-5.

undertakings detailed in the *View*. One might almost say that the poetic vision of Irena and Artegall is interpreted in the treatise. In book five also, in a passage strongly reminiscent of Virgil's famous address to the Romans (*Aeneid* 6, 851-3), Spenser condemns his contemporaries for failing to colonise the New World thereby frustrating their own national destiny:

> But this to you, O Britons, most pertaines,
> To whom the right hereof it selfe hath sold;
> The which for sparing litle cost or paines,
> Loose so immortall glory, and so endlesse gaines. (IV. 11. 22)

The civic attainments of Britons and Fays have begun to diverge. Ideally, however, Elizabeth's own reputation contrasts strikingly with that of Burbon (Henry IV) and Geryoneo (Philip II) whose lawless imperial ambitions have destroyed them,

> Witnesse may *Burbon* be, whom all the bands,
> Which may a Knight assure, had surely bound,
> Vntill the loue of Lordship and of lands
> Made him become most faithlesse and vnsound:
> And witnesse be *Gerioneo* found,
> Who for like cause faire *Belge* did oppresse,
> And right and wrong most cruelly confound:
> And so be now *Grantorto*, who no lesse
> Then all the rest burst out to all outragiousnesse. (V. 12. 2).

This moment of 'witnessing' is characteristic of a poem which frequently freezes the temporal progress of the romance and the history it 'shadows' to dwell upon the timeless significance of the moral *exemplum*. As such insights are snatched out of time, the 'Book of Fame' becomes a moral directory. It is in this sense that Clio, the Muse of history, is asked to enroll Elizabeth's ancestors in the 'great Volume of Eternitie' (III. 3. 4). Despite the erosion of human records evidenced in the chamber of Eumnestes, the registers of providence remain impervious to time and decay. The 'immortall booke of fame' which serves to 'eternize' the names of those who support Cleopolis (I. 10. 59) is effectively identified by Guyon's Palmer with the 'heauenly Registers' of the elect (II. 1. 32), the Book of Life mentioned so often in Revelation. To regard fame as the ultimate goal of the quest is to limit Spenser's intention unduly.[85] The books of the poem are entitled 'Legendes', a term, as Drayton pointed out, anciently used 'in an Ecclesiastical sense, and

85 Isabel Rathborne, *The Meaning of Spenser's Fairyland* (New York, 1937), pp. 142-3.

restrained therein to things written in Prose, touching the Lives of the Saints'. He fully approved of Spenser's transference of the word from prose to verse on the grounds that the 'Argument of his Bookes' is 'of a kind of sacred Nature' comprehending 'things as well Divine as Humane'.[86] Properly understood, there need be no incompatibility between personal honour and the service of God. Sainthood is the perfect expression of their synthesis, the 'blessed end' ordained for the elect and the Christian equivalent of the deification of classical heroes.[87] Thus, making a 'pleasing analysis' of past, present, and future, Spenser attempts to interpret 'the truth of a foolish world' in the light of the spiritual reality beyond it.[88]

The romance narrative constitutes a gigantic temporal labyrinth through which the questing knights make an uneasy and uncertain way towards a mysterious, elusive centre. Despite their difficulties and disappointments, the implication of the work's total structure, of which book one serves as a convenient paradigm, is that a final resolution of its manifold complexities will ultimately emerge according to the old adage that truth is the daughter of time. Examinations of the traditional iconography used to illustrate this principle — Father Time, opposed by a winged monster, releasing a young lady from imprisonment in a cave — have demonstrated how time takes on a Christlike nature, effecting the rescue in a manner reminiscent of the Harrowing of Hell.[89] George's championship of truth against the dragon of Hell and Death is certainly suggestive of the traditional woodcuts, and the wayfaring Una has aptly been described as 'a picture of truth wandering in unredeemed time'.[90] Since she leads George back to Eden, of which her father is king, she is the daughter of time in more senses than one, and the episode constitutes perhaps the fullest possible development of St Paul's injunction to 'redeem the time' (Ephesians 5:16). However, we are seldom allowed forget that George is an English knight whose championship of truth stems from his devotion to Christ *and* Gloriana. It is a very patriotic Apocalypse to which we draw near. During the sixteenth century both Mary Tudor and Elizabeth were variously cast as truth or truth's deliverer, and one can detect a strong element of this in Spenser's poem.[91] Elizabeth herself was to be compared to George in Gerard de Malynes *Saint George for England* (1601),

86 *Works*, edited by J.W. Hebel, 5 vols (Oxford, 1961), II, 382.

87 Ernst Robert Curtius, *European Literature and the Latin Middle Ages*, translated by Willard R. Trask (London, 1953), pp. 167-70.

88 Sidney, *Apology for Poetry* in *Elizabethan Critical Essays*, I, 170.

89 Fritz Saxl, 'Veritas Filia Temporis', in *Philosophy and History: Essays presented to Ernst Cassirer* (Oxford, 1936), pp. 197-222 (p. 204).

90 Catherine Rodgers, *Time in the Narrative of 'The Faerie Queene'*, Salzburg Studies in English Literature (Salzburg, 1973), p. 35.

91 Saxl, pp. 206-210. For Elizabeth as Una see Robin Headham Wells, *Spenser's 'Faerie Queene' and the Cult of Elizabeth* (London, 1983), pp. 29-51.

and there is an intriguing posthumous depiction of the queen 'as a St George figure vanquishing the hydra [presumably Rome] and liberating Truth from her cave'.[92] Elizabeth was fond of representing herself as the child of providential time, and her 'mystical marriage' to her kingdom is imaged both in Una's marriage to George and, in the larger world of romance, Arthur's intended alliance with the Fairy Queen.[93] In all such cases the underlying order of affairs fosters a mood of optimism and enhances the value of human endeavour.

It is by perceiving such patterns and projecting them into the future that the poet himself shares the 'sharpe foresight' of the prophet and that Mt Parnassus may be compared with Mt Sinai (I. 10. 53-4). To the extent that poetic inspiration resembles the 'extatick stoure' of Merlin and his kind, the poet may be termed *vates*, 'which is as much as a Diuiner, Fore-seer, or Prophet'.[94] In Plato's *Phaedrus* the discussion of prophetic madness leads directly to the inspired madness of the poet, 'glorifying the countless mighty deeds of ancient times for the instruction of posterity'.[95] Similarly for Neo-platonists such as Ficino, true poetic inspiration was closely allied to the prophetic vision which 'comprehends the three parts of time in one'.[96] Like a prism, Spenser's allegory resolves providential illumination into the three primary shades of human perception: past, present and future. The timeless Platonic 'idea' of eternity can be articulated only through the rhetoric of tense. Merlin's narrative voice is indistinguishable from that of Spenser. Britomart meets her creator in the enchanted cave.

92 *Saint George for England*, sigs. A2-A3, reproduced in *Spenser Allusions in the Sixteenth and Seventeenth Centuries, 1580-1700*, edited by William Wells, 2 pts (Chapel Hill, 1971-2), I, 84. Roy C. Strong, *Portraits of Queen Elizabeth I* (Oxford, 1963), pp. 156-7.

93 For Elizabeth's 'marriage' see William Camden, *The History of the Most Renowned and Victorious Princess Elizabeth*, edited by Wallace T. MacCaffrey (Chicago, 1970), pp. 29-30.

94 Sidney, *Apology* in *Elizabethan Critical Essays*, I, 154.

95 *Phaedrus* (244a-245b), translated by R. Hackforth, in Hamilton and Cairns, p. 492.

96 Kristeller, p. 312.

CHAPTER TWO

'Wicked Time'

> Wicked *Time*, who with his scyth addrest,
> Does mow the flowring herbes and goodly things,
> And all their glory to the ground downe flings,
> Where they doe wither, and are fowly mard:
> He flyes about, and with his flaggy wings
> Beates downe both leaues and buds without regard,
> Ne euer pittie may relent his malice hard.
>
> (III. 6. 39)

I. *Time as Destroyer*

Spenser was obsessed by the passage of time. From the boyhood verses contributed to John Van der Noodt's *Theatre for Voluptuous Worldlings* (1569) to the *Mutabilitie Cantos* he remains time's laureate. But time is thankless. Like fortune, with which it is often associated, it remains entirely impartial working equally against the beautiful and the ugly, the elect and the damned. Yet it is also the medium in which illusions are shattered and truth revealed.[1] The passage of time highlights the 'vanity' — to use one of Spenser's favourite words — of worldly success. As Northrop Frye points out, vanity was the term chosen by the translators of the Authorised Version to render the Hebrew word 'hebel'. It thereby required 'a derived sense of "emptiness", the root meaning of the Vulgate's *vanitas.*' The author of Ecclesiastes therefore presents the notable paradox that, 'all things are full of emptiness'.[2] Spenser made that paradox his own and his writings present a depressing panorama of mortality and death, even by the standards of an age fascinated by the contrast between fleeting success and inevitable decay. Before ever we meet Prince Arthur, we are reminded of his death. His victories are past, and all that remains are the magic arms preserved in the Land of Faerie, and the fame kept alive by the labours of his poet (I. 7. 36). Ultimately even fame proves unreliable.

1 On these two aspects of time see Samuel C. Chew, *The Pilgrimage of Life* (Port Washington, New York, 1973 — first published 1962), pp. 12-22.

2 *The Great Code* (London, 1982), p. 123.

The classic expression of time's destructiveness is provided by Aristotle in the *Physics* when he asserts that,

> we are wont to say that time crumbles things, and that everything grows old under the power of time and is forgotten through the lapse of time. But we do not say that we have learnt, or that anything is made new or beautiful, by the mere lapse of time; for we regard time in itself as destroying rather than producing, for what is counted in time is movement, and movement dislodges whatever it affects from its present state.[3]

Christian Aristotelians might draw an appropriately spiritual conclusion, and from the end of the fifteenth century the traditional attitudes of the *contemptus mundi*, endorsed by scholasticism, were further reinforced by the teachings of the Florentine Neoplatonists for whom the realm of nature was 'a place of unending struggle, ugliness and distress, when contrasted with the celestial, let alone the supercelestial world'. Whereas on the one hand Neoplatonism lent a philosophical background to the aesthetic appreciation of beauty, it also promoted 'the unfathomable dissatisfaction' with the created universe which is the hallmark of the later work of Michelangelo.[4] Spenser does full justice to the productions of time both natural and man-made, and from this viewpoint the world of *The Faerie Queene* is one of exquisite landscapes and valiant heroes, a world with which the poet himself is 'nigh rauisht' (Proem VI. 1). Yet everything he depicts exists in a whorl of flux. The element of permanence and stability so important to the Medieval and Renaissance mind is nowhere to be found. Cleopolis may be a monument to the civic achievements of man but it too is subject to time.[5] Macrocosm and microcosm share the same ultimate fate, all that differs is the period of respite.

When Arthur and Guyon enter the House of Alma they are greatly impressed by the design of the fabric and their admiration is deserved. For a brief time they share the passion of the young Michelangelo for the beauty of the human form, 'all so faire, and fensible withall' (II. 9. 21). But 'fensible' cloaks a latent threat — 'No fort so fensible. . . . But that continuall battery will riue,/Or daily siege through dispuruayance long' (III. 10. 10) — and the materials of which the edifice is comprised are 'like to that *Aegyptian* slime,/Whereof king *Nine* whilome built *Babell* towre'. We dwell, Job reminds us, in 'houses of clay, whose foundation is in the dust' (4:19). The human body was fashioned from the 'slime' of the earth ('de limo terrae',

3 *Physics* (IV. 221a-b), translated by Philip H. Wicksteed and Francis M. Cornford, 2 vols (London, 1929-34), I, 403-5.

4 Erwin Panofsky, *Studies in Iconology*, revised edition (New York, 1962 — first pub. 1939), pp. 134, 180.

5 'Romance has no continuing city as its final resting place.' Northrop Frye, *The Secular Scripture* (Cambridge, Mass., 1976), p. 172.

Genesis 2:7) and ironically it is from this same slime that man constructs his monuments. Depending upon the nature of the men involved, the outcome may be either Cleopolis or Babel, civic order or civic chaos. In either case there is something pathetic in the attempts of living clay to achieve a vicarious immortality by fashioning inanimate clay to its own glory, and more pathetic still in the return of both to their original condition:

> But O great pitty, that no lenger time
> So goodly workemanship should not endure:
> Soone it must turne to earth; no earthly thing is sure.

The grim pun in the last line suggests that not even the primary elements are unassailable. The final solution can lie only in an escape from the succession and duration of time, essentially an escape into eternity.

From Verlame, the 'spoil of time', to Cleopolis, summit of earthly glory, the 'walled towne' (I. 1. 41) or city remained one of Spenser's most important symbols. Central to his view of history are the three great focal points of human civilization: the Troy of Homeric epic; Rome, the second Troy founded by the descendants of Aeneas; and London, or Troynovant, founded by the legendary Brutus. Cleopolis is none of these, but the perfect image of what all three aspired to be. Yet even Cleopolis is deemed inferior to the New Jerusalem, 'the Citie of the great king. . . . Wherein eternall peace and happinesse doth dwell' (I. 10. 55). In the final analysis, Malbecco's 'balefull mansion', perpetually in danger of collapse, and perpetually shaken by the 'roring billowes' of a 'boystrous' sea, comes to symbolise all temporal fortresses. Troy and Rome have become images of physical and moral corruption, and even should Troynovant, against all odds, fulfil its ultimate potential, perfection would nevertheless elude it. Meditation carries George beyond the temporal world of *The Faerie Queene* just as the *Visions of the Worlds Vanitie*, appearing as the poet begins 'to enter into meditation deepe', present him with images of earthly mutability *sub specie aeternitatis*. While man must live and work in the earthly city, he must also remain aware of its transitoriness. Such is the message of the very first sentence of St. Augustine's *City of God*, composed in response to the fall of Rome:

> Most glorious is and will be the City of God, both in this fleeting age of ours, wherein she lives by faith, a stranger among infidels, and in the days when she shall be established in her eternal home. Now she waits for it with patience, 'until righteousness returns to judgment' [Psalms 94:15]; then she shall possess it with preeminence in final victory and perfect peace.[6]

6 *The City of God*, translated by George E. McCracken, Loeb Classical Library, 7 vols (London, 1957-72), I (1957), p. 11.

The earthly city is rocked in the mobility of time ('temporali mobilitate') but the heavenly city is established beyond time through divine grace ('divina gratia'). For this reason, Lucifera's 'stately Palace . . . Whose wals were high, but nothing strong, nor thick' is crowned by a 'diall' which 'told the timely howres' (I. 4. 4). Since 'thriftlesse howres' characterize the lives of those within, 'timely' constitutes a piece of black humour (I. 5. 51). The sundial — or, possibly, the only mechanical clock in the Spenserian canon — is a 'diall of princes', in Sir Thomas North's phrase, for those who can interpret it aright.

Time, as man experiences it, is consequent upon the Fall. Since then, time is 'out of joint' and must, in the words of St Paul, be somehow 'redeemed' (Ephesians 5:16). There is much evidence in *The Faerie Queene* that Spenser's pervasive view of history, despite the scientific optimism of his contemporary Francis Bacon, is one of continual decline. The 'incorrupted Nature' of Eden (I. 11. 47) has suffered the 'curse' of the Fall which in practical terms is the curse of moral and physical mutability (VII. 6. 6-7). As a result, for example, Guyon and the Palmer see,

> Most vgly shapes, and horrible aspects,
> Such as Dame Nature selfe mote feare to see,
> Or shame, that euer should so fowle defects
> From her most cunning hand escaped bee;
> All dreadfull pourtraicts of deformitee. (II. 12. 23).

Nature has begun to produce its own antithesis. The Bower of Bliss corresponds to the 'blacke bowre of sorrowe' from which 'great Pan' attempts to save man in the September eclogue of *The Shepheardes Calender* (1. 97). In keeping with the Apocalyptic pessimism of the age, Spenser frequently suggests that such decline is both progressive and inevitable. The most notable instance is the proem to book five where the malaise affects the use of language, the 'instrument of society', thereby accelerating moral decay:

> For that which all men then did vertue call,
> Is now cald vice; and that which vice was hight,
> Is now hight vertue, and so vs'd of all:
> Right now is wrong, and wrong that was is right. (Proem, 4)

The complaint is double-edged since language remains the principal medium for the expression of our notions of time. The two would appear to have entered a state of mutual degradation. By corrupting language time effectively depraves manners which in turn pervert the 'times'. Hence Spenser's earlier point in associating human flesh with the tower of Babel. However facile such a viewpoint may now appear, a sobering indication of its centrality to Spenser's political and philosophical outlook is to be found in his treatise on Ireland where he attributes the degeneracy of the first Norman settlers to their progressive adoption of the Celtic language: 'the wordes are the Image of the minde So as they procedinge from the minde the minde must be nedes affected with the wordes So that the speache beinge Irishe the harte must nedes be Irishe for out of the abundance of the harte the tonge speakethe' (*Prose*, 119). Consequently, as the guardian of language, the poet is locked in a peculiarly personal battle with the forces of time. Ironically, however, his enemy is also his inspiration. Aesthetically speaking, time would be far less fascinating had it remained unfallen and Spenser is imaginatively complicit in the destruction he laments. His poem is as much satire as celebration and the two have a disconcerting habit of usurping one another's official function. There are moments when the heroes seem like vandals, moments when the villains shine. Wicked time makes for good verse.

II. *Golden Age and Fallen City*

Supporting his arguments with reference to Bodin, Gabriel Harvey complained that Spenser overlooked the claims of his own century by insisting that the 'Golden Age' formed part of a now irretrievable past:

> You suppose the first age was the goulde age. It is nothinge soe. Bodin defendith the goulde age to flourishe nowe, and owr first grandfathers to have rubbid thorowghe in the iron and brasen age at the beginninge when all thinges were rude and unperfitt in comparison of the exquisite finesse and delicacye, that we are growen into at these dayes.[7]

The tone of Harvey's letter is humorous and bantering yet it serves to illuminate a prevalent mode of Spenser's thought, the mode so vividly captured in *Colin Clovts Come Home Again* where the golden age of Elizabethan panegyric proves unable to survive the experience of the Elizabethan court. Of the many 'golden ages' evoked in *The Faerie Queene* none are permanent. Cleopolis is inferior to the New Jerusalem, time stalks the Gardens of Adonis, Calidore's pastoral paradise is destroyed by brigands and Meliboe, its rustic philosopher, is murdered. Earthly places where time appears to stand still prove dangerous. The Bower of Bliss is merely a Fools' Paradise though three times compared to Eden (51, 58, 70).[8] Its seductive 'Song of the Rose' tellingly rhymes 'time' with 'crime' (II. 12. 75). By choosing to remain with Acrasia, Verdant dissipates his precious youth,

7 *Works*, edited by A.B. Grosart, 3 vols (London, 1884-5), I, 146.

8 On the tradition of the false paradise see A. Bartlett Giamatti, *The Earthly Paradise and the Renaissance Epic* (Princeton, 1966) pp. 255-90.

retreating from the mainstream of time into a stagnant pool. Guyon functions to propel the inmates of the Bower back into the dynamism of the moral quest and ends the canto anxious to continue his journey, 'whilest wether serues and wind' (87). Similarly, by rescuing Amoret from the solipsistic world of the House of Busirane where time's endless repetitions take on the qualities of recurrent nightmare, Britomart releases her from an essentially unnatural timewarp. Spenser's insistent message is that any attempt to achieve permanence within a fallen world is destined to fail, a message which renders suspect the promise of 'perpetuall reformation' in Ireland through war and colonization. Much of the repressed psychological tension of *A View of the Present State of Ireland* is born of this intellectual impasse. Similarly, despite his constant praise of Elizabeth and his hopes for the future glory of England, Spenser's deeper neuroses call both in question. Having foretold the coming of the Virgin Queen in book three, Merlin becomes too emotionally disturbed to continue his prophecy — whether through excessive joy or excessive grief remains uncertain (III. 3. 50). In practical terms, of course, he could scarcely have gone much further since Spenser has reached his own time and is consequently as ignorant as his heroine, Britomart. He tactfully avoids nominating his choice of successor despite the obvious temptation afforded by the story-line. Nevertheless the poem has here reached a characteristic Spenserian crux. Vision ends in confusion and uncertainty since Merlin's limitations are those of the poet himself. Art cannot impose coherence upon reality: even within the world of romance narrative the subject of Ireland was, six years later, to prove virtually intractable.

In 1492, the year Columbus caught his first glimpse of the New World, Marsilio Ficino wrote to the mathematician Paul of Middelburg proclaiming the arrival of a new Golden Age. By way of evidence he adduced the revival of learning and the arts, the invention of printing, and the general ethos of optimism associated with the Humanist movement.[9] He was to be echoed many times during the sixteenth century. There was the Golden Age of Pope Leo X, of Francis II, of Charles V, of Philip II, of Henry IV, and of England's own 'Gloriana'. Yet running counter to all these trends was the insistence of the Reformers, particularly Calvin, upon man's innate depravity. Erasmus's treatise on the freedom of the will was answered by Luther's treatise on the will in bondage.[10] At the same time the early enthusiasm for the primeval innocence of the New World gave way to the more realistic appraisal of later travellers.[11] An apparent outpost of Eden came to be regarded as a savage

9 Harry Levin, *The Myth of the Golden Age in the Renaissance* (New York, 1969), pp. 38-9.

10 For the significance of this controversy see *Luther and Erasmus: Free Will and Salvation*, edited by E. Gordon Rupp and Philip S. Watson (London, 1969), pp. 1-32.

11 Hugh Honour, *The New Golden Land* (New York, 1975), pp. 53-8.

continent of bestiality and sin. In his famous essay 'Of the Cannibals' Montaigne contrasts the savagery and wildness of the New World with the stale, corrupt sophistication of the old. Neither emerges unscathed. The 'savage men' who cross the paths of the questing knights in *The Faerie Queene* reflect very similar attitudes on Spenser's part. His race of satyrs preserves Una for her beauty and grace but their admiration turns to idolatry and she fails to bring them to a recognition of the truth she represents. The savages of Book Six are marauding cannibals, yet some of their worst characteristics are all too evident in the behaviour of degenerate knights. The wild man who aids Calepine and Serena is recognised as a special case, a child of noble antecedents the secrets of whose history were doubtless to be revealed in some later book.[12] The literature of the New World can only have confirmed Spenser's opinion that the Age of Gold was long past. Like the early Church Fathers he appears to have identified it with the unfallen state of Adam. Predictably, Guyon draws his patterns of virtue from the 'antique world' which,

> in his first flowring youth,
> Found no defect in his Creatours grace,
> But with glad thankes, and vnreproued truth,
> The gifts of soueraigne bountie did embrace:
> Like Angels life was then mens happy cace. (II. 7. 16)

Mammon replies that Guyon must leave 'the rudenesse of that antique age/ To them, that liu'd therein in state forlorne' and become a man of his own time willing to 'engage' his life for gold. Thus the metal loses its symbolic significance and commercial values replace virtuous ideals. The new age of gold is the age of money.[13] In book four authorial didacticism endorses Guyon's arguments, rendering the moral doctrine even more uncompromising. One notes the recurrence of the term 'soueraigne' in both passages bespeaking the ideal, if unattainable, relationship between monarchy and first principles:

> But antique age yet in the infancie
> Of time, did liue then like an innocent,
> In simple truth and blamelesse chastitie,
> Ne then of guile had made experiment,
> But voide of vile and treacherous intent,
> Held vertue for it selfe in soueraine awe. (IV. 8. 30)

12 Isabel G. MacCaffrey, *Spenser's Allegory: The Anatomy of Imagination* (Princeton, 1976), p. 408.
13 Victor Harris, *All Coherence Gone* (London, 1966), p. 114.

According to the topos whereby names reveal nature — a staple of both biblical exegesis and secular allegory — the following stanza asserts that 'when the world woxe old, it woxe warre old/(Whereof it hight)'. The process of degeneration realises the destiny implicit in the name. The older it grows the more disastrously the world fulfils its dark potential. The 'dialectical' force of such etymologies is attested by Zachary Coke in *The Art of Logick* (1654) using an identical example: '*World* so called of *War-old*, because the older it is, the War or worse it is'.[14] The other meaning of 'warre' would not have escaped Spenser's notice: violence is the inevitable consequence of decline. The events of *The Faerie Queene* occur not in time's 'infancie' but in an age of forceful, violent heroes analogous to that which Hesiod interpolated into the traditional four ages of gold, silver, bronze, and iron in order to accommodate national pride.[15] Spenser provides an equivalent accommodation for Arthurian chivalry and, through the medium of historical allegory, for Tudor aspiration. His heroes operate in an age 'fruitfull' in 'rancknes' as do their Tudor antitypes.[16] Neither group is assured of success. Sir Walter Raleigh believed that 'good and Golden Kings make good and Golden Ages', but in the world of *The Faerie Queene*, as in that of sixteenth-century Europe, it is the *iron* man Talus who proves indispensable to the patrons of justice.[17] The Golden Age is incompatible with sinful time and man is doomed to inhabit a corrupt environment of which the fallen city is the supreme exemplar.

Time is associated with motion, change, and instability and, therefore, with the wheel of fortune. In *The Ruines of Time* the spirit of Verlame describes how she has become, 'the worlds sad spectacle, and fortunes scorne' while Spenser comments adversely in *The Faerie Queene* on Agape's desire to lengthen her sons' lives, 'knowing the miserie of their estate' (IV. 3. 1). Graphic illustrations of such attitudes are provided by the woodcuts of *A Theatre for Voluptuous Worldlings* to accompany which Spenser provided a series of epigrams translated from Du Bellay, later reproduced with minor variations in his volume of *Complaints*.[18] The theme of this section of the *Theatre* is the transitoriness and instability of temporal happiness. The woodcuts alternate between scenes of triumph and scenes of disaster in a sequence of antithetical images which must have left an indelible impression

14 *The Art of Logick* (1654), p. 77. Discussing the corruption of the clergy in the September eclogue of *The Shepheardes Calender* Diggon remarks, 'They sayne the world is much war then it wont' (108).

15 Giamatti, pp. 17-20.

16 Levin, pp. 14-5.

17 *The History of the World* (London, 1614), p. 155.

18 *A Theatre*, sigs. Bi^{v}-Dvi^{r}. For a full discussion of Du Bellay's work see Julia Conaway Bondanella, *Petrarch's Visions and their Renaissance Analogues* (Madrid, 1978), pp. 49-72.

on the mind of their schoolboy translator. The image of the triumphal arch in the fourth epigram, for example, may be regarded as the archetype of all the ill-fated triumphal buildings — such as the palace of Lucifera — which recur throughout *The Faerie Queene*. Its sudden destruction typifies the uncertainty of human aspiration at its most godlike:

> On each side purtraid was a Victorie,
> Clad like a Nimph, that wings of siluer weares,
> And in triumphant chayre was set on hie,
> The auncient glory of the Romaine Peares.
> No worke it seem'd of earthly craftsmans wit,
> But rather wrought by his owne industry,
> That thunder-dartes for *Ioue* his syre doth fit.
> Let me no more see faire thing vnder sky,
> Sith that mine eyes haue seene so faire a sight
> With sodain fall to dust consumed quight.
> (*Visions of Bellay*, 4)

That the arch should be Roman is most appropriate. Du Bellay's Rome symbolised both the splendour and the inevitable decay of the material world; in fact, '*Rome* was th'whole world, and al the world was *Rome*' (*Ruines of Rome*, 26). The 'eternal' city is the prey of time 'which all things doth devour':

> And though your frames do for a time make warre
> Gainst time, yet time in time shall ruinate
> Your workes and names, and your last reliques marre.
> (*Ruines of Rome*, 7)

Time is perhaps unique in creating the medium of its own action, but the phrase 'time *in time* shall ruinate' also implies the odd 'timeliness' of the devastation, recalling the play on death's 'timely' harvest in *The Shepheardes Calender*. Against this background Du Bellay explored the paradox of decline as evidenced in the monuments of the Roman past at once awe-inspiring and pathetic. He traces the cyclical progress of a group of insignificant shepherds' cottages through centuries of empire back to their 'first being' with the advent of the papacy, casting the pope in the traditional role of spiritual pastor. But there are greater cycles still into which even such momentous events are ultimately subsumed. The collapse of empire is merely an anticipation of Creation's inevitable return to its constituent elements:

> So when the compast course of the vniuerse

In sixe and thirtie thousand yeares is ronne,
The bands of th'elements shall backe reuerse
To their first discord, and be quite vndonne:
The seedes, of which all things at first were bred,
Shall in great *Chaos* wombe againe be hid.
(*Ruines of Rome*, 22)

For those of the Reformed outlook Rome held the additional fascination of being the seat of Antichrist, the great worldly Babylon presumptuously posing as the spiritual Jerusalem. As such, it could easily be presented as the supreme product of materialistic illusion. In Spenser's hands, therefore, Du Bellay's epigrams begin to develop associations never intended in the original.[19] To mention but one instance, the cyclical progress from shepherds to popes becomes grimly ironic. There is a central opposition in the world of *The Faerie Queene* between the forces of Roman Catholicism, enmeshed in the web of time, and those of Reformed Christianity, looking beyond the recurrent successions of temporal affairs to a timeless and changeless state of rest. This contrast is evident in the manner in which Duessa and Una first introduce themselves. Duessa '*was*, (O what now auaileth that I was!)/Borne the sole daughter of an Emperour' (I. 2. 22): self-indulgent nostalgia confounds an identity peculiarly vulnerable to the passage of time. By contrast, Una asserts an unalterable self-knowledge in the present tense:

The forlorne Maiden, whom your eyes haue seene
The laughing stocke of fortunes mockeries
Am th'only daughter of a King and Queene.
(I. 7. 43)

That 'am' is unmistakably emphatic, sharing something of the atemporal force of Revelation's 'I am he that liveth. . . . I am alive for evermore' (1:18). Spenser was disposed from his youth to see the matter in Apocalyptic terms. The poetic section of *A Theatre for Voluptuous Worldlings* ends with four 'Visions from Revelation' — perhaps by Spenser himself — the second and fourth of which contrast Augustine's two cities. The latter describes the 'holy Citie of the Lorde' just as St John imagined it, but the former concludes with the resounding assertion, 'Now for a truth great Babylon is fallen'.[20]

19 Alfred W. Satterthwaite, *Spenser, Ronsard, and Du Bellay: A Renaissance Comparison* (Princeton, 1960), pp. 93-112.

20 On the question of Spenser's authorship see *The Minor Poems*, II (Variorum edition), pp. 279-80, 611-627.

III. *Experience, Contingency and Despair*

The third woodcut accompanying the 'mutabilitie' sonnets of Van der Noodt's *Theatre for Voluptuous Worldlings* depicts a 'sharped spire/Of diamant' which upholds the ashes of a 'mightie Emperour' in a golden urn, 'the metall that we honour most'. When the spire collapses in a sudden storm thereby destroying the vicarious immortality of its anonymous owner the irony of the situation is heavy: it was indeed 'a worthie tombe for such a worthie corps'.[21] Nevertheless, the imagery recurs in the beautiful sonnets lamenting the death of Sir Philip Sidney with which Spenser chose to conclude *The Ruines of Time*. Here the ashes of the 'great Prince' are encased in a golden ark supported by a 'brazen pillour standing hie . . . for endles memorie/Of him, whom all the world did glorifie'. Earth and sky contend for the honour of possessing Sidney and the dispute is settled by the arrival of Mercury, messenger of the gods, who takes the ark 'aboue the skie' in order to confer a 'second life' upon the poet's ashes (659-672). Once again the speaker 'for dole was almost like to die' but his sense of loss is to be distinguished from his former sense of futility. The sonnet acknowledges Sidney's escape from time, but only in terms of an escape from the 'architecture' of earthly fame. Unless the 'ark' becomes the ark of the covenant, the poet's sepulchre remains as ostentatiously brittle as the emperor's.

The central event in Christian history facilitating the necessary transformation is that of the incarnation, the moment when the fusion of divine and human natures began the redemption of time: Nicodemus's apocryphal account of the Harrowing of Hell impressed its significance upon the religious mind. The difficulty, however, was that the effects of the incarnation were not immediately perceptible in the course of 'redeemed' history which remained subject to the curse of contingency. The issue is raised in the 'Briton Moniments' examined by Prince Arthur in the House of Alma. In many respects these chronicles make depressing reading since all the vicissitudes of misfortune are there. The stanza relating to Cymbeline brings us to the birth of Christ:

> Next him *Tenantius* raigned, then *Kimbeline*,
> What time th'eternall Lord in fleshly slime,
> Enwombed was, from wretched *Adams* line
> To purge away the guilt of sinfull crime:
> O ioyous memorie of happy time,
> That heauenly grace so plenteously displayd;
> (O too high ditty for my simple rime.)
> Soone after this the *Romanes* him warrayd;
> For that their tribute he refusd to let be payd. (II. 10. 50)

21 *A Theatre*, sigs. Ci^v-Cii^r.

'What time th'eternall' is virtually oxymoronic and 'fleshly slime' consciously recalls the fabric of both the House of Alma and its corrupt counterpart, the Tower of Babel. Miraculously, two contrary dimensions of existence intersect through the medium of 'grace'. As in the 'Song of the Rose' the rhyme again associates 'time' with 'crime' but to a wholly different effect since the emphasis now falls upon time's purgation. Thus the very source of corruption is made to yield is own antidote. Nevertheless, celebration is tempered by the sombre resonance of the vocabulary. Christ appears in a 'happy time' of 'ioyous memorie', 'ioyous' in a strictly spiritual sense for the elect but not necessarily for others and certainly not for Cymbeline who finds himself embroiled in a war with Rome. The stanza is well structured to convey the conflicting sensations of its message. We start unremarkably as if the list of kings is to continue unbroken. Two are named in the first line and a third recalled in the first two words. As the stanza begins, time is proceeding rapidly along its appointed course when suddenly eternity intervenes in a strangely ambivalent way. From one point of view the incarnation is just another temporal event ('What *time* . . .') and the nature of our 'fleshly slime' is not noticeably altered by the advent of the Messiah, indeed it appears all the more loathsome in comparison. A sense of claustrophobia is evoked by the process of 'enwombing', and the 'wretchedness' of the whole 'line' stretching back to the time of Adam is particularly stressed. Lines 3-6 celebrate the intervention of God just as the poet turns to tell us that this is not his present theme. The aesthetic experience of reading the account is made to represent the historic experience. We might have expected the incarnation to be the subject of many stanzas just as we might have expected — as many Millenarians did — a perceptible change in the pattern of history. Neither is the case. History, like the poem, moves remorselessly on. 'Soon after' the birth we return to the ordinary course of temporal affairs. Not Christ but Caesar's tribute preoccupies the concluding couplet.

Nonetheless a new era had begun, an era commonly regarded as a mere prelude to Doomsday.[22] As the sixteenth century moved to its close the sense of impending dissolution intensified. So many certainties had been shaken during the past hundred years that events seemed to have reached a critical stage. Foxe's sense of sudden insight at the discovery of the dreaded Antichrist beneath the papal robes is typical of this experience.[23] Originally Luther

22 Don Cameron Allen, 'The Degeneration of Man and Renaissance Pessimism', *Studies in Philology*, 35 (1938), 202-27 (pp. 213-4).

23 'For who would ever have judged or suspected in his mind, the bishop of Rome (commonly received and believed, almost of all men, to be the vicar and vicegerent of Christ here on earth) to be antichrist, and the great adversary of God, whom St Paul so expressly prophesies of in these latter days to be revealed by the brightness of the Lord's coming, as all men now for the most part may see it is come to pass?' *The Acts and Monuments of the Church*, edited by M. Hobart Seymour (London, 1838), p. 499.

had paid only scant attention to the Book of Revelation but, forced to defend his position against persistent Catholic attacks, he became increasingly aware of its usefulness in theological debate.[24] The notion that the events described symbolically by St John were being realised in their own lifetimes held obvious attractions for the Reformers, adding a sense of urgency to their endeavour by allowing them to cast contemporary occurrences of an otherwise undistinguished character in dramatically universal terms. Such, at least, was the broad social view, but for individual Christians the difficulty lay in assessing the nature of their true allegiance in the light of a personal experience likely to prove just as frustrating and disillusioning as that of the non-elect, and perhaps even more so. It is Mammon's daughter Philo*time*, the dispenser of worldly honour, who, as the covert pun in her name suggests, is the poem's great lover of time. A similarly submerged time-pun undercuts the 'honour' of Arthur's squire *Tim*ias.

The tardiness of Doomsday — as if the final pageant wagon had gone astray — lent encouragement to the vicious, even as it disheartened the godly. In old age knights might become hermits (I. 10. 64) but in the meantime desire for spiritual peace had somehow to be accommodated to the debilitating expense of militant energy. The psychological trick was to despair of all but grace (I. 10. 21); the moral danger was despair of grace itself. Both Christianity and Neoplatonism posed the difficult problem of the choice between the active and the contemplative life — in medieval terms the choice between the chivalric and the monastic code. Although the Reformers held monasticism in disrepute, they acknowledged the need for spiritual reflection with the result that a blending of the two life-styles came to be regarded as the ideal. At the outset of book one St George has chosen the active life but his spirit is weak and he plunges headlong into a series of disasters. During his debate with Despair only the promise of his predestined election restores his confidence: 'why shouldst *thou* then despeire, that *chosen* art?' (I. 9. 53).

Despair argues that the active life is rendered futile by the imperfections of its human agents since sin is inevitable in a fallen world. Drawing upon George's personal experience, he exploits the Calvinist doctrine of man's innate depravity and the consequent insufficiency of supposed 'good works':

> Witnesse the dongeon deepe, wherein of late
> Thy life shut vp, for death so oft did call;
> And though good lucke prolonged hath thy date,
> Yet death then, would the like mishaps forestall,
> Into the which hereafter thou maiest happen fall. (I. 9. 45)

24 Norman Cohn, *The Pursuit of the Millennium* (London, 1957), pp. 80-1, 242-3.

In urging George to commit suicide he appeals from the 'weariness' of the quest, the lassitude and frustration felt by all Spenser's heroes, to the 'eternall rest' of the dead. Logically the argument is self-contradictory, but its appeal is primarily emotional, designed to intensify George's sense of depression. Gradually he is led to number himself among the damned, amongst those predestined to destruction before world or time existed. As Calvin defined it, predestination is,

> God's eternal decree, by which he compacted with himself what he willed to become of each man. For all are not created in equal condition; rather, eternal life is fore-ordained for some, eternal damnation for others. Therefore, as any man has been created to one or the other of these ends, we speak of him as predestined to life or to death.[25]

The self-destruction of one 'predestined . . . to death' could, therefore, be regarded as a manifestation of the eternal will fulfilled in created time:

> Is not his deed, what euer thing is donne,
> In heauen and earth? did not he all create
> To die againe? all ends that was begonne.
> Their times in his eternall booke of fate
> Are written sure, and haue their certaine date. (I. 9. 42)

With the fatalism which serves as the hallmark of the poem's villains, Despair argues that for George this critical moment has now arrived.[26] This is the infamous 'devil's syllogism' attacked by Luther and a host of English Reformers from Latimer onwards. It is the syllogism employed by Marlowe's Faustus as he argues himself out of salvation.[27] If time cannot be 'redeemed' by good works it cannot be redeemed at all, 'let none aske whence, or why'. Despair's strongest argument is George's own experience of the vicissitudes of the quest. There is nothing in George's life, no special mark of approval or favour, that might lead him to suspect that his opponent is wrong — quite the contrary, 'witnesse the dongeon deepe'. Despair perverts the practice of spiritual 'witness' (1 John 5:9) in order to undermine George's confidence and posit a world-order guided solely by 'fickle fortune', a world in which George owes his continued survival to 'good lucke'. This was one of the great dangers of the Reformed viewpoint since distrust in providence led ultimately

25 *Institutes of the Christian Religion*, translated by Ford Lewis Battles, edited by John T. McNeill, Library of Christian Classics, 2 vols (Philadelphia, 1960), II, 926.

26 Susan Snyder, 'The Left Hand of God: Despair in Medieval and Renaissance Tradition', *Studies in the Renaissance* 12 (1965), 18-59 (pp. 23-4, 33, 41-2).

27 *Ibid.* pp. 30-1.

to desperation. The psychology of Spenserian characters is largely determined by their attitude to time:

> for this is a real wrestling school in which God tests our faith, for every day obstacles arise to impede His counsel up and down through all creation. What then is to be done? If only faith will ascend to the level of divine power, it will without great trouble overcome all agents that seem to oppose it.[28]

In the House of Holiness George is aptly referred to as 'the man that would not liue' (I. 10. 27), and the problem of despair and suicide is one which recurs throughout the poem. Perhaps the most remarkable instance, and the one which affects modern readers most forcefully, is the fate of Spenser's Cordelia. In this version of events Cordelia succeeds in defeating her sisters and in restoring Lear to the throne. Her 'entire affection' would, therefore, appear to have been rewarded and after Lear's death she reigns 'peaceably' for many years, 'and all mens harts in dew obedience held'. Finally, however,

> her sisters children, woxen strong
> Through proud ambition, against her rebeld,
> And ouercommen kept in prison long,
> Till wearie of that wretched life, her selfe she hong.
> (II. 10. 32)

Not merely do the forces of evil triumph, but their virtuous counterparts are led to self-destruction, unable to make sense of history. Cordelia grows so 'wearie' of the 'wretched' passage of time that she finally seeks release in death. Arthur finds George in much the same mental state: 'O who is that, which brings me happy choyce/Of death . . . O welcome thou, that doest of death bring tydings trew' (I. 8. 38). Such is the 'happy' choice — with a possible pun on 'hap' as misfortune — despair affords, and were it not for Una's insistence upon the positive aspect of predestination, transforming the fatalism of doom into the fatalism of salvation, George would undoubtedly have shared Cordelia's tragedy. Indeed, it is notable that Una snatches the knife from his hands, thereby making it physically impossible for him to kill himself, *before* she begins to reason with him.

The figure of despair would be familiar to Spenser's readers from the tradition of the morality play. Towards the end of Skelton's Magnyfycence, for example, just after the hero has declared himself 'wery of the worlde', Dyspare makes his entrance:

28 John Calvin, *Concerning the Eternal Predestination of God*, translated by J.K.S. Reid (Cambridge, 1961), p. 168 (see also pp. 165-7).

> Dyspare is my name, that Adversyte dothe felowe,
> In tyme of dystresse I am redy at hande;
> I make hevy hertys, with eyen full holowe.
> Of farvent Charyte I quenche out the bronde;
> Faythe and Good Hope I make asyde to stonde.
> In Goddys Mercy, I tell them, is but foly to truste;
> All grace and pyte I lay in the duste.[29]

Having brought Magnyfycence to admit that he cannot hope to merit the grace of God, he implies that he cannot receive mercy either. At this point he is joined by Myschefe who offers a choice between a knife and a halter. 'Have done at ones', says Dyspare, 'without delay'. As Magnyfycence is on the point of driving the knife through his breast, Good Hope snatches it from his grasp and begins to convince him of his error. The scene Spenser depicts was obviously a traditional one.[30] The crucial difference is that whereas Good Hope, as much an aspect of Magnyfycence's psyche as a divine gift, dispenses Christian counsel at great length, Una contents herself with a terse statement of George's election (I. 9. 53). Hope is the gift of a later canto.

Time's deadliest ally is the morbid psychology generated by man's experience of its apparently absurd transience. Thus, in an even more basic sense than St Augustine intended, time 'exists' within the human mind. Despair's dagger is closely akin to time's scythe, his cave is merely one of the darker caverns of George's skull. Appropriately it remains unclear whether stanza 42 (the subject of which is the vexed question of providential control of human 'times') forms part of despair's argument or George's reply. The two figures are becoming indistinguishable. Despair can slay itself only in George's person.

Despair is born of the inability to fathom contingency. Amavia, for example, commits suicide following her husband's death unable to reconcile herself to divine will. Guyon finds her, 'with feeble hands . . . stretched forth on hye,/As heauen accusing guiltie of her death' (II. 1. 49). Because she cannot find the meaning she wishes to find in life, she assumes none exists. Pondering her fall, Guyon is led to revile 'fortune, and too cruell fate' while at the same time distancing himself from the criticism of heaven which appears to Amavia to form the logical conclusion to such complaints. Temperance lends detachment opening up new perspectives upon Amavia's tragedy. She now emerges as an 'image of mortalitie/And feeble nature cloth'd with fleshly tyre' (II. 1. 57). The fault is hereby internalized: those

29 *Four Morality Plays*, edited by Peter Happé (Harmondsworth, 1979), p. 300.

30 Samuel S. Chew, 'Time and Fortune', *ELH*, 6 (1939), 83-113 (pp. 93-4); See also *Mankind* (804-10) in *Four Tudor Interludes*, edited J.A.B. Somerset (London, 1974) pp. 47-8.

'feeble' hands, robust in their own destruction, are self-disabled. Even so, Guyon refuses to condemn Amavia upon an act proceeding from 'anguish' rather than 'crime'. 'After death the tryall is to come' and Amavia, buried honourably despite the usual practice with suicides, is left to her 'eternall doome'. However, the whole tenor of *The Faerie Queene* is against her in its insistence upon the necessity for endurance. Later in the same book Impotence and Impatience both destroy themselves after the defeat of their champion Maleger thereby defining the qualities which led to Amavia's destruction. The desperate desire for death is perhaps the most intimate peril to confront the questing knights. A latent eroticism informs the dialogue with despair just as a latent violence informs the luxuriance of the Bower of Bliss. The agents of decadent time are invariably seductive and the poetry itself is frequently seduced. The tension hereby produced is not primarily dialectical but emotional: Spenser experiences rather than asserts the power of the great enemy. For a time he becomes its sponsor. But those times are amongst the most poetically powerful in the entire poem and from this turbulent paradox the epic draws its human strength.

Upon learning of the defeat of George, even Una, the personification of Truth, is led to desire the comfort of 'eternall night' complaining, almost in defiance of her allegorical role, of how the 'cruell fates the carefull threeds vnfold,/The which my life and loue together tyde' (I. 7. 22) — a harrowing image of the slow, painful unravelling of happiness as the frayed strands of life and love are pulled apart leaving nothing of significance behind. The ancient image of life as a tapestry was never better employed. Una has become the 'laughing stocke of fortunes mockeries' (I. 7. 43) and such 'griefe' commonly 'breedes despaire' (41). On this occasion it falls to Arthur to assert that, 'Despaire breedes not . . . where faith is staid'. By placing her faith in Arthur as the instrument of God's grace, Una recovers to see George 'redeemd . . . from bands' (I. 9. 1), and the opening of the tenth canto enforces the point that the victory is solely God's. As the knight who 'of his cheere did seeme too solemne sad' (I. 1. 2), George is temperamentally prone to depression from the outset, but such melancholy, as Robert Burton was later to argue, is symptomatic of the human condition. Despair's own attempt at suicide proves futile — he cannot be destroyed only abandoned. Many more will come to his cave, few will be elect.[31] Throughout the poem providential

31 One of the most astonishing suicides in the Spenserian canon occurs in *The Visions of Petrarch* a sequence of sonnets which had formerly appeared as 'epigrams' in *A Theatre for Voluptuous Worldlings*. Sonnets three and four tell of the destruction of a heavenly tree ('of Paradise/Some noble plant') and poetic spring ('Whereto approched not in anie wise/The homely shepheard, nor the ruder clowne;/But manie Muses') both of which seem eternal in their perfection. The 'rufull memorie' of the catastrophe wounds the speaker to the soul and his reaction is dramatised by the phoenix of sonnet five. Both in

theories of redemption fascinate Spenser in direct proportion to the difficulty of applying them to common experience. The narrative patterns of his work bespeak a mind constantly analysing, and even doubting, its own presuppositions and prejudices. Again and again the romance reintroduces complexity just at the moment when matters seem to be reaching a conclusion. Despair is endemic in the very structure of the form.

IV. *Time vs. Fame*

Epic poetry juxtaposes the brevity of life and the immortality of fame thereby enhancing the role of the poet as the celebrator of heroic virtue.[32] During the Renaissance, the opinions of Falstaff to the contrary, honour remained the cornerstone of the chivalric code, and praise the just reward or 'meed' of honour.[33] Theoretically, everyone agreed that virtue was its own reward: Calidore assures Artegall, for example, that a knight cannot become less honourable in himself for being publicly maligned. Nevertheless, Cleopolis, as its name suggests, is the city of fame (I. 10. 59) and in the modern sense of the term most of the poem's young knights are in the process of 'making their names' in Fairyland.[34] In the House of Alma Prays-desire is identified as Arthur's motive force, inextricable from his pursuit of Gloriana, 'glory' in Spenser's 'generall intention'. He rides with Guyon 'to hunt for glorie and renowmed praise' (III. 1. 3).

In Sidney's view the poet surpasses the work of the historian by inter-

Christian and pagan thought the phoenix was regarded as a symbol of immortality and resurrection, but here, 'spying the tree destroid, the water dride', it kills itself, 'as in disdaine'. The manner of the creature's death — piercing its breast with its beak — renders the passage a travesty of one of the most famous Renaissance emblems of the crucifixion, that of the pelican piercing its breast to feed its young on its blood. The significance of the phoenix is that it is both unique and immortal, periodically rising from its own ashes renewed and rejuvenated. Its wilful self-destruction upon encountering the vanities of time is therefore all the more remarkable. Despairing of the world, it rejects the eternal mutability of Adonis leaving the poet in sonnet seven to long for the 'happie rest' of death. This is the note upon which Spenser's volume of 'complaints and meditations' ends: 'When ye these rythmes doo read, and vew the rest,/Loath this base world, and thinke of heauens blis' (*Visions of Petrarch*, 7). On the phoenix as a symbol for the renewal of time see R. Van den Broek, *The Myth of the Phoenix* (Leiden, 1972), pp. 98-132. See below pp. 149, 154.

32 On the 'aeternitas' of fame as a poetic convention see Ernst Robert Curtius, *European Literature and the Latin Middle Ages*, translated by Willard R. Trask (London, 1953), pp. 476-7.

33 Jacob Burckhardt, *The Civilization of the Renaissance in Italy*, introduced by Benjamin Nelson and Charles Trinkaus, 2 vols (New York, 1958), I, 151-62.

34 Isabel Rathborne, *The Meaning of Spenser's Fairyland* (New York, 1937), pp. 45-59; Angus Fletcher, *The Theory of a Symbolic Mode* (New York, 1964), pp. 121-2; Thomas H. Cain, *Praise in 'The Faerie Queene'* (London, 1978), passim.

preting contingency in the light of the spiritual reality beyond it.[35] This is the doctrine to which Spenser adheres placing his own 'historicall fiction' squarely in the tradition of the 'antique poets historicall', Homer and Virgil, and invoking Clio wherever necessary.[36] For him, poetry is 'the Nourse of time, and euerlasting fame' (I. 11. 5) unrolling 'the records of antiquitie' (IV. 11. 10). It is in this sense that we must interpret Clio's lament in *The Teares of the Muses*. To the Muse of History it should matter little whether the deeds she chronicles are good or bad. The 'Briton Moniments' read by Prince Arthur record both, often with apparent indifference. Spenser is thinking of Clio specifically as she inspires the epic poet. It is the 'song' that matters:

> So shall succeeding ages haue no light
> Of things forepast, nor moniments of time,
> And all that in this world is worthie hight
> Shall die in darknesse, and lie hid in slime:
> Therefore I mourne with deep harts sorrowing,
> Because I nothing noble haue to sing.
> (*Teares of the Muses*, 103-8).

Calliope, not Clio, is the proper muse of heroic poetry but, as Lotspeich points out, in the Spenserian canon their functions are virtually identical, an assertion vindicated by the protracted and inconclusive controversy regarding the identity of the Muse invoked in the proem to book one.[37] There is no way of deciding between them and in *The Teares of the Muses* they lament two aspects of the same situation.

In the House of Alma, Arthur and Guyon discover both the power and the paradoxical weakness of man's collective memory. Entering the third chamber of the mind they encounter Eumnestes, an 'old oldman, halfe blind,/And all decrepit in his feeble corse',

> This man of infinite remembrance was,
> And things foregone through many ages held,

35 *Elizabethan Critical Essays*, edited by G. Gregory Smith, 2 vols (Oxford, 1904), I, 170.

36 Edwin B. Benjamin, 'Fame, Poetry, and the Order of History in the Literature of the English Renaissance', *Studies in the Renaissance*, 6 (1959), 64-84; S.K. Heninger, 'The Aesthetic Experience of Reading Spenser', in *Contemporary Thought on Edmund Spenser*, edited by Richard C. Frushell and Bernard J. Vondersmith (Carbondale, 1975) pp. 79-98.

37 Henry Gibbons Lotspeich, *Classical Mythology in the Poetry of Edmund Spenser* (Princeton, 1932), p. 84. Clio was often depicted iconographically with a trumpet 'to celebrate the achievements of famous men'. See Arthur B. Ferguson, *Clio Unbound: Perception of the Social and Cultural Past in Renaissance England* (Durham, North Carolina, 1979), p. 4.

> Which he recorded still, as they did pas,
> Ne suffred them to perish through long eld,
> As all things else, the which this world doth weld,
> But laid them vp in his immortall scrine,
> Where they for euer incorrupted dweld. (II. 9. 56)

This is the positive side of the picture, although we might well feel more encouraged were the sage not quite so decrepit nor his chamber so 'ruinous and old'. As it is, he appears to be perishing 'through long eld' himself, as time carries its relentless battle to the very heart of the forces opposing it. Even the comfort of the 'immortall scrine' is seriously impaired by the appalling condition of the manuscripts the visitors find scattered at random throughout the chamber 'some in long parchment scrolles,/That were all worme-eaten, and full of canker holes'.[38] These records are clearly inferior to the 'heauenly Registers' in which George's name is 'enrolled' amongst those of the saints (II. 1. 32).[39] A note of frustration, even of futility, is struck with the description of the sage 'tossing and turning' his books 'withouten end', constantly forgetting what he wants and constantly reminded by Anamnestes whose duty it is to find records 'lost' or 'laid amis'. There is an element of nightmare about the whole thing, as if we had suddenly entered the world of Beckett's *Endgame*. Which is exactly why poets are needed: to renew, perpetuate, and glorify, to ensure that the heroism of the past is not, as Calliope complains, 'all corrupted through the rust of Time'. Ideally she wishes to see 'the auncestrie/ Of th'old Heroes memorizde anew' (*Teares of the Muses*, 433-40). Thus the poet serves as the world's Anamnestes.

Proceeding directly from the Chamber of Memory to his own British chronicle, Spenser notes that the 'argument' is 'worthy of *Maeonian* quill', no less than Homeric grandeur is required (II. 10. 3). He is, therefore, fulfilling the task he identifies as the supreme labour of the epic poet. 'What odds', he had made Calliope ask,

> Twixt best and worst, when both alike are dedd;
> If none of neither mention should make,
> Nor out of dust their memories awake?
> (*Teares of the Muses*, 448-50)

As 'due praise' is 'the spur of doing well', it falls to her, the 'nurse of virtue' and 'golden trumpet of eternity', to 'deify' mortal men, to write the saintly 'legends' of which *The Faerie Queene* itself is comprised.

Spenser's most important statement of the poet's role as a purveyor and

38 Chew, p. 15.

39 On sainthood and fame see Curtius, pp. 167-70.

perpetuator of fame is to be found — ominously — in *The Ruines of Time*. There, while lamenting the phenomenon of universal decay, the spirit of Verlame pauses to consider the possibility that art may withstand the encroachments of age. Surrounded by ruins, she rejects the claims of architecture and sculpture — 'for how can mortal immortality give?' — in favour of poetry:

> All such vaine moniments of earthlie masse,
> Deuour'd of Time, in time to nought doo passe.
>
> But fame with golden wings aloft doth flie,
> Aboue the reach of ruinous decay,
> And with braue plumes doth beate the azure skie,
> Admir'd of base-borne men from farre away.
> (*Ruines of Time*, 419-24)

Only through fame can a man expect his memory to endure and only poetry can guarantee fame, 'poetry', that is, in the broad sense in which Sidney used the term. Oblivion is the fate of those who die unsung. Verlame's advice to the powerful is that they should patronise poetry in the hope of immortality. As daughters of Memory and Jove ('the father of eternity'), the Muses are uniquely empowered to lend mortals a share in the life of the gods:

> Then who so will with vertuous deeds assay
> To mount to heauen, on *Pegasus* must ride,
> And with sweete Poets verse be glorifide.
> (*Ruines of Time*, 425-7)

Particularly to be praised is Sir Francis Walsingham ('good Melibee') who 'hath a poet got/ To sing his living praises being dead'. In the work of Thomas Watson he will live 'in spite of enuy'. Such, at least, is the ideal, and its vigorous assertion in a poem which actively solicits patronage comes as no surprise. The matter is complicated, however, by the notion of poetry's own mortality.

Spenser faces this problem in the fourth book of *The Faerie Queene* when he turns to Chaucer as his source for the fable of Cambell and Triamond. The June eclogue of *The Shepheardes Calender* includes a lament for 'the God of shepheards *Tityrus*' (identified as Chaucer by E.K.) who taught Colin how 'to make', but consoles itself with the notion that whereas 'all hys passing skil with him is fledde' — particularly effective is the delicate ambiguity of 'passing' — his fame 'doth dayly greater growe' (ll. 81-92). Yet although the author of the *House of Fame* is himself 'on Fames eternall beadroll worthie to be fyled', the fact remains that not even his own works have escaped the ravages of time:

> But wicked Time that all good thoughts doth waste,
> And workes of noblest wits to nought out weare,
> That famous moniment hath quite defaste,
> And robd the world of threasure endlesse deare,
> The which mote haue enriched all vs heare.
> (IV. 2. 33)

In this case Spenser hopes to restore the supposedly lost *Squire's Tale* 'through infusion sweete' of the Chaucerian spirit which 'doth in me survive', but the problem remains. What guarantee is there that *The Faerie Queene* itself will survive? On his own admission it is less likely to do so than *The Canterbury Tales*. Verlame's confidence now seems strangely misplaced. It is not at all clear that poetry, any more than architecture or sculpture, lasts 'till the worlds dissolution' as the envoy to *The Shepheardes Calender* suggests. Indeed the proem to book four comments bitterly upon the poor reception of the poem's first instalment.

That Spenser was experiencing difficulty in completing *The Faerie Queene* is suggested in the *Amoretti* where he admits to Lodowick Bryskett that:

> Great wrong I doe, I can it not deny,
> to that most sacred Empresse my dear dred,
> not finishing her Queene of faery,
> that mote enlarge her liuing prayses dead.
> (Sonnet 33)

Should the poet fail, the striking oxymoron of line four may prove to be little more than a hollow rhetorical flourish, or worse still an ironic epitaph. Fame depends on feeble human talent and the poet is weary of 'tedious toil'. The question posed in *The Ruines of Time* — 'how can mortal immortality give?' — now applies itself to poetry also, and the surprising introduction of Colin Clout, Spenser's fictional *alter ego*, into the 'Legend of Covrtesie' heralds a striking demonstration of the fragility of art. In effect what Spenser has done is to create within his own imaginative world an image of the forces which sustain it. Calidore stumbles upon Colin as he achieves the zenith of aesthetic insight but since the Graces come of their own accord the shattered vision cannot be recalled. 'Vaine is the art that seekes it selfe for to deceiue' (IV. 6. 40).

The concentric circles of naked maidens, 'raunged in a ring, and dauncing in delight' (VI. 10. 11) resemble the concentric rings of the spheres as they 'dance' about the point of eternal rest. As the centre of Colin's emotional and poetic universe, his lady precariously occupies that still point until the illusion is destroyed. For a few brief moments the harmony of art reflects that of the universe. In the words of Plotinus:

> We are like a company of singing dancers, who may turn their gaze outward and away, notwithstanding they have the choirmaster for centre; but when they are turned towards him, then they sing true and are truly centred upon him. Even so we encircle the Supreme always, and when we break the circle, it shall be our utter dissolution and cessation of being; but our eyes are not at all times fixed upon the Centre. Yet in the vision thereof is our attainment and our repose and the end of all discord, God in his dancers and God the true Centre of the dance.[40]

Plotinus speaks not only of the order of the cosmic dance but also of the great difficulty in sustaining mortal concentration upon its focal point, and this is the problem which receives such dramatic illustration on Mt Acidale. The fragility of art is impressed upon us at the moment of its greatest triumph and the episode ends in lamentation.

In thus emphasising the ultimate vanity of art and fame, Spenser is contributing to a distinguished literary tradition. In Petrarch's *Trionfi* the 'Triumph of Death' is followed by the 'Triumph of Fame', but this in turn gives way to the 'Triumph of Time': 'And time dissolves not only visible things,/But eloquence, and what the mind hath wrought'.[41] Similarly in Stephen Hawes *Pastime of Pleasure*, Time disputes the claims of Fame to confer immortality upon mortals. Even in those instances where Fame is apparently successful it merely sustains itself *in time* and is therefore insecure:

> Withouten tyme is no erthely thynge
> Nature/fortune/or yet dame sapyence
> Hardynes/clergy or yet lernynge
> Past/future/or yet in presence
> Wherfore I am of more hye preemynence
> As cause of fame/honoure and clergy
> They can nothynge without hym magnyfy.[42]

40 *Enneads* (VI. IX. 8), as cited by Edgar Wind in *Pagan Mysteries in the Renaissance*, revised edition (London, 1958), p. 209.

41 *The Triumphs of Petrarch*, translated by Ernest Hatch Wilkins (Chicago, 1962), p. 100. Tudor translators especially emphasised time's hostility to fame. See Henry Parker, *The Triumphs of Petrarch* (1554), edited by Stafford Henry Earl of Iddesleigh (London, 1887), pp. 86-92.

42 *The Pastime of Pleasure*, edited by William Edward Mead, Early English Text Society (London, 1928), p. 218.

Like all his fellow men, the poet must come to terms with time admitting that the fame he confers is as insecure as the art through which he confers it.[43] As the 'Legend of Covrtesie' ends, Calidore muzzles the Blatant Beast in order to 'shut vp his blasphemous tong,/ For neuer more defaming gentle Knight' (34), but in marked contrast to book one this is a victory in which the poet cannot share. Unlike St George's dragon, the Blatant Beast is not destroyed but gets 'into the world at liberty againe' (38) either through 'wicked fate' or 'fault of men' — one remembers Artegall's earlier admonition that men blame their own folly on fate (V. 4. 28). Despite the efforts of all the knights 'borne in Britaine land' the Beast proves impossible to recapture. A reason for this is implied in the description of Detraction who, along with Envie, first introduces the Beast to the poem. As Spenser depicts her, she is a relative of 'griesly Lachesis' who grudgingly spins the slender threads of life in book four:

> A distaffe in her other hand she had,
> Vpon the which she litle spinnes, but spils,
> And faynes to weaue false tales and leasings bad,
> To throw amongst the good, which others had disprad.
> (V. 12. 36)

Apparently original to Spenser, this iconography serves to suggest that detraction and the infamy it occasions are all but inseparable from our mortal condition. If one accepts the Augustinian view that the past 'exists' only as memory, the erosion or distortion of its records, whether historical or poetic, becomes tantamount to the obliteration of epochs of human experience. The struggle for fame is a struggle for survival. But what of Spenser's own complicity with detraction? What of his skilful distortion of key aspects of Elizabethan policy in Ireland and Belgium, of his gross misrepresentation of the trial and death of Mary Queen of Scots which caused such deep offence to 'Gloriana's' heir?[44] Is it possible that Bonfont and Malfont are one and the same person seen from different political perspectives, a sense quite contrary to the conscious moral allegory (V. 9. 26)? Spenser's doubts are as integral to his 'vision' as his beliefs. His imagination is at once too penetrating and too sincere to betray complexity to dogma. In *The Faerie Queene* he not merely reflects the struggle between creativity and decay, he lives it. Thus the many failures in conscious intent prove artistically fascinating in their own right. The most intriguing quests are those that remain unresolved.

43 For similarly pessimistic attitudes towards fame in Montaigne and Fulke Greville, see Benjamin, pp. 81-2.

44 For further discussion see Richard A. McCabe, 'The Masks of Duessa: Spenser, Mary Queen of Scots, and James VI', *English Literary Renaissance*, 17 (1987), 224-42.

Just as book six nears its conclusion, the second last stanza suddenly reverts to the present tense transferring the Beast from its Arthurian setting to contemporary England (VI. 12. 40). The chronological time-sequence of the poem is shattered and the romance vision vanishes as disconcertingly as that of the Graces. Indeed, the collapse of private vision on Mt Acidale heralds the disintegration of public confidence. The Blatant Beast comes rampaging down the centuries and finds Spenser himself in his path. The poem affords no more dramatic demonstration of the relevance of its allegory, nor is there any equivalent in the epic tradition. The 'mirrour' of art cracks as the figures emerge into life. Despite all the celebration of heroic fame, it is the Beast that proves immortal.

CHAPTER THREE

'Iust Time'

> Most goodly glee and louely blandishment
> She to me made, and bad me loue her deare,
> For dearely sure her loue was to me bent,
> As when iust time expired should appeare.
> (I. 9. 14)

I. *The Arthurian Moment*

The movement of *The Faerie Queene* both in geography and time is backwards to the point from which we first set out. The last book, as Spenser tells us, is the beginning.[1] In order to give us 'as well the times as the actions' an historian would have begun with the annual feast of Gloriana and proceeded from there to the various quests. The poet, however, goes straight to the critical moment employing it as a focal point for his 'pleasing analysis' of past, present and future — 'pleasing' aesthetically because of the resulting artistic form, and 'pleasing' didactically because order is thereby imposed upon the chaos of life.[2] In Bacon's words,

> Because true history propoundeth the successes and issues of actions not so agreeable to the merits of virtue and vice, therefore poesy feigns them more just in retribution, and more according to revealed providence . . . And therefore it was ever thought to have some participation of divineness, because it doth raise and erect the mind.[3]

But Spenser's is the poetry of crisis proper. The formal disposition of his material into books of twelve distinct cantos belies its complexity just as the division of years into twelve calendar months ignores aberrant seasonal variations. Struggling to emerge through this conflict of form and matter, Spenser's 'pattern' needs some point of providential reference. An analogy may be drawn with biblical exegesis for much of which the moment of the incarnation provides the focal point for interpretation. Through various

1 *The Faerie Queene*, edited by A.C. Hamilton (London, 1977), p. 738.
2 See J.G.A. Pocock, *The Machiavellian Moment* (Princeton, 1975), p. 25.
3 Bacon, *Works*, III, 343.

techniques of typology it establishes 'recourse to the thinges forepaste' by fulfilling the prophecies and prefigurations of the Old Testament, while its centrality to Apocalyptic prophecy lends it a unique significance in the business of 'divination'.

The time of the poem's action has been chosen very carefully since Arthur is the legendary ancestor of Elizabeth whose 'most excellent and glorious person' is shadowed in the poem. Indeed, the 'Arthurian moment' is central to Spenser's conception of the progress of British history, providing it with a sort of secular incarnation. It is the moment towards which all of past history has been moving, Arthur providing the vital link between the primitive age of the giants and that of the Elizabethan court. Yet the Arthur of Spenser's poem is not the Arthur of the Chronicles, nor even the romance hero of *Arthur of Little Britain*, but the young Prince Arthur as yet ignorant of his own identity. Only on completion of these twelve adventures can be become the famous founder of the Round Table. Like George, he too is in the process of proving himself, of winning the glory he pursues. Spenser focuses, therefore, upon crucial moments of decision, upon that tide in the affairs of men which 'taken at the flood' leads on to greatness. In this he was typical of his age for, as Agnes Heller argues, 'during the Renaissance . . . the *whole value-content of action became a function of knowing the times*. The reason and purpose of action came to nothing if someone acted blindly in opposition to the concrete demands of the historical moment'.[4] Hence Glauce can advise Britomart: 'Daughter, I deeme that counsell aye most fit,/That of the time doth dew aduauntage take' (III. 3. 52).

According to this view, the secret of success lay in harmonising the rhythms of one's life with those of history. The critical 'moment' of decision could therefore span several years: 'the point in time is actually *an interval of time*'.[5] Nevertheless, the poem draws a sharp moral distinction between Glauce's perceptive advice and the Machiavellian intrigues of Burbon (Henry IV) who 'temporizes' with God in book five. Burbon plans to resume his Protestant faith 'when time doth serue', but to this attitude Artegall opposes the chivalric doctrine that 'knights ought be true, and truth is one in all' (V. 11. 56). Clearly when the 'aduauntage' sought is purely material and the hazard is faith, to 'temporize' is to prefer the products of time to those of eternity. With scathing irony Spenser describes Burbon's ambition as 'sacred', in the sense of accursed. Sir Turpine's obsession with the proper timing of his endeavours is of a similarly debased nature (VI. 7. 3-22).

The chronology of *The Faerie Queene* held many surprises for the con-

4 Agnes Heller, *Renaissance Man*, translated by Richard E. Allen (London, 1978), p. 175.
5 *Ibid.*, p. 179.

temporary reader.[6] The proem to book one asserts that the subject of the poem is the love of the great 'Briton Prince' for 'fairest Tanaquill'. Those who had read the 'Letter to Raleigh' would doubtless identify the prince with Arthur and the lady with Gloriana. They might even suppose the 'gentle knight' of the first stanza to be the poem's promised hero. As the canto proceeds, however, anyone familiar with medieval pageantry would easily deduce the identity of St George, a figure whose 'historical' existence was believed to precede that of King Arthur by about two hundred years. According to the best authorities, George suffered martyrdom in 303 A.D. whereas Geoffrey of Monmouth asserts that Arthur's death occurred in 542 A.D.[7] Neither the chronicles nor the romances associate the two, bringing them together in time and place was very much Spenser's invention. By thus telescoping the accepted historical chronology, he enabled himself to unite the two figures who epitomised the British nation, the patron saint of British Christianity and the founder of British chivalry. Remarkably it is the chivalric prince who saves or, as the poem has it, 'redeems' the saint: Spenser's analysis is conducted very much in the light of Tudor policy which effectively subordinates church to state. As the poem proceeds it becomes clear that George has been moved forward to the Arthurian period. Both Merlin and Artegall figure prominently in the Galfridian account and it was through the latter, Arthur's half-brother, that the Tudor line pretended descent. Tristram, the Questing Beast, and Britomart's father, King Ryence (King Royns) would all be familiar from Malory. For the purposes of Spenser's poem, George is a Saxon knight born of an 'ancient race/Of Saxon kings' who,[8]

> haue with mightie hand
> And many bloudie battailes fought in place
> High reard their royall throne in *Britane* land,
> And vanquisht them, vnable to withstand.
>
> (I. 10. 65)

In the 'Briton Moniments' Arthur reads how Vortigern introduced the Saxons to England in order to usurp his dead brother's throne by depriving his nephews of their rightful inheritance. The rest of the chronicle is pre-

6 For the general treatment of time in romances see Northrop Frye, *The Secular Scripture* (Cambridge, Mass., 1976), p. 136.

7 *The Catholic Encyclopaedia*, 16 vols (New York, 1907-1914), VI (1909), 453-5. *The History of the Kings of Britain* (XI. 2), translated by Lewis Thorpe (Harmondsworth, 1966), p. 261. All further references are to this edition.

8 'In S. *Georges* English birth the Poet followes the vulgar errour, of purpose, to fit his fabulous morall argument the rather'. Tristram White, *The Martyrdom of Saint George of Cappadocia: Titular Patron of England, and of the most Noble Order of the Garter* (London, 1614), sigs. A2r-v.

occupied with the continuing hostility between the two races right down to the age of Arthur's father, Uther Pendragon. George and Arthur should properly be enemies. Furthermore, the arms in which Britomart sets out from her father's castle are those of the Saxon Queen Angela whom Glauce has seen fighting against Uther at the battle of Menevia (III. 3. 55). These arms, we are told, were captured by the Britons in a raid just a 'few dayes' prior to Glauce's narration. Ironically, therefore, Britomart rides forth as the Saxon queen from whom the Angles take their name. The exact time of her departure is declared in some detail:

> Ye see that good king *Vther* now doth make
> Strong warre vpon the Paynim brethren, hight
> *Octa* and *Oza*, whom he lately brake
> Beside *Cayr Verolame*, in victorious fight,
> That now all *Britanie* doth burne in armes bright.
> (III. 3. 52)

Unfortunately this is somewhat less precise than it seems since Spenser has conflated two separate battles. The use of 'now' and the present tense indicates that the war is still in progress and that Octa and Oza (Geoffrey of Monmouth's Octa and Eosa) are still living. But Spenser adds that Uther 'lately brake' the Saxon leaders 'beside Cayr Verolame'. Herein lies the confusion. Uther fought two battles with Octa and Eosa, the first shortly after the battle of Menevia in which Angela was, on Glauce's evidence, one of the principal combatants. Victorious at Menevia, Uther learned of the death of his brother King Aurelius and succeeded to the throne. Turning his attention to the aggression of Octa and Eosa he defeated them after a hard-fought campaign at the battle of Mount Damen. The Saxon leaders were taken prisoner and incarcerated. This is the battle which Spenser erroneously located at 'Cayr Verolame' or St Albans. The next episode in Uther's career was his illicit passion for the wife of his ally King Gorlois which resulted in the birth of Prince Arthur.[9] Many years later Octa and Eosa escaped from prison, raised support on the continent, and returned to wreak a devastating revenge. This, therefore, is the current war to which Glauce refers, this is the troubled 'time' of which she urges her charge to take advantage. The chronology is perfect for Arthur and Artegall would then be the young adults the poem portrays. In Geoffrey's account Arthur's half-sister Anna is just old enough to be given in marriage. Uther's defeat of Octa and Eosa at St Albans resulted in their deaths and ended the war.[10] Spenser has mistakenly trans-

9 Geoffrey of Monmouth (VIII. 18-20), pp. 202-8.

10 *Ibid.*, (VIII. 21-23), pp 208-210. See the account of the siege in *The Ruines of Time* (113-9).

ferred the first battle to the scene of the second and foreshortened the intervening time. Otherwise one would have to suppose that the Saxon leaders survived the final battle despite the contrary evidence of the chronicles. Despite such difficulties, however, the intention remains clear. We are to understand that Britomart sets forth towards the end of the reign of Uther Pendragon while 'all *Britanie* doth burne in armes bright' as the aging king is struggling against the forces of Octa and Eosa for the second time. It is the 'moment' upon which the future of Arthurian Britain depends.

II. *Narrative Chronology*

According to the 'Letter to Raleigh', 'the Faery Queene kept her Annuall feaste xii dayes, vppon which xii seuerall dayes, the occasions of the xii seuerall aduentures hapned'. This would suggest a virtually simultaneous beginning of all twelve adventures at a single festival analogous to the twelve days of Christmas. However, the account given by Guyon suggests an annual feast of just one day, 'the day that first doth lead the yeare around' with a possible compliment to Elizabeth's Accession Day (II. 2. 42). One is then faced with the implication that the adventures may have begun upon successive years, an idea strengthened by the sequential nature of the narrative: Calidore tells Artegall that 'where ye ended haue, now I begin' (VI. 1. 6).[11] Guyon tells Medina that the celebration he attended occurred three months previously (II. 2. 44), yet he has encountered George at the conclusion of the first quest. It would seem unlikely that the whole of book one plus the first two cantos of book two have lasted less than three months. Indeed, apart from any of his other activities, George has spent at least three months in the Dungeon of Ignorance: 'for now three Moones haue changed thrice their hew,/ And haue been thrice hid vnderneath the ground' (I. 8. 38). In other words at least three moons have passed through the cycle of new moon, full moon, and waning moon since the combat with Orgoglio although some commentators believe that the period in question is nine months (thrice three). Guyon can hardly have attended the same feast as George. In fact, it is impossible to reconcile the notion of a single feast of twelve days with Guyon's assertion that the beginning of his quest coincided with the beginning of the festival (II. 2. 43). The 'Letter to Raleigh' would have it begin on the 'second day'. Furthermore when one considers the necessary lapse of time occasioned by Arthur's successive adventures as he rides from book to book, it seems even less likely that Artegall (encountered by the Prince after his second parting from Britomart) could have set out at the same time as

11 For a convenient synopsis of the controversy see Josephine Waters Bennett, *The Evolution of 'The Faerie Queene'* (Chicago, 1942), p. 36; On the association with Elizabeth's Accession Day (17 November) see Alastair Fowler, *Spenser and the Numbers of Time* (London, 1964), p 170.

either George or Guyon — however dilatory he may have been (V. 11. 39).[12] As the poem stands, whatever the prefatory material may claim, it is easier to suppose a series of feast days on successive years.

Nevertheless, the attractions of a simultaneous beginning must have weighed heavily with Spenser since it could easily be manipulated to create the deliberately — even defiantly — illogical illusion that the twelve quests are both sequential and concurrent. The pattern of the poem would then reflect both the 'eternal present' of its divine overseer and the transient flux of its mortal participants. Classical epic tends to reinforce the linear structure of time, classical romance tends to fracture it. Because *The Faerie Queene* hovers uneasily between both forms, the lack of correspondence between the 'Letter to Raleigh' and the extant poem may indicate an unresolved dilemma in Spenser's art, amounting to a refusal to forgo the imaginative possibilities of either viewpoint. Critical analysis is thus burdened with problems which would not have greatly exercised Renaissance readers. Spenser does not supply sufficient information for the construction of a coherent time-scheme for the poem as a whole. As so often in romance narrative, the matter is left vague.[13] It remains interesting, however, to consider the periods of duration occasionally specified for despite the great wandering of which we hear so often, months rather than years are invariably involved.

Arthur tells Una in book one that nine months have elapsed since his dream-vision (9. 15). As George has then spent at least three months in prison it may roughly have coincided with Gloriana's feast. In book two he tells Guyon that his quest has lasted a year (9. 7). This means that in the time-scale of the poem only three months pass from the delivery of George to that of Guyon. Since George meets Guyon at the outset of book two having successfully completed his quest, all the intervening events — the encounter with despair, the sojourn in the House of Holiness, the struggle with the

12 'While the action of each of the other books occupies the space of a year, the actions of Books Three and Four (delimited temporally as they are by the seven-month terms of Florimell's and Amoret's imprisonments) *together occupy only one year*.' Fowler, pp. 169-70. The astrological information supplied at I. 2. 1 (long before George's three month imprisonment) makes the season summer; that at II. 2. 46 makes it winter. It would, therefore, be highly unlikely that George and Guyon had attended the same feast given the latter's reference to the mere three months which have since elapsed. If the 'day' to which Guyon refers is indeed 17 November it would be impossible.

13 Assuming that the twelve quests run concurrently from a single twelve-day festival, S.K. Heninger is forced to conclude that 'the chronological sequence is only illusory, like all sense impressions. Or less severe (and more likely), the action is both chronological and atemporal.' 'The Aesthetic Experience of Reading Spenser' in *Contemporary Thought on Edmund Spenser*, edited by Richard C. Frushell and Bernard J. Vondersmith (Carbondale, 1975), pp. 79-98 (p. 93). More likely still is Spenser's failure to reconcile his chronological details.

dragon, the marriage to Una, the discovery of Mortdant and Amavia, the intrusion of Braggadocchio, the combat with Furor and Pyrochles, and the descent to the Cave of Mammon — occur within those three months. This would scarcely have been the reader's impression had Spenser not chosen to be so precise. George's stay in the House of Holiness seems rather protracted when one considers the sequence of spiritual states through which he passes, though in another sense the whole episode seems strangely outside normal time. Even so, it must be admitted that most of the other happenings account for only a few days. Some of them, such as the combat with Furor and Pyrochles are conducted in a few hours. When we count the days of action, three months seem more than sufficient, but the implied weariness of the apparently endless travelling 'through voide, wastefull ground' creates an impression of much longer duration. It seems longer to the knights themselves, partly because they too are ignorant of the total time-scheme of the poem. His vision has encouraged Arthur in the belief that his meeting with the fairy queen is imminent but repeated disappointments prove otherwise. Promising to be with him when 'iust time' has 'expired', she gives no indication as to when this might be. He is in the position of the early Christians awaiting a supposedly imminent Apocalypse inexplicably delayed. Time, the medium of the poem's fulfilment, is also that of its characters' frustration. Gloriana will reappear when Arthur may 'justly' be said to have earned such a reward and from this point of view the event seems indefinite or even conditional. But 'iust' has connotations of exactitude. The Fairy Queen speaks of a moment appointed by destiny. When the duration of Arthur's quest exactly corresponds to the fated lapse of time, when the measure of both is 'iust' or proportionable, events will move to a predestined conclusion. Arthur's ignorance is exacerbated by the assurance that the outcome is not indefinite, that precise timing is an element of moral justice. The attribution of justice to time is central to Spenser's vision since it is the virtue which 'defines' morality (V. 7. 1) emerging 'most sacred . . . of all the rest,/ Resembling God in his imperiall might' (5 Proem, 10). In the *Fowre Hymnes* Christ is simply 'the Iust' (III. 154).

When he meets Guyon in book two, Arthur feels no nearer his goal than he was in book one and this sense of frustration is understandably intensified in the more confusing and apparently episodic atmosphere of books three and four. In accordance with the Augustinian theory of time the weariness of disappointed expectation is easily transferred to the period of its experience, and the consciously repetitive nature of the language together with the calculated recurrence of similar incidents, create an impression of protracted duration, an interminable sequence of days and nights.[14] Gradually we are

14 *Confessions*, translated by R.S. Pine-Coffin (Harmondsworth, 1961), p. 276.

led to confuse distance and time with mood as Spenser manipulates the experience of both knights and readers. A series of revisions made to the second edition of the first three books illustrates this process. In the original version Prays-desire alludes to the 'three years' Arthur has spent searching for Gloriana (II. 9. 38) thereby contradicting what he himself had told Guyon some stanzas earlier. In 1596, however, 'three years' was altered to 'twelve moneths' and the chronology is thereby preserved since the two knights reach the House of Alma just a short while after the conflict with Pyrochles and Cymochles, in fact by the evening of the same day. This might well be dismissed as the correction of a minor error of detail were it not that Arthur had originally told Guyon that not one but seven years had passed since his vision (II. 9. 7). By 1596, therefore, Spenser had decided to insist both on the brevity of the actual timespan and the contrary impression it has left on the minds of the protagonists.

Had Arthur continued to date all subsequent events from the moment of vision we might have constructed a full time-scheme for the entire work, an exercise now impossible. It is as though the vision recedes the closer one approaches it. Although Guyon returns to the House of Alma after his defeat of Acrasia to rejoin Prince Arthur, we are not informed how long this takes. The demands of the narrative require no more than a day or two. The friends set out together and encounter Britomart 'at last' after an apparently long, but actually unspecified, period of time:

> Long so they trauelled through wastefull wayes,
> Where daungers dwelt, and perils most did wonne,
> To hunt for glorie and renowmed praise;
> Full many Countries they did ouerronne,
> From the vprising to the setting Sunne.
>
> (III. 1. 3)

The poem does not encourage us to relate the chronology of Britomart's adventures to those of her fellows, yet we are constantly reminded that in all cases the periods involved are relatively short. Britomart spends only one night in Castle Joyeous and the whole of cantos two and three mark less than a single day in the action of the poem, though dealing by way of flashback with the entire history of Britomart's love for Artegall. Despite the impossibility of constructing a definite chronology from the periods of duration specified hereafter they continue to invite the impossible as if to enforce its abandonment. For example, Amoret spends seven months in the House of Busirane and Florimell seven months in the dungeon of Proteus. But seven months from when? Such numbers may, of course, be credited with symbolic significance and numerologists claim to have discovered highly complex systems of allusion to more esoteric periods of measurement, such as the astrological year, by counting the number of stanzas and even lines between significant occurrences.[15] However, many of the calculations involved are of a rather unreal order of complexity, even for highly educated Renaissance readers. Qualities matter more than quantities, time in the head more than time in the hour-glass. The precise calibration of time by clocks, calendars and astrological charts is of less importance than the perception of rhythmic correspondences between natural and supernatural sources of renewal.

This being the case, despite the absence of specific dates the dawning of a new day or the onset of night are frequently described in the most elaborate and striking terms:

> By this the Northerne wagoner had set
> His seuenfold teme behind the stedfast starre,
> That was in Ocean waues yet neuer wet,
> But firme is fixt, and sendeth light from farre
> To all, that in the wide deepe wandring arre:
> And chearefull Chaunticlere with his note shrill
> Had warned once, that *Phoebus* fiery carre
> In hast was climbing vp the Easterne hill,
> Full enuious that night so long his roome did fill.
> (I. 2. 1)

This is not merely a matter of epic decorum. Here, for example, the description is thematically appropriate to the narrative since it is just at this moment that Archimago's 'accursed messengers of hell' return to report their failure with St George having spent an 'ill succeeding night' (2). The 'stedfast starre' behind which the 'Northerne wagoner' sets his 'seuenfold teme' is therefore symbolic of St George's still unshaken faith, a faith that guides all who oppose Rome's seven hills. As it is almost daylight, the danger would seem to have passed and 'chearefull Chaunticlere' duly announces the approach of the sun. One notes, however, that Chaunticlere's voice is 'shrill' and that he 'warns' of the coming day as if there were a note of anxiety or forboding mixed with his cheerfulness. St George has successfully resisted the first temptation but there is more to come. One is perhaps reminded of St Peter's experience with another daybreak. By the time 'faire *Hesperus* in

15 Flower, pp. 58-9, 139, 221. For example, none of Spenser's contemporaries could have read the poem as a 'planetary week' of seven books (pp 227-8) since the existence of the *Mutabilitie Cantos* remained unknown until 1609. See below, chapter six, fn. 51. The title-pages of both the 1590 and 1596 editions focus the reader's attention on the number twelve not seven — as do the *Amoretti* (80).

highest skie/Had spent his lampe, and brought forth dawning light' (6), George has abandoned Una and gone his way alone. As a result, the hopes of a new day are disappointed and the human drama is lent universal significance by being played out on a cosmic stage. Owing to George's sin the ideal relationship between the movements of the heavens and the actions of man is disrupted. From now on his time is 'out of joint'. Una is described 'rising forth out of her baser bowre' just at the moment when 'the rosy-fingred Morning faire' (7) rises from her saffron bed but there is no one to appreciate the spiritual implications of either vision because George's 'eye of reason was with rage yblent' (5). Una continues in her role of 'woman clothed with the sun' but since George is now 'blind' his actions are out of phase with those of his heavenly guide. Only after his sojourn in the House of Holiness does he regain a sense of harmony with the created universe. On the third morning of his combat with the dragon macrocosm and microcosm come miraculously into line:

> The ioyous day gan early to appeare,
> And faire *Aurora* from the deawy bed
> Of aged *Tithone* gan her selfe to reare,
> With rosie cheekes, for shame as blushing red . . .
>
> Then freshly vp arose the doughtie knight,
> All healed of his hurts and woundes wide,
> And did himselfe to battell readie dight.
>
> (I. 11. 51-2)

Now it is not the 'shrill' note of an ambivalent dawn chorus but the 'merry note' of a 'mounting larke' that routs the 'cheareless darke'. Fulfilling the providential plan for the good of salvation, George and the sun rise together in Eden. Genesis and Revelation coalesce.

The Faerie Queene is pervaded by images of return but also by images of childhood and youth. The two fit well together since the ultimate return, as the Reformers insisted, is to the moral standards of the world's 'infancie' (IV. 8. 30). Linear progress is illusory to the extent that all moral and civil advancement represents a partial return to the conditions of a distant past, a movement recalling Christ's injunction to become like little children (Matthew 18:3). Paradoxically, however, man's spiritual childhood may be attained only at the price of physical maturity and death: 'Be not children in understanding', warned St Paul (1 Corinthians 14:20). All of the poem's major protagonists are young, but their youth is sexually and morally ignorant and we meet them in the process of growing up. It is a 'youthfull' St George who rushes rashly into the Cave of Error and an immature, self-ignorant Britomart who finds herself distracted by the first motions of sexual desire.

For those who are 'chosen', time functions primarily as the medium of spiritual trial and self-discovery, of a quest through life for a lost spiritual innocence. The structure of the poem helps enforce this impression, particularly in the edition of 1596 where continuity and temporal succession are insisted upon so strongly. There is a pattern to spiritual development and each new quest begins at the point where its predecessor ends, the implication being that there is a necessary temporal connection between the two. Holiness fosters temperance, temperance chastity, chastity friendship, and so on until the capture of the Blatant Beast. The design is most evident in the person of Arthur. His is the work of perfection and each success, as both Una and George point out, brings him closer to his goal. Many of his enemies, notably Maleger and Corflambo, are clearly internal opponents. Furthermore, though ignorant of his own identity and commonly referred to as 'infant' or 'child', he gains in experience as he proceeds. Reading the 'Briton Moniments' in the House of Alma, where he also encounters his own motive force in Prays-desire, he gathers the information vital to his future role as British king. In book five, albeit unwittingly, he encounters his half-brother Artegall and willingly enters the service of Mercilla, one of Gloriana's principal surrogates. The 'iust time' that must elapse before their union evidently coincides with the duration of the twelve moral adventures. Arthur's mind, we are told, 'did trauell as with chylde,/Of his old loue, conceau'd in secret brest' (IV. 9. 17). Like George, he is 'with child of glorious great intent' seeking to deliver himself of 'th'eternall brood of glorie excellent' (I. V. 1). This is perhaps the most subtle use of the child imagery in the poem since, as Plato pointed out, children after the spirit are preferable to childen after the flesh (*Symposium*, 209d). Arthur is giving birth to his own heroic character thereby recapturing the 'flowring *youth*' of the '*antique* world' (II. 7. 16). A child of both Renaissance and Reformation he embodies time's greatest paradox.

It is doubtless appropriate that we should be unable to follow the exact chronology of events into books three and four since the whole pattern of Ariostan polyphonic narrative works to suggest a world in which the multiplicity of events cannot easily be correlated, an effect essential to the experience of these books both for the protagonists themselves and for the readers who follow them. We get lost together. Spenser's intention is underscored by what amounts to a distortion of the narrative time-scheme in the Marinell episode. At the beginning of book three Arthur, Guyon, and Timias rush off in pursuit of Florimell leaving Britomart to await their return a 'certaine space' before continuing her quest alone. After visiting Castle Joyeous she separates from her new companion, the Redcross Knight, and encounters Marinell whom she greviously wounds and leaves for dead. The chronological sequence of events is clear: Florimell's flight, the visit to Castle Joyeous, and the combat with Marinell. A problem arises, however, when

Florimell's dwarf tells Arthur that the reason for his lady's flight from the court of the Fairy Queen was the news of Marinell's injury. The latter occurred five days before the dwarf's meeting with Arthur, the former only four days. This account cannot be reconciled with the events of the poem where Florimell's flight clearly precedes her lover's fall. If we accept the dwarf's word, Florimell has no reason for being where she is — in flight or otherwise — in canto one: a timely warning this against the dangers of attempting to fabricate elaborate systems of chronology from this point onwards. Aesthetic effect is what matters most even at the price of occasional chronological discrepancy. Despite the impression of tedious duration, events are actually treading so hotly upon one another's heels that we must not complain if an effect appears to precede its cause. And the dwarf, after all, may be misinformed! As in the case of Shakespeare's *Othello*, there is really no problem unless the reader insists upon treating fiction as fact thereby distracting himself from the work's real significance.[16] As one might expect in an allegorical poem, there are many obvious occasions upon which the time-schemes of the narrative, as related to different characters, are rendered conspicuously incompatible in order to reflect the particular nature of the vice or virtue then in question. After the death of Pyrochles, for example, Atin flies to the Bower of Bliss encompassing in a few hours a journey Guyon finds both long and laborious. It is clearly Atin's allegorical character that speeds the journey.[17] The land of Faery has its own peculiar time-scheme and affords many similar instances.

III. *Time, Progress and Faery*

In his commentary upon the June eclogue of *The Shepheardes Calender* E.K. dismisses the fairies out of hand, linking the 'rancke opinion' of their existence with the superstitions of popery: 'the truth is, that there be no such thinges, not yet the shadowes of the things'. Yet the fairies are used to charming effect in the eclogue itself and return, despite the strictures of Gabriel Harvey, to enrich *The Faerie Queene*.[18] With Spenser it is not a question of existence or non-existence — a point much disputed by his contemporaries — but of aesthetic utility.[19] The fairies, like the classical gods

16 *Othello*, edited by M.R. Ridley (London, 1958), pp. lxvii-lxx. For a provocative study of Spenser's narrative techniques (including narrative inconsistencies) see Jan Karel Kouwenhoven, *Apparent Narrative as Thematic Metaphor: the Organization of 'The Faerie Queene'* (Oxford, 1983), pp. 72-130.

17 Robert Rawdon Wilson, 'The Deformation of Narrative Time in *The Faerie Queene*', *University of Toronto Quarterly*, 41 (1971), 48-62

18 *Prose*, p. 472.

19 Keith Thomas, *Religion and the Decline of Magic*, second edition (Harmondsworth, 1973), pp. 701-34. Minor White Latham, *The Elizabethan Fairies* (New York, 1930), pp. 41-62.

and Graces, are useful for a poem such as his, and this usefulness is taken to justify their presence. They also have the added advantage of a long native pedigree.

King Arthur was no stranger to Fairyland. His association with Morgan-la-Fay has its roots in Celtic mythology, and a vast literature had grown up on the continent, as in Britain itself, upon these topics.[20] By the sixteenth century the Arthurian legends were virtually inseparable from fairy lore. Spenser's Arthur rides easily out of Britain into Fairyland, but to imagine his entering the land of diminutive creatures popularised in *A Midsummer Night's Dream* is peculiarly anachronistic. Shakespeare's vision of the fairy race was very much the product of his own invention: according to the prevailing view they were of mortal appearance and normal human size and could be either helpful or malignant. One of their most dreaded activities was the substitution of malign changelings for healthy human children.[21] Such are the personal histories of George (I. 10. 65) and Artegall (III. 3. 26) and the sinister aspect of the legend persists, though officially suppressed, to confront Tudor 'myth' with Tudor experience. Had not Gloriana's service 'allmoste *changed*' Arthur Grey's 'naturall disposicion' (*Prose*, p.160)?

Fusing the two meanings of the term 'iust' Arthur tells Una that he has no idea as to his real identity but that Merlin has promised that 'time in her *iust* terme the truth to light should bring'. Almost as soon as he was born he was taken 'vnfit' from his 'mothers pap' and 'streight deliuered to a Faery knight,/To be vpbrought in gentle thewes and martiall might' (I. 9. 3). He is now in pursuit of the Fairy Queen who has slept beside him in a dream, a perplexing dream since the print of her body was left beside him on the grass.[22] The fairy mistress was a common theme of romance literature, but Spenser has ingeniously emphasised the clash of illusion and reality thereby

20 Lucy Allen Paton, *Studies in the Fairy Mythology of Arthurian Romance*, revised edition (New York, 1960). See also Isabel E. Rathborne, *The Meaning of Spenser's Fairyland* (New York, 1937), pp. 142-206, 211-221; Thomas P. Roche, *The Kindly Flame: A Study of the Third and Fourth Books of Spenser's 'Faerie Queene'* (Princeton, 1964), pp. 31-50.

21 Latham, pp. 68-80, 148-60. See also Sverre Arestad, 'Spenser's *Faery* and *Fairy*', *MLQ*, 8 (1947), 37- 42. Arestad argues that Spenser employs the term 'faery' in two quite distinct senses, one of which entails little or no association with the supernatural beings of folklore. He calls attention to the mortality of Spenser's fairies (pp. 41-2). However, his argument suffers from the admission that Spenser himself never distinguishes orthographically between the two and his own distinctions become untenable when applied to Gloriana. See also Edwin Greenlaw, 'Spenser's Fairy Mythology', *SP*, 15 (1918), 105-22 (pp. 114-5, 118). For some contrary evidence of diminutive fairies before Shakespeare see *A Midsummer Night's Dream*, edited by Harold F. Brooks (London, 1979), pp lxx-lxxv.

22 For the interpretation of dreams see C.S. Lewis, *The Discarded Image* (Cambridge, 1964), pp. 54, 63-5.

exciting speculation concerning the nature of the quest and its final goal.[23] The sexual component of Arthur's desire (Corflambo) impedes his 'conception' of honour and renders Gloriana's nature as equivocal as that of England's virgin but seductive queen. A further complication is that, apart from Gloriana, the fairies of the poem seem virtually indistinguishable from the human characters. Should it be argued that Guyon's 'demonic energy' is the product of his fairy origins, the same can scarcely be said of Calidore, and in any case it is Arthur who rescues Guyon, not Guyon Arthur.[24] Neither Guyon nor Calidore display the supernatural powers of Archimago, and throughout their various combats seem just as vulnerable as George or Artegall. When fairy powers are stressed, as in the case of Agape, the figures involved, as their names suggest, are virtually personifications.

Spenser's creation of a separate fairy race has led some critics to postulate a distinction in the poem between the 'order of grace' and the 'order of nature' as demonstrated for example, in the alleged contrast between St George and Guyon.[25] Guyon is said to represent the perfection of the natural order, an order shown to be inadequate as book two continues. Yet when Guyon falls an angel protects him and Arthur, acting in accordance with the will of Providence, delivers him. In what sense then do George and Guyon differ? For most of book one George is mistaken for a fairy knight. This is what he believes himself to be. Like Guyon he has already been to Cleopolis and seen Gloriana. Herein lies the crux of the matter since it is claimed that Cleopolis endorses 'classical and this-worldly values' excluded from all 'Christian commendations of the Active Life': in urging George to resume his quest, Contemplation advises him 'to become a pagan again for a while'. As in modern science-fiction, it is argued, the fairies constitute an alternative 'humanoid' race which never fell but were created with 'some moral and metaphysical evil built into them by virtue of their corruptible matter'.[26]

As Guyon is the poem's first fairy knight of any importance (excepting Satyrane) it was essential that Spenser should establish his moral credentials from the outset, just as he had done with St George. In Guyon's case the need was even more pressing since fairies were often regarded by Spenser's

23 Paton, p. 1.

24 On 'daemonic energy' see Angus Fletcher, *Allegory: The Theory of a Symbolic Mode* (New York, 1964), pp. 26-69 (p. 51).

25 A.S.P. Woodhouse, 'Nature and Grace in *The Faerie Queene*', *ELH*, 16 (1949), pp. 194-228. For a corrective to Woodhouse's view see Harry Berger, *The Allegorical Temper: Vision and Reality in Book II of Spenser's 'Faerie Queene'* (New Haven, 1957) chapters 2 and 3. See also Anthea Hume, *Edmund Spenser: Protestant Poet* (Cambridge, 1984), pp. 145-61; Patrick Cullen, *Infernal Triad* (Princeton, 1974), pp. 68-96.

26 Carol V. Kaske, 'Spenser's Pluralistic Universe', in Frushell and Vondersmith, pp. 121-49 (pp. 128, 131, 136, 146, 148).

contemporaries as devils and fairyland as Hell.[27] The easiest solution was to make Guyon a Christian. When first we meet St George we are made aware of his religious allegiance by the symbol of the cross emblazoned on his shield and breast-plate, 'the deare remembrance of his dying Lord'. It is this same symbol that causes Guyon to abandon his ill-advised attack upon George and beg his pardon (II. 1. 27). In order that there should be no mistake about the significance of this incident, Spenser has Guyon refer to the cross as, 'the sacred badge of *my Redeemers* death' a phrase clearly designed to echo the description of the armour in book one. If Guyon venerates Christ as God, he cannot be excluded from the religious world of George, and if he regards Christ as his personal saviour he cannot be a member of an unfallen race, humanoid or otherwise. As Richard Hooker explains, 'Christ, although a Redeemer only unto men, might notwithstanding be revealed unto angels as their Lord, without any reference at all to sin, which the knowledge of Christ a Redeemer *doth necessarily presuppose*'.[28] This is the point of the incident. It is the common bond of Christianity that unites George and Guyon at the beginning of book two. Their virtues are not exclusive but complementary. This is why Guyon's Palmer can praise George so highly and hope for a similar end to their own adventures. It would be allegorically impossible for '*heauenly* Contemplation' to advise George to be a pagan no matter for how short a time. He urges him to resume the quest because he acknowledges no inconsistency between the service of Gloriana and that of God. Rather he suggests that George's final years must be dedicated to the contemplative life, a life he may approach only through the fulfilment of the active quest. Just as Guyon honours the cross on George's shield, George honours the 'faire image of that *heauenly* Mayd' that decks Guyon's arms. They are united in their service of Cleopolis also (II. 1. 28).

If any analogy is to be drawn between Spenser's depiction of Fairyland and the narrative methods of modern science-fiction, the creation of 'totally different humanoid races, perhaps unrelated either to Adam or to Christ' is clearly not the correct one.[29] Fairyland may be strikingly dissimilar to Britain

27 Thomas Warton, *Observations on the 'Faerie Queene' of Spenser*, 2 vols (London, 1762), I, 61-2; Lewis, *Discarded Image*, pp. 134-5.

28 *Works*, edited by John Keble, 3 vols, seventh edition (London, 1888), II, 568. The interpretation closest to my own is that of Robert Hoopes, '"God Guide thee, Guyon": Nature and Grace Reconciled in *The Faerie Queene*, Book II', *RES*, 5 (1954), 14-24. However, whereas Hoopes has chosen to concentrate on the Palmer's benediction, I emphasise Guyon's own acknowledgement of the doctrine of redemption. The opposing view is represented by amongst others, Sherry L. Reames who declares quite baldly that 'Guyon is not a Christian. He places his faith in reason rather than in grace'. See 'Prince Arthur and Spenser's Changing Design' in Kenneth John Atchity, ed., *Eterne in Mutabilitie: The Unity of 'The Faerie Queene'* (Hamden, Connecticut, 1972), p. 191.

29 Kaske, p. 146.

but the knights errant of the two worlds are indistinguishable. If there is an Archimago in Fairyland, there is a Merlin in Britain, and even Gloriana finds her equivalent in England's Elisa. As in More's *Utopia* we arrive in an exotic landscape only to discover beings identical to ourselves creating a civilization in many respects superior to our own. Yet superior as this civilization may be, its individual members prove just as vulnerable to the ravages of time and fortune. Indeed there are times when one detects something of a dichotomy between Spenser's description of the fairy race and that of its individual members: the long-suffering, unfortunate Florimell is no less a member of the fairy court than Guyon or Calidore. Particularly important in this respect is what the fairy knights tell us of the circumstances of their own lives. For example, the plight of the orphan child of Mortdant and Amavia moves Guyon to comment on the pitiful condition of mortal existence: 'Such is the state of men: thus enter wee/Into this life with woe, and end with miseree' (II. 2. 2). The crucial word here is 'wee'. Guyon identifies with the plight of the 'luckless babe' which thereby becomes emblematic of all life, whether fairy or Briton. Recognising no distinction between his own condition and the 'state of men', he describes himself to Mammon as, 'I, that am fraile flesh and *earthly* wight' (II. 7. 50). Similarly, Artegall recognises no distinction between his own human condition and that of his adopted race. He too is a changeling: Merlin explains that although he lives in Fairyland he is 'no *Fary* borne, ne sib at all/ To Elfes, but sprong of seed terrestriall,/ And whilome by false *Faries* stolne away,/ Whiles yet in infant cradle he did crall' (III. 3. 26). While Merlin discriminates between the Fairy race and 'seed terrestrial', he appears to mean no more by this phrase than 'seed of those who live in Briton'. He cannot imply any radical difference between the nature of the Fairy race and that of man since he proceeds to tell us that Artegall believes himself to be of fairy origin and that nothing in his experience of life has altered that belief: 'ne other to himselfe is knowne this day,/ But that he by an Elfe was gotten of a Fay'. Of further interest in Merlin's remarks is his reference to 'false *Faries*'. Apparently not all 'elves' are of Guyon's moral stature, and once we admit this the idea of a separate unfallen race again collapses.

Much has been written of the contrast between the British and Fairy chronicles read by Arthur and Guyon in the House of Alma. The general consensus is that fairy history displays a type of civic perfection alien to fallen men. Such a view has much to commend it.[30] The succession of fairy kings is perfect; there are no civil wars, no rebellions, and no cultural setbacks. Despite this, the 'Antiquitie of Faerie' is no less a history than the 'Briton Moniments' because the notion of progress is incompatible with that of

30 Berger, pp. 87-8, 108-114.

perfection. To regard the fairy kings as improving the situation they inherit is to acknowledge the relative imperfection of the inheritance. Furthermore, even the most trouble-free succession is succession still. Gloriana has not always been fairy queen and there is no reason to suppose her destined to remain in that station indefinitely. She is merely the fairy monarch whose reign coincides with the life of Arthur. Yet, according to book one, she is fated to survive him, bringing his lance 'to Faerie lond, where yet it may be seene, if sought' (I. 7. 36). The passage does not claim that Gloriana herself is still to be seen, but many feel that this is implied both here and, more generally, in the 'particular intention' of the poem's design. The point is of special relevance to the historical allegory since it involves the continuity of the British monarchy, but on the level of romance narrative Gloriana's resulting longevity would appear to sort ill with the constant emphasis upon her mortality and that of her ancestors. Elfinor 'who was in Magick skild' — not, one notices, a feature of all or even most of the fairy line — dies and 'leaves' three sons who each die in their turn. Similarly 'Elferon' did 'vntimely dy' and the phrase rings heavily. Even in fairyland there rise the same notes of sorrowful complaint that pervade Spenser's elegy on Sidney. Time stalks the land of Faery too and Guyon chooses his words carefully when he refers to Gloriana's 'rare perfection *in mortalitie*' (II. 2. 41). 'Immortality' would fit the rhyme, but was impossible.

A number of plausible solutions deserve attention. In the first place one might argue that Gloriana spans the centuries in the sense that Elizabeth represents the culmination of the Briton monarchy. Spenser is wary of actually identifying the two characters. Rather he tells his sovereign very precisely that she will find her ancestors amongst the Britons (II. 10. 4), but her own image amongst the fays (1 Proem, 4). Thus Gloriana would become an icon of earthly monarchy as it perpetuates itself from age to age, an idea examined in greater detail in chapter four. Spenser could then be seen as employing the popular celebrations of Elizabeth as fairy queen to highly patriotic effect.[31] A second explanation might be found in traditional fairy lore. That time moves more slowly in fairyland than elsewhere is a common motif of Celtic literature.[32] Human travellers returning after what seems to have been a relatively short stay find that centuries have elapsed. To preserve the moral allegory, Spenser would have to suppress the darker side of the legend: Arthur, Britomart, and Artegall are clearly intended to return to their own place and time once their present adventures have concluded. Fairyland

31 Frances A. Yates, *Astraea: The Imperial Theme in the Sixteenth Century*, second edition (Harmondsworth, 1977), pp. 97-101; *Entertainments for Elizabeth*, edited by Jean Wilson (Trowbridge, 1980), pp. 29-31, 115-6, 129-31.

32 Paton, pp. 2-3; John Erskine Hankins, *Source and Meaning in Spenser's Allegory* (Oxford, 1971), p. 201.

is the place or time of their youth. However, if this is indeed the explanation for Gloriana's longevity, it must be inferred from the reader's previous acquaintance with fairy romance. At no time does Spenser offer it as his own solution. An investigation of his sources produces better results.

The characterization of Gloriana is distinguished by four salient features: 1. Exquisite physical beauty; 2. Benign intentions towards those in whose lives she intervenes; 3. Mortality; 4. Spiritual grace, 'for she is heauenly borne, and heauen may iustly vaunt' (I. 10. 59). In fact Gloriana is Christian. Such a peculiar combination of characteristics is far to seek within Celtic folklore but lay readily to hand in *Huon of Burdeux*, translated by Lord Berners in 1534. Direct reference to the work is made within *The Faerie Queene* itself. Spenser makes a point of telling us that Guyon took his knighthood 'of good Sir *Huons* hand,/ When with king *Oberon* he came to Faerie land' (II. 1. 6). The fairy monarch Oberon is a remarkable creation by any standards. As the most beautiful of living creatures, he enchants Huon on their first encounter although fear of the allegedly infernal nature of the fairy race postpones their speaking. But Oberon's intentions are benign and he dispels Huon's suspicions by constant reference, sincerely intended, to the Christian God to whom he attributes his power and influence. He accompanies one of his lesser miracles with the sign of the cross and displays open hostility to those who renounce Christianity for paganism.[33] As far as his spiritual makeup is concerned, he is neither devil nor angel. Indeed he tells Huon, 'I am a man as other be'.[34] Despite his youthful appearance, however, it emerges that he was born in 40 B.C. but is still alive and reigning in the time of Charlemagne.[35] Yet however long his life, it is almost done. Throughout the romance there is frequent reference to his approaching death, the event with which the narrative concludes. Its manner is particularly noteworthy being intended to sanctify faery once and for all. Oberon dies 'makyng his prayers to our lorde Iesu cryste' and 'recommendyng his sowle to god, the which incontynent was borne in to paradyce by a greate multytude of angelles sent fro our lord Iesu chryst, who at ther depertynge made such shynynge and clerenes in the palays that . . . they knewe suerly that kynge Oberons sowle was saued'.[36] Heavenly Contemplation would have few qualms in recommending the service of such as Oberon and it seems clear that this must have been Spenser's ultimate source — particularly as the fairy

33 *The Boke of Duke Huon of Burdeux*, edited by S.L. Lee, Early English Text Society, Extra Series 40, 41, 43, 50, 2 vols (New York, 1973 — first published 1882-7), I, 67-71, 76, 81. See J.R. MacArthur, 'The Influence of *Huon of Burdeux* upon *The Faerie Queene*', *JEGP*, 4 (1902), 215-38.

34 *Ibid.*, I, 69.

35 *Ibid.*, I, 73.

36 *Ibid.*, I, 605.

chronicles list Oberon as Gloriana's father (II. 10. 76). Her name may have been suggested by that of Gloryande or Gloriant, 'the good knyght of the Fayery' who intercedes for Huon incessantly throughout the romance.[37]

There have been many theories as to the exact significance of Spenser's Fairyland. For Isabel Rathborne it is the land of fame and its inhabitants 'members of the same race [as ourselves] under different conditions'. Fairyland, she suggests, is 'a mythical land of fame where departed heroes, the ancestors of his royal and noble patrons, enjoy an extended, if not an immortal life, closely resembling their heroic lives on earth'.[38] In this view Miss Rathborne is supported by John Hankins who employs Francesco Piccolomini's discussion of heroic virtue to enforce the same point. In effect, he sees Spenser as creating a land fit for his chivalric heroes.[39] An interesting variation of this idea is Carol Kaske's suggestion that Fairyland represents the 'realm of education', the realm in which the Christian Britons acquire 'vertuous and gentle discipline'. Hence the many personifications they encounter on the way since personification is 'a notoriously didactic mode of allegory'.[40] A more specific interpretation is that of Edwin Greenlaw who associated fairyland historically with the Ancient Britons and geographically with Wales, the homeland of the Tudor family.[41] Michael O'Connell developed the allegorical implications of this notion when he claimed that Fairyland was not 'a simple shadowing of Tudor rule but an idealization of it'.[42] By contrast Isabel MacCaffrey sees Fairyland as 'the mirror of Elizabethan England as the "antique Images" of history are mirrors of every unfolding present moment'. However, her special interest in Spenser's 'anatomy' of the imagination leads her to conclude that Fairyland is 'the human imagination itself, hospitable to solicitations from the world without and the world within'. It is a place 'that lives within the mind' as the proem to book six seems to suggest. On this reading, neither Guyon nor Calidore has a history

37 *Ibid.*, I, 70, 167, 537-7. Spenser may have conflated the knight Gloryande with the fairy lady Gloriande who gives the power of healing to the magic horn received by Huon (p. 66). This horn probably contributed to the description of that carried by Timias (I. 8. 3) for along with its beneficial properties it can also be used to occasion uncontrollable panic (pp. 67-8). The 'vses manifold' of Spenser's horn may be a reminiscence of the long list of properties ascribed in *Huon* (p. 66).

38 Rathborne, pp. 142-3, 206.

39 Hankins, pp. 46-50.

40 Kaske, pp. 144-5.

41 *Studies in Spenser's Historical Allegory* (Baltimore, 1932), 193-8. Britomart, however, rides *from* 'South-wales' (III. 2. 18) to 'Faery lond' (III. 3. 62).

42 Michael O'Connell, *Mirror and Veil: The Historical Dimension of Spenser's 'Faerie Queene'* (Chapel Hill, 1977), p. 81.

— a point which seems contradicted by the Fairy chronicles.[43] More promising is the assertion of Angus Fletcher that 'the interaction of the two modes of heroic existence, faery and Briton, is an interaction of two aspects of time, its recurrent forms and its linear, evolutionary forms'.[44]

Let us, therefore, approach the problem from what Spenser himself says of it. The proem to book one tells us that the poet intends to open the hidden 'antique rolles',

> Of Faerie knights and fairest *Tanaquill*,
> Whom that most noble Briton Prince so long
> Sought through the world, and suffered so much ill.
> (1 Proem, 2)[45]

At the conclusion Spenser addresses himself to Elizabeth who is 'the Mirrour of grace and Maiestie diuine' thereby implying that her just mode of government reflects (like a mirror) the grace and majesty of God. She may, therefore, be termed 'goddess' after the biblical phrase which identifies divinely appointed rulers as earthly gods (Psalms 82:6; Exodus 22:9). Elizabeth is the poet's immediate inspiration and he longs to create a poetry worthy of her. In *The Faerie Queene* she will find her own 'glorious *type*', and this is surely the key to our interpretation. The 'Letter to Raleigh' tells us that in the poet's 'generall intention' Gloriana signifies 'glory', but that in his 'particular intention' he 'conceiue[s] the most excellent and glorious person of our soueraine the Queene, and her kingdome in Faery land'. Elizabeth, as one individual monarch, partakes of the universal glory which all of the heroes strive to attain. That ultimate glory resides in God of whom

43 *Spenser's Allegory* (Princeton, 1976), pp. 69, 74, 209, 409. MacCaffrey develops ideas first postulated by Samuel Taylor Coleridge, *Miscellaneous Criticism*, edited by Thomas Middleton Raysor (London, 1936), p. 36.

44 *The Prophetic Moment: An Essay on Spenser* (Chicago, 1971), p. 68. See also Josephine Waters Bennett, 'Britain among the Fortunate Isles', *SP*, 53 (1956), 114-40.

45 Tanaquil was the faithful, enlightened wife of Lucumo, the first Tarquin, whom she helped to the throne. She plays a very significant role in Livy's account of the early history of Rome as an interpreter of omens concerning the future of the state. In other words, she functions as the instrument of a preordained fate (I. 34). It was largely through her efforts that Servius Tullius, one of the key figures in the development of Roman society, was recognised as a future king (I. 39), and finally succeeded to the throne on the assassination of her husband Tarquin (I. 41). The point of using the name Tanaquil here, instead of the more customary Gloriana, would seem to be that Prince Arthur's union with the Fairy Queen will finally confirm his own claim to the British crown. Tanaquil, who has clearly recognised him as a man of destiny, will be the instrument of his imperial glory. Skelton had compared Lady Margaret, Countess of Richmond, mother of Henry VII to Tanaquil. See *Complete Poems*, edited by Philip Henderson (London, 1931), p. 466.

the queen is merely an earthly reflection. On the Mount of Contemplation George sees beyond the reflection — beyond Cleopolis — to the very source of glory. He looks into heaven.

Fairyland is a land of 'types', a place or state in which matters appear *sub specie aeternitatis*. Hence the appropriateness of Spenser's allegorical method. Elizabeth sees not herself but her type in Gloriana, and not England but England's type in the fairy realm. What distinguishes the 'Briton Moniments' from the fairy chronicles most clearly is the cumulative progress of the fairy race. All of their kings inherit, consolidate, and advance the total achievement of all previous reigns. By contrast, British kings constantly subvert the gains of their forbears. Successful monarchs are often forced to begin virtually *ab ovo* only to have their renewed efforts frustrated by their heirs or contemporaries. In this respect the unbroken progress of the fairy kings corresponds to that attitude towards time inspired by the scientific optimism of Francis Bacon and Giordano Bruno. To those of this outlook, 'it is by living through others' years, by appropriating the technical and scientific expertise of earlier generations, that man becomes the child of time'.[46]

In Spenser's fable the race of fairies is created by Prometheus, although it is a 'man' he is credited with creating. This man finds a 'fay' in the Gardens of Adonis, centre of cyclical life and energy in the poem, and their descendants form the race of which Guyon and Gloriana are members. Allegorising the pagan myth, Ficino identifies Promethus with the third office of divine intelligence, with that aspect of 'providence' which concerns itself with lower things ('inferiora') filling the soul with rational principles ('rationes'). As a result of such activity, the soul imitates the triple nature of its creator, developing powers of contemplation, reason, and phantasy. From these arise the gifts of philosophy, prudence, and artistic skill. Although a higher office of divine intelligence, identified with Jove, is credited with inspiring concepts of law and civic order, Prometheus (or Providence) provides the medium through which such concepts reach the human world. As the universal distributor ('largitor') of divine gifts, 'Prometheus gives us an ingenious quickness of mind. But as the intermediary and preparer ('medius . . . et praeperator'), he turns our intelligence and reason towards wisdom, and towards civic skills too, especially since the intelligence and the reason are stimulated and prepared in us for more important things by the agency of the primary human skills'.[47] As we have seen, divine providence is intimately related to human prudence which imitates the higher power in working

46 Heller, p. 184.

47 *The 'Philebus' Commentary*, translated by J.B. Allen (Berkeley, 1975), pp. 240, 244; Fulgentius identifies Prometheus with the divine foresight instrumental in the creation of man. See *Fulgentius the Mythographer*, translated by Leslie George Whitbread (Ohio, 1971), pp. 71-2.

through time. Alert to such implications, Natalis Comes identifies Prometheus with time itself, 'for time is the master and inventor of all things and all arts as is claimed for Promethus'.[48] He is also associated with 'mens' or foresight, an idea supported by Bacon.[49] Foresight is regarded as the ability to anticipate contingency. Living for the present alone, the first men had no conception of futurity. Experience, however, made them more provident ('prudentiores') and led to the discovery of fire, the basis of all artistic skill and the element with which Spenser's Prometheus animates his creation. Comes credits him with the infusion of the intellectual powers from which all public and private knowledge takes its origin ('e quibus bona consilia, et prudentia tum in rebus privatis, tum etiam in publicis administrandis, et rerum humanae vitae necessarium inventiones exurgunt'). Prometheus drew men from their wild woodland life to the life of the cities ('ad urbaniorem vitam e sylvis'), and significantly, in Spenser's account, the supreme creation of the fairy race is the city of Cleopolis.[50] The myth of Prometheus may be interpreted as the development of human 'providence' through experience. The fairies are the children of Baconian time. Nevertheless, their progress is not wholly the product of self-reliance. 'Faery' and 'fay' are cognate with 'fate', and the evolution of the fairy race realises the intentions of divine providence in the world of time and matter. Spiritual forces operate through mortal agencies.

The suffering of 'Prometheus' subsequent to the descent of the divine spirit into the world of matter is emphasised in all Neoplatonic accounts of the myth from Plotinus to Ficino, but Spenser is alone in terminating the agony in death thereby making mortality a necessary consequence of the cosmic process.[51] However, the prevalence of death in their world does not impair the progress of the Fairy race since they live through other's years. The dead bequeath their success to the living who increase it and in their turn bequeath an even greater inheritance to their own children. Such is the quality of fairy time: time as the medium of simple linear progress without any of the reversals and inconsistencies of human time, associated as it is with the wheel of fortune. Fairy civilization is not diminished by the death of its individual members. It represents man's most cherished dream for his own social development. Though mortal, the fairies have attained the supreme civic achievement, but it is both misleading and unnecessary to regard them as paragons of the natural

48 *Mythologiae* (Venice, 1567 — first published 1551), fol. 100v.

49 *Ibid.*, fol. 101r; Bacon, *Works*, VI, 746-7. For a full discussion of the development and interpretation of the Prometheus myth see Olga Raggio, 'The Myth of Prometheus: Its Survival and Metamorphoses up to the Eighteenth Century', *JWCI*, 21 (1958), 44-62.

50 Comes, fol. 101r.

51 Raggio, pp. 53-4. The earliest commentator to notice Spenser's insistence upon the death of Prometheus was John Jortin, *Remarks on Spenser's Poems* (London, 1734), p. 68.

order excluded from grace. Unlike More's Utopians, whom Spenser probably had in mind, these fairies are Christian from the outset: by the time Hythlodaeus *leaves* Utopia most of its inhabitants have been converted. Spenser has simply moved the process one stage back as Bacon was later to do in his *New Atlantis*.

In the light of all this, Elizabeth may well see her 'owne realms in the lond of Faery'. What she sees, in effect, is the goal towards which her kingdom is supposedly moving. Like Plato's republic it exists as an ideal. In order to achieve it, one must first conceive of it intellectually as Arthur 'conceiues' of glory and his creator 'conceiues' of him. In courtly compliment Spenser suggests that under 'covert vele' and 'shadowes light' the poem reflects the established glory of Elizabeth's own kingdom. In so far as the ideal has already been achieved, this is true. All civic progress is towards Cleopolis and Elizabeth has done more than most in establishing order and stability. Yet she cannot have her attention focussed upon Cleopolis without also being made aware of all that remains to be achieved. The compliment insinuates a vision of unfulfilled potential and, as Spenser was well aware, unmerited praise can ultimately prove as corrosive as direct satire. In the world of the poem the crowns of England and Fairyland remain separate though Arthur aspires towards their union. Theoretically, this has now been achieved since the Queen of England is also the 'fairy queen'. Ideally fiction and reality should now converge as the 'particular' and 'general' intentions of the allegory fuse. Unfortunately, however, the ideal itself remains part of the poetic fiction. As often as not, in the world of real politics, Elizabeth betrays Gloriana and the desired unity fragments. Colin Clout's nightmare vision of the Elizabethan court haunts and occasionally obscures fairyland. Like all idealists, Spenser is dissatisfied with the present, and not least with its complacency. Ironically, Elizabeth can never become fairy queen as long as she believes she already is. To earn the compliment she must reject it.

What Spenser has done in creating his fairy chronicle is to imagine what might have been had the English proved 'children of time' in the sense the fairies have. The chronicle represents the fulfilment of Christian man's earthly potential. Spenser emphasises the fairies' mortality in order to suggest that their perfection is *not* alien to man. As a result they are not generally credited with magical powers but achieve their goals through natural means. Nor are they born into a perfect world but have to fight to establish their civilization against the forces of evil and disruption. Hence their battles with 'wicked *Gobbelines* in bloudy field', a detail which might have come from Arthur's chronicle. Working in accordance with right reason and justice and in co-operation with one another, men may hope to emulate the fairy race. Not by coincidence does Arthur read the history of Britain in fairyland, a history that will in time inspire the creation of Camelot and the Round Table.

All worthwhile quests impinge on fairy terrain, all worthwhile knights mature in fairyland.

IV. *The Value of Empire: Time's Monuments*

The diverse episodes of the 'auncient booke, hight *Briton moniments*' are unified in the person of their reader. Since the story they have to tell culminates in the arrival of Arthur himself, the account breaks off at the reign of his father Uther Pendragon. Arthur is the next chapter, the living embodiment of Britain's future. From the viewpoint of Spenser's contemporaries, however, Arthur's life was itself part of distant history. Consequently the poem finds its ultimate point of reference in their own lives. This immediacy of concern is signalled by the invocation of a queen whose 'realme and race' derive from the 'renowmed Prince',

> Who mightily vpheld that royall mace,
> Which now thou bear'st, to thee descended farre
> From mightie kings and conquerours in warre,
> Thy fathers and great Grandfathers of old,
> Whose noble deedes aboue the Northerne starre
> Immortall fame for euer hath enrold;
> As in that old mans booke they were in order told. (4)

Despite the chronological distance of the descent, it is as if Arthur himself had placed the mace in Elizabeth's hands.

The first nine stanzas of the account present the gradual emergence of Britain's identity first as a separate geographical entity and finally as a separate self-governing 'imperium'. In stanza five the land is a 'saluage wildernesse,/Vnpeopled, vnmanurd, vnprou'd, vnpraysd', not even an island but an indistinguishable part of the continental mainland. Only in stanza six does it acquire the name of Albion, after the white cliffs of Dover. At first it was inhabited by a 'saluage nation . . . Of hideous Giants, and halfe beastly men,/That neuer tasted grace' (7). These were 'naked without shame' not innocently like Adam and Eve, but ignorantly like wild animals. The stage of history Spenser here describes, employing terminology reminiscent of his description of Ireland, is that evoked in Montaigne's essay 'Of the Cannibals' but without the saving grace of natural virtue. The Giants represent man in his sinful fallen state cut off from divine mercy. This point is made allegorically by tracing their origin to the union of Dioclesian's homicidal daughters with 'feends and filthy Sprights'. Spenser denies the veracity of the legend even as he relates it, but the impression of moral turpitude it creates lingers in the mind. The story is given in such detail that by the end of stanza eight we have almost forgotten its dismissal, and stanza nine follows as if

Spenser had himself endorsed it. The natural order has been overturned and the result is 'monstrous error'. As in the Gardens of Adonis, a state of chaos precedes the influence of creative forces. The Giants so 'pollute' the 'gentle soyle' with their 'filthiness' that even the earth herself rejects their 'vnkindly [unnatural] crime'. Thereafter an almost Lucretian vision of savage 'pre-history' gives way to destined progress. 'Monstrous error' is opposed by 'fatall error'.

By depriving the Giants of their 'vniust possession' Brutus re-enacts the arrival of the Jews in a promised land populated by 'giants' in comparison with whom the children of Zion seemed like grasshoppers (Numbers 13:33). The defeat of these Giant imposes the beginnings of civic order upon the country. The various battles confer names on the hitherto uncharted landscape and the survival of these names to Elizabethan times serves as a testimony to the enduring quality of the civilization so founded. Later in book three Paridell refers to the destruction of the 'Geaunts broode' as,

> A famous history to be enrold
> In euerlasting moniments of brasse,
> That all the antique Worthies merits far did passe.
>
> (III. 9. 50)

He further points out that Brutus was the founder of Troynovant [London], thereby placing its foundation many centuries before that of Rome. The 'Briton Moniments', however, content themselves with asserting the establishment of the British 'throne' and the spread of empire 'to the vtmost shore' (10). When Brutus dies he divides his 'imperiall state' between his three sons and from this point on the account plunges into the frustrating difficulties of domestic politics. Nevertheless, this first section stands as an epitome of the entire story. We witness the slow emergence of civilization from barbarity as Britain separates itself from 'the *Celticke* mayn-land' and gains a distinct identity. Such severance fuels the dynamism of empire as Brutus in a sense resurrects Troy in imitation of his kinsman Aeneas. The imperial destiny Virgil claims for Rome is, therefore, by implication attributed to Britain. Occupancy of the throne imposes a moral duty to extend the Briton empire.

With the history of Locrine moral complications begin to creep into the account (14-20). At first the king emerges as a royal saviour defeating the 'straung' nations who 'ouerflow'd all countries farre away,/ Like *Noyes* great flood'. However, returning 'proud of victorie', he 'insolent wox through vnwonted ease. . . . And fell to vaine voluptuous disease' (17). Victorious in war, he defeats himself in peace — an object lesson to indolent Elizabethans. Guendoline's rebellion leads to his own incarceration and to the murder of his mistress and illegitimate daughter: 'such was the end, that to disloyall loue did fall' (19). This authorial comment invites us to see the episode in purely moral terms: the wages of sin are death. Yet the fact remains that the 'faire Sabrina', Locrine's daughter, was 'innocent of all' — she is the virgin spirit invoked in Milton's *Comus*. Her death raises the problem of contingency in the most forceful way. Her name, it is true, lives on in that of the river, but hers is the immortality of slaughtered innocence. Topography encodes not solely the great victories of civilization but also its most lamentable failures.

A further complication is that the pitiless queen who 'first taught men a woman to obay' might in other respects be regarded as a type of Elizabeth. Her make-up is complex. She combines remorseless vengeance with personal sacrifice, freely surrendering the throne to an 'vnworthie' son who fills it with shame only to bequeath it to another as unworthy as himself. The moral issues are becoming murky, and consciously so. Spenser appears to have had no source in the early chronicles for the evil character he attributed to Madan. He preferred the later versions.[52] Throughout Arthur's career the insistence is on worthiness, but here amongst his own ancestors are uncovered records of the foulest crimes, no less part of his heritage than the glorious victories of which so many 'braue moniments' also remain. The chronicles expose the personal histories behind the great names deftly counterpointing success with failure to entangle great movements of history in the vagaries of private passion. The implications for contemporary history are implicit but paramount.

The 'heritage of lasting peace' ushered in by Brute's ruthless if needful force produces Bladud who 'in arts/Exceld at *Athens* all the learned preace' (25). He is credited with introducing classical learning to England and with the construction through 'wondrous faculty' of the health-giving spring at Bath. In a perfect world-order the story should end here with the grandson of the second Brutus confirming the heritage of peace by bringing 'health to euery forreine nation' (26). One might almost mistake Bladud for one of Guyon's fairy kings until 'contending to excell/The reach of men' he destroys himself in a vain attempt to fly. The great father of civilization ends as a second Icarus, a symbol of the vanity of human wishes. His intellectual achievements end in folly, and his 'fall' ushers in the disastrous reigns of Lear and Gorboduc. In the scheme of Spenser's narrative Bladud is directly related to Britomart since it is he who fashioned the magic lance that preserves her throughout her various battles (III. 4. 60). She inherits all that is best in him, all that gives health and life, but his demise remains inextricable from his power. The lance Britomart carries advises her not to be 'too bold', to be content to act within 'the reach of men'. Spenser is here touching on the

52 Carrie Anna Harper, *The Sources of the British Chronicle History in Spenser's 'Faerie Queene'*, (Philadelphia, 1910), p. 63.

Marlovian problem of attaining a proper balance between aspiration and potential. Bladud's fall, like that of Simon Magus, prototype of all aspiring wisards, teaches the lesson of human limitations, a necessary prelude to reading the Fairy chronicles.

The two histories that immediately follow make an oblique comment upon Bladud's calamity since they both demonstrate the self-destructive forces of human nature at work within the family, the centre of human society. Wyden's 'mercilesse' and 'pittilesse' murder of her son brings to a grim close the account of '*Brutus* sacred progenie,/ Which had seuen hundred yeares this scepter borne,/ With high renowme, and great felicitie' (36). The reader is tempted to interpret this ironically, particularly after allusions to 'the greedy thirst of royall crowne,/ That knowes no kindred nor regardes no right' in the previous stanza. Yet Spenser's tone is not ironic; the effect he wishes to produce is even more unsettling. There is no need to take 'sacred' as 'accursed', nor even to question the 'great felicitie' involved. The line of Brutus *is* the chosen line, and his people the chosen people. What we have read, calamitous as it seems, constitutes the only 'felicitie' available to such men within time and history. Mercy and pity actually impede Mercilla. As in the Old Testament, the chosen race comes to grief, yet despite the ill success of Brutus's descendants they represent an order of which they remain largely unaware even in their downfall. Their eventual self-destruction, as children turn against parents and parents against children, leaves the state bereft of leadership and breaks the precious continuity of the kingly line. We have returned yet again to the Elizabethan problem of the succession:

> The noble braunch from th'antique stocke was torne
> Through discord, and the royall throne forlorne:
> Thenceforth this Realme was into factions rent,
> Whilest each of *Brutus* boasted to be borne,
> That in the end was left no moniment
> Of *Brutus*, nor of Britons glory auncient. (36)

The book Arthur reads is entitled 'Briton Moniments', but all such material monuments have perished. The pattern of slow emergence into national identity established by the earliest part of the chronicle is obscured as the wheel comes full circle, returning us to a state resembling primeval confusion. Yet no sooner has the chronicle reached its nadir when Dunwallo, 'the gracious *Numa* of great *Britanie*', founds a new system of government based on law or 'pollicie'.[53] Spenser implies that the process of renewal necessitates the collapse of the old order since Dunwallo, like his classical precursor,

53 Livy, I. 19. *The Early History of Rome*, translated by Aubrey de Sélincourt (Harmondsworth, 1960), p. 38. Brutus would, therefore, correspond to Aeneas and Dunwallo to Numa.

institutes an enlightened concept of monarchy fundamentally alien to that which had previously obtained:

> For till his dayes, the chiefe dominion
> By strength was wielded without pollicie;
> Therefore he first wore crowne of gold for dignitie. (39)

'Dignity' has replaced naked strength yet 'pollicie' remains ambivalent. The seemingly senseless self-destruction of the ruling house now proves to have been a necessary factor in the providential evolution of Arthur's inheritance.[54] From the ashes of the royal family there arises a new order purporting to be based on the rule of law. Not surprisingly, as in the case of Numa Pompilius, such innovations are attributed to divine revelation. In theory the religious aspect of monarchy sustains its civic importance and the crown becomes as much a symbol of justice as of power. Until the coming of Caesar (49), the new line maintains a level of civilization comparable to that of the fairy chronicles. Unlike Bladud, for example, Dame Mertia, wife of Dunwallo's great-grandson, exercises an entirely beneficent influence as,

> A woman worthy of immortall prayse,
> Which for this Realme found many goodly layes,
> And wholesome Statutes to her husband brought;
> Her many deemd to haue beene of the Fayes,
> As was *Aegerie*, that Numa tought;
> Those yet of her be *Mertian* lawes both nam'd and thought. (42)

It is Mertia's absolute dedication to justice and the rule of law that gives rise to the legend of her fairy origins. But the comparison with 'Aegerie' might well alert the cynical to uncomfortable similarities with what Machiavelli regarded as the first recorded exploitation of religious belief for political ends. Nevertheless, though fairy myth be fairy guile, such legends fleetingly associate the troubled history of the ancient Britons with Gloriana's ideal civic state, or in other words, with visions of its own potential fulfilment. There is no magic involved though much policy. Mertia's 'prayse' not her person proves immortal, and Dunwallo survives only in the dignity of the

54 Harper, pp. 93-4. For the view that 'the existence of a divine, coherent plan' working throughout Spenser's chronicle is suggested by the numerological arrangement of the stanzas see Jerry Leath Mills, 'Spenser and the Numbers of History: A Note on the British and Elfin Chronicles in *The Faerie Queene*', *Philological Quarterly*, 55 (1976), 281-7 (p. 284).

crown he redeems: '*Dunwallo* dyde (for what may liue for ay?)'.[55] Such immortality is open to all and the 'dew successe' of the king's descendants (despite the troubles of 'pitteous Elidure') forms yet another link with the fairy chronicle where this very principle guarantees the stability and order of the fairy state. Only the perfidy of Androgeus, 'false to natiue soyle', gives the Romans a foothold in Britain, and affords Spenser the opportunity of pointing another topical moral: 'Nought else, but treason, from the first this land did foyle'. The history of Dunwallo's successors represents the very best that humanity can hope for: the establishment of impartial laws, royal fertility, rightful inheritance, and a victorious foreign policy. The incidence of all such blessings in the one house is unusual to say the least, and their perilous fragility is emphasised by the successful invasion of Julius Caesar (spiritual kinsman to Philip II) whose 'hideous hunger of dominion' assisted by the treachery of the 'enuious' Androgeus overturns all that has been attained. Despite this, the civic achievements of the House of Dunwallo distinguish it from that of Brutus, and 'endlesse moniments' are left in its wake. 'Pollicie' works.

The period of Roman dominion which ensues lasts 'till *Arthur* all that reckoning defrayd' (49). The Prince, of course, cannot recognise himself in this future redeemer, yet the phrase indicates how the fate of successive dynasties culminates in his own personal history. The fall of the ruling house initiates an era of oppression and slavery, but it too is made appear essential to the providential plan. Even 'treason' forms part of the pattern. The 'Briton Moniments' speak of the future as if it were already chronicled. Arthur has not yet begun to reign but the phrase concerning him is given in the past tense. Thus chronicle and prophecy combine to telescope the normal sequence of temporal events. In any case, the birth of Christ during the reign of Cymbeline (50) and the adoption of Christianity by Lucius (53) have the effect of bringing Roman and Briton closer together until finally the Emperor Constantine is produced from their union (59-60).

By closely interweaving the strands of native and European history, Spenser universalizes the significance of the British success thereby placing his countrymen at the very centre of providential concern. Yet for those locked in the day to day struggles of life history proceeds relentlessly. No sooner has the second Constantine vanquished the 'spoilefull Picts' than the ambitions of Vortigern introduce the Saxon menace. Since the slaying of Vortigern by the sons of Constantine, Uther and Ambrose, is foretold by Merlin in Geoffrey of Monmouth, it is doubly appropriate that the eventual union of Saxon and Briton — suggested in the person of Spenser's St George

55 *Discourses on the First Decade of Livy*, I. 11; Ernst H. Kantorowicz, *The King's Two Bodies: A Study in Medieval Political Theology* (Princeton, 1957), pp. 336-42.

— should become a major theme of Merlin's prophecy in book three.

The last remarkable image of the 'Briton Moniments' is that of Stonehenge. It was at Stonehenge that the Saxon Hengist slaughtered 'three hundred Lordes ... Of British bloud' whose 'dolefull moniments ... Th'eternal markes of treason' may still be seen in the great stone circle. And it was also at Stonehenge 'by the heath' that Arthur's uncle King Aurelius was laid to rest after his treacherous poisoning. According to Geoffrey of Monmouth, Stonehenge is the Briton name for the Giants' Ring brought from Ireland on Merlin's advice on account of its medicinal properties to dignify the ancient cemetery at Mt Ambrius. In later times Arthur's father, Uther Pendragon, credited by Holinshed with 'serpentine subtiltie', was also buried inside the ring.[56] What Spenser has done, is to associate the greatest national 'moniment' with infamy. In the course of his chronicle we move from the Britons' victory over the Giants to the entombment of the murdered Aurelius within the Giant's ring. The descendants of Brutus, the Giant-slayer, lie within the great stones as all human endeavour lies within the shadow of gigantic corruption. Stonehenge is a monument both to honour and to infamy and the curse of human history is that the two cannot be disentangled. The monuments of time bear a disconcerting resemblance to its ruins

The 'Briton Moniments' end 'abruptly' but very deliberately upon the word 'succeeding' 'without full point, or other Cesure right'. Like the reader of a long, intriguing novel who suddenly finds the last page missing, Arthur feels cheated. Man longs for closure, for a resolution that will unify all the diverse incidents of life, but this is precisely what history denies him. The chronicle ends in the tense with which *The Faerie Queene* begins, past continuous. In thus confronting the historian's 'bare was', Spenser highlights the difference between life and art. The chronicle cannot conclude since each moment, as St Augustine pointed out, passes even as we think of it. Spenser breaks his chronicle in mid-sentence thereby creating an image of history itself. 'By succession', the race, like Adonis, is 'made perpetuall' (III. 6. 47). But who will perpetuate the Tudor dynasty? Arthur's anxiety is also the reader's.

The 'succeeding' events which the 'Briton Moniments' anticipate are those of Arthur's own lifetime. One of the principal differences between him and Guyon is that he remains ignorant of his own identity, and therefore cannot appreciate the personal relevance of the final word nor of the auspicious pun contained within it. Nevertheless his gratitude to his, as he thinks, adopted country proves his worthiness: 'how much to her we owe, that all vs gaue,/ That gaue vnto vs all, what euer good we haue'. The 'fatall error' which led

56 Geoffrey of Monmouth (VIII. 10-12, 24), pp. 196-8, 211; *Chronicles of England, Scotland and Ireland*, 6 vols (London 1806-8), I, 570.

Brutus to the chosen land finds its antitype in the tortuous but equally 'fatal' wanderings of the Prince as he comes into his ancient inheritance. Fate and error are inextricable. To man fate is error, to God error is providence. Tasso accounted the forms of epic and romance particularly suitable to the demonstration of such complex relationships.[57] Thus by insinuating chronicle into romance-epic, Spenser implies a coincidence of structure. Allegorical fiction projects the patterns of history into exaggerated images of themselves thereby facilitating imaginative exploration of their formative forces. But the process is dangerously circular since the 'patterns' themselves are born of allegorical habits of exegesis. Read in the 'fleshly' House of Alma, the Briton Chronicles partake of human fallibility and remain as potentially delusive as the Celtic 'romances' dismissed in *A View of the Present State of Ireland.* Much of Spenser's material, as he well knew, was designated 'fabulous' and 'beyond credit' by Holinshed (*Prose*, p. 82).

The notion of history as a sort of providential romance ensured the fascination of the form for generations of Renaissance writers, yet as Spenser tells Raleigh, romance is also a notoriously escapist genre 'the which the most part of men delight to read, rather for variety of matter, then for profite of the ensample'. Thus under certain circumstances 'historicall fiction' might caricature the patterns it was meant to explore and providential history emerge —especially in the wake of Guicciardini and Machiavelli — as an equivalent exercise in escapism. Spenser engineers such circumstances himself by juxtaposing two radically contrasting, though related, chronicles within a fictional narrative which draws upon both without reconciling them. In the absence of a Magus, such as Merlin, to inform their response, Arthur and the reader are left to form their own judgements, the latter in the knowledge that the Round Table too was destined to collapse. The effect is disconcerting. Interpreted as visions of Tudor history (or Tudor Myth) encapsulating the providential 'conceit' informing the Briton chronicles, the Fairy narrative bridges the time-gap between Arthur and Elizabeth yet remains strangely inadequate to the vibrant, if often destructive, individualism of their Briton counterparts. As yet Spenser would seem to have struck no workable balance between the private and public domains.

Guyon's chronicle 'ne yet has ended' — the tense is notable — when Arthur's breaks off. The Fairy chronicles largely ignore the problems of life to concentrate upon the achievement. When Elfinor died, for example,

> He left three sonnes, the which in order raynd,
> And all their Ofspring, in their dew descents,

57 *Discourses on the Heroic Poem*, translated by Mariella Cavalchini and Irene Samuel (Oxford, 1973), pp. 16-17.

Euen seuen hundred Princes, which maintaynd
With mightie deedes their sundry gouernments;
That were too long their infinite contents
Here to record, ne much materiall:
Yet should they be most famous moniments,
And braue ensample, both of martiall,
And ciuill rule to kings and states imperiall. (74)

The details are not 'much materiall' for the simple reason that plentiful 'ensamples' have already been supplied in Arthur's chronicle, as in his own exploits. Here the overall pattern takes precedence over specific incidents, and Spenser subordinates his interest in individuals to his interest in the race. Society itself is the principal 'character' of this account. The bequest of Prometheus (Providence in Time) sets man apart as a separate species. In the fairy chronicle he exploits his advantages to the full.

The 'seuen hundred Princes' have often been related to the seven hundred years of Brutus's line, but the essential difference is that theirs are years of unimpeded progress whereas the others end in chaos. Despite the troubles of individual fairies the success of their state remains unimpaired. When 'faire *Elferon* . . . did vntimely dy' his place was 'doubly' supplied by his younger brother Oberon. There is, of course, a clear parallel here with Tudor history since Henry VIII also doubly supplied the place of Prince Arthur 'in spousall, and dominion' (75). However, the parallel ignores the fact that Henry's marriage to Katharine of Aragon was later judged incestuous and ended in tragedy. Moreover its final result was to cast the all-important question of succession into grave doubt and divide the country into endless factions. In Fairyland matters are managed with far greater foresight:

He dying left the fairest *Tanaquill*,
Him to succeede therein, by his last will:
Fairer and nobler liueth none this howre,
Ne like in grace, ne like in learned skill;
Therefore they *Glorian* call that glorious flowre,
Long mayst thou *Glorian* liue, in glory and great powre. (76)

In Fairyland Tanaquill is undisputed heir to Oberon and succeeds directly to the throne. This is history as God might see it, with all the inessentials removed and the pure divine plan, the great structure of redemption, visible as the true and only reality. Writers such as John Foxe struggled to interpret English history in such terms. The atmosphere of epiphany which he casts over the birth of Elizabeth — recalled in the moving prophecy attributed to Cranmer in Shakespeare's *Henry VIII* — points in this direction but the character of her forbears proved so intractable as to occasion constant qualification.[58] The providential historian cannot vie with the providential poet. The chronicles of Faerie constitute a vision of history which tantalisingly 'shadows' real events. Man is invited to realise the vision within the chronicle of his own times, arranging matters of 'policy' and succession in a rational, deliberate manner thereby creating his own fairy myth in history as Spenser has done in fiction.

In the famous *Dialogue* between Cardinal Pole and Thomas Lupset, Thomas Starkey concluded that good fortune was necessary to the happiness of the earthly republic while virtue of itself was insufficient.[59] In the fairy chronicles Fortune appears to work for the good of the fairy race all the time and its benefits are immediately manifest. At first this would appear to render their mode of existence alien to the conditions of human life, yet this is not in fact the case. It is not merely that individual fairies suffer defeat and disappointment but that, rightly considered, Fortune also works for the total good of man. In the fourth book of *De Consolatione Philosophiae* Boethius argues that all fortune would be perceived as beneficial were it not that man's lack of spiritual vision renders its usefulness unclear. He proceeds to suggest that if we could view the course of history through the eyes of God we would have to agree that bad fortune did not exist.[60] In this respect, Spenser's fairy chronicle constitutes a fictive image of fortune's ultimate benevolence. This is not to ignore the problem of pain but to reassess its function in the great scheme of things. When the plan lies fully revealed evil will be subsumed into the pattern of providence, and the history of the chosen few will disclose itself as one of unbroken progress towards the ultimate glory symbolised by the Fairy Queen. Once one agrees to read the Briton chronicles through those of faery there is 'linear' progress after all. The cycles of Renaissance historiography spiral upwards towards a still point. 'Savage' anarchy gives way to monarchy established by brute force. Thereafter comes monarchy by rule of law, preferable to its predecessor but more fragile. Its enemy is Rome, first as enslaving empire then, more insidiously, as corrupting religion. Thereafter comes the Apocalypse, and the monarchy of grace. Yet as he reads the history of his own race, man finds himself in the position of Prince Arthur,

58 *The Acts and Monuments of the Church*, edited by M. Hobart Seymour (London, 1838), p. 534. Just as Spenser's fairy chronicles make Elizabeth her father's sole and immediate heir, Shakespeare's Cranmer smoothes the difficulties of the succession by suggesting Elizabeth's mystical generation of James, her spiritual son and sole heir (*Henry VIII*, V. 4. 39-47). For Tanaquil as king-maker see above p. 99.

59 *A Dialogue between Reginald Pole and Thomas Lupset*, edited by Kathleen Burton (London, 1948), pp. 66-9.

60 *The Consolation of Philosophy* (Book 4, Prose 7), translated by Richard Green (Indianapolis, 1962), pp. 97-9.

unsure of his relationship to the great scheme and unaware of the full meaning of the text. Only in moments of supreme revelation does he awake to a sense of life's hidden spiritual source.

V. *Isis Church and Time's Justice*

Moments of spiritual illumination hallow the time, and often the place, in which they occur. Consequently, to the Medieval and Renaissance mind, time is 'uneven': there are sacred times just as their are sacred places. Indeed the word temple is etymologically associated with 'tempus'. Thus the Christian calendar sets certain times apart — feast days, holy days, anniversaries of great religious events — although such distinctions are by no means exclusively Christian. Pagan man regularly re-enacted the great paradigms of myth in elaborate rituals designed to reunite him with the primary forces of creation. The times of these rituals were sacred times in which the participants in a sense became the contemporaries of the powers with which they sought identity.[61] Britomart undergoes such an experience in the Temple of Isis, or Isis Church as the epigraph terms it, subtly fusing ancient myth with contemporary Christianity to suggest the fundamental unity of all religious experience — an idea congenial to the Neo-Platonists. Like doorways in time, prophetic dreams effect the 'vacatio' of soul from body necessary to communion with the divine intelligences. In such a state, according to Ficino, the mind communes with providence.[62]

In the euhemeristic interpretation explained, but subsequently rejected, by Plutarch, Isis and Osiris emerge as paragons of justice and equity 'deified' after death by their admirers.[63] Their further significance is explained by Spenser himself:

> *Isis* doth the Moone portend;
> Like as *Osyris* signifies the Sunne.
> For that they both like race in equall iustice runne. (V. 7. 4)

As the two heavenly bodies which determine its computation, the sun and the moon regulate the course of human time dividing the year in 'equall iustice' between them.[64] Since the principle of equity governs temporal

61 Mircea Eliade, *The Sacred and the Profane*, translated by Willard R. Trask (New York, 1959), pp. 75, 87, 99. See also Eliade, *The Myth of the Eternal Return*, translated by Willard R. Trask (Princeton, 1954), p. 7.

62 Ficino, *Opera*, 2 vols (Basle, 1576), I, 288-93. For his translation of Synesius's *De Somniis* see II, 1968-1978.

63 Of Isis and Osiris, 23.

64 According to Plutarch, Isis (moon) seeks Osiris (sun) during the long winter nights (52), and the sun functions to restore the moon after eclipse (55). Isis and Osiris are also to be regarded as the male and female principles of generation.

existence the Litae or Hours (Spenser appears to conflate the two) fittingly surround Mercilla's throne. Originally the Horae served as goddesses of water and sky but eventually developed, through their relationship to time, into 'the guardians of natural law and of the divine Order which causes the same thing to recur in Nature in an unalterable sequence'.[65] In the *Mutabilitie Cantos*, for example, the Howres function as 'Porters . . . Of heauens gate . . . Which they did dayly watch, and nightly wake/By euen turnes, ne euer did their charge forsake' (VII. 7. 45). Even dealing is the hallmark of time. Not surprisingly, therefore, Talus, whose ignorance of equity would profane the temple, is denied access to Isis Church. Britomart enters alone since her immediate purpose of redeeming Artegall (Justice) from bondage casts her in the role of Isis to his Osiris. Their union, both as 'historical' characters and allegorical representatives of Justice and Equity, secures the future of the British imperium. This is particularly appropriate in the light of book three for according to the ancient myth after the archetypal destroyer Typhaon had murdered Osiris, his wife Isis restored him to life and imprisoned his enemy. Typhaon, however, was never completely destroyed and his influence remained responsible for the evil and corruption in the world.[66] In Merlin's prophecy Britomart is fated to see her husband undone by 'practise criminall/ Of secret foes' (III. 3. 28), but not before the conception of his son. By this means she performs the function of Isis in restoring him to life, for the child is no less than, 'his Image dead,/That liuing him in all actiuity . . . shall represent' (III. 3. 29). In the fulness of time he shall emerge 'like as a Lyon, that in drowsie cave/ Hath long time slept' to regain his father's throne.[67] As he will then need to harness the forces Talus represents, the episode again illustrates Spenser's ambivalent attitude to political violence. Talus's presence would desecrate the Temple but the imperial vision experienced within it both necessitates and 'justifies' his employment by the central Briton characters. Like time itself, violence is both creative and destructive. As divine providence justifies time in both its aspects, so human providence, partaking of the divine, justifies violence.

In creating the Temple, or Church, of Isis, Spenser drew upon the long tradition of Medieval legal allegory with its manifold depictions of the 'Templum Iustitiae' and the 'goddess' of justice herself. Aulus Gellius provides a seminal source in his presentation of Iustitia as 'an awe-inspiring virgin with penetrating eyes and with some venerable grief in her dignity' attended by a perfect judge known as 'Iustitiae antistes' or the 'priest' of

65 Sigmund Freud, *The Standard Edition of the Complete Psychological Works*, translated by James Strachey and Anna Freud, 24 vols (London, 1953-73), XII (1958), 297.

66 *Isis and Osiris*, 30, 55.

67 Plutarch particularly emphasises the role of Horus as avenger. *Isis and Osiris*, 19.

justice.[68] Medieval lawyers such as Ulpian were very fond of representing themselves as 'priests' and this undoubtedly explains much of the reverence attributed to the priests of Isis in Spenser's description.[69] As a result, the 'idol' of Isis, unlike that set up by the blasphemous Geryoneo, is not profane, and Britomart prostrates herself before it without any sense of impropriety to worship justice, one of the supreme aspects of God. The iconography of the idol is characteristic of former Medieval and Renaissance depictions of the same subject.[70] The emphasis upon the centrality of reason, explored in the myth of the vine (V. 7. 10-11), is also typical of such treatments since reason forms the basis of human justice; passion has helped enslave Artegall. The association between intoxication and delusive dreams was traditional.[71]

Falling asleep 'under the wings of Isis', Britomart begins to enter the sacred time of cosmic myth. While 'her earthly parts with soft delight/ of sencelesse sleepe did deeply drowned lie', she receives a vision of the type that does not deceive declaring 'the course of all her fortune and posteritie'. This last detail is vital since it links the experience to Merlin's prophecy. Nevertheless, the present revelation differs in kind from the former. Merlin revealed the historic pattern of British history, the slow and painful emergence of unity through centuries of civil war and political disturbance. His listeners, though moved, remained detached from his account, unable to share his prophetic ecstasy. In the temple, however, Britomart experiences personal revelation. The first stage in this process, a prelude to the re-enactment of the paradigmatic marriage, is her virtual identification with the goddess to whom she has prayed a short while previously:

> All sodainely she saw transfigured
> Her linnen stole to robe of scarlet red,
> And Moone-like Mitre to a Crowne of gold,
> That euen she her selfe much wondered
> At such a chaunge, and ioyed to behold
> Her selfe, adorn'd with gems and iewels manifold. (V. 7. 13)

The word 'transfigured' is doubtless intended to recall Christ's experience but the occasion is altogether less tranquil. Just as Britomart becomes queen there occurs a fiery cataclysm 'that all the Temple put in ieopardy/Of flaming, and her selfe in great perplexity'. Although the crocodile (Osiris) swallows the flames, he then turns upon Britomart herself until the 'goddesse' beats

68 Kantorowicz, pp. 107-111 (p. 109).

69 *Ibid.*, 118-21, 139-40.

70 Jane H. Aptekar, *Icons of Justice: Iconography and Thematic Imagery in Book V of 'The Faerie Queene'* (New York, 1969), pp. 87-107.

71 *Isis and Osiris*, 6.

him back.[72] At this stage there would seem to be two female participants, the goddess and her surrogate, but in the following stanza Britomart clearly supplies the place of Isis as the lover of Osiris by conceiving the crocodile's child, 'a Lion of great might;/That shortly did all other beasts subdew'. The lion, as the high priest explains, is Britomart's son, and his explanation is obviously intended to recall Merlin's similar description.

The difference now is that Britomart has herself entered the world of myth. Now it is the gods who act as interpreters assigning her an appropriate role in the mythic pattern. The priest explains the symbolism of the vision as he would explain the cosmic myth itself leading Britomart from 'errour blind' to penetrating insight. His address to the 'Magnificke Virgin' may be intended to recall the opening words of the 'Magnificat' recited in honour of the Virgin Mary, as British history once more emerges as the secular equivalent of scripture:

> For that same Crocodile doth represent
> The righteous Knight, that is thy faithfull louer,
> Like to *Osyris* in all iust endeuer.
> For that same Crocodile *Osyris* is. (V. 7. 22)

According to one version of the legend, Osiris was the father of Hercules Spenser's mythical model for Artegall.[73] The correspondence is thus complete.

Just one night has passed in the action of the romance but within these few hours has been re-enacted the ancient paradigm of cosmic justice. It defines Britomart's role in the context of the cosmic spiritual reality underlying and sustaining the seemingly episodic events of the romance. Paradoxically the dream is more 'real' that its interpretation, indeed no interpretation can fully encompass it. Since, according to Plato, spiritual things are more 'real' than material, the translation of timeless symbols into temporal equivalents is fundamentally regressive. Prophetic sleep constitutes an awakening of the soul (*Phaedo*, 83). Britomart's dream 'interprets' her life. Its centrality to the poem's historical concern is entirely fitting since the burden of the whole book, from the address to Elizabeth in the proem to the attempt to 'reform' Ireland in canto twelve, is the embodiment of supreme earthly justice in the British monarchy.

Britomart's return to the world of the narrative marks a deliberate anticlimax. The purpose of the vision is not to detain her in Isis Church but to inspire the completion of her quest. This distinguishes it from the masque she

72 This reflects Plutarch's Apocalypse, *Isis and Osiris*, 47, 75.

73 Jean Seznec, *The Survival of the Pagan Gods*, translated by Barbara F. Sessions (Princeton, 1972 — first pub. 1953), p. 26.

encounters in the House of Busirane, where Amoret, too, takes part in a sort of mythical pageant but of a singularly destructive, enervating kind. Whereas in the Temple of Isis the elements of disorder are made to subserve the forces of creation, the antimasque elements of Cupid's procession overturn the forces of concord to produce devastation (III. 12. 25). Britomart sees her vision while her '*earthly* parts' lie 'deeply drowned' in sleep, but the Masque of Cupid is preceded by 'a most delitious harmony' that 'the feeble senses wholly did confound,/And the *fraile soule* in *deepe* delight nigh *dround*' (III. 12. 6). The vision of Isis releases the soul from the body but the masque entraps it ending not merely in death, but 'death with infamie', corroding the immortality of its victim's name. The masque proceeds 'as on the ready flore/Of some Theatre' not in a temple since it presents a distorted image of life at a second remove from reality rather than an insight into the very nature of things. When Britomart encounters her, Amoret has already spent seven months in the House of Busirane re-enacting the same degrading ritual night after night. Not surprisingly, 'lewd *Losse of Time*' figures prominently in the pageant. What we are dealing with here is not the sacred time of the temple, but the endlessly repetitive, punitive time of the damned as described in the recurrent horrors of Dante's *Inferno*.

By liberating Amoret, Britomart completes a necessary stage in her own sexual development, releasing the energies destined to participate in the constructive cycles of the Gardens of Adonis and further the course of empire. Scudamour can no more win his way into the House of Busirane than Talus into the Temple of Isis, just as Scudamour could no more prevent the capture of Amoret than Talus could prevent the enslavement of Artegall. Their natures are too closely associated with the respective problems for this to be possible. Only Britomart, combining the virtues of lady and knight, of chastity and love, of justice and equity, can keep the epic action moving along its destined course. Dispelling the illusions of Busirane is a necessary prelude to enjoying the insights of Isis. As in the case of Arthur and George, maturity transforms Britomart's sexual fantasies into political visions. Hers is the 'sacred *throne*' of a 'chaste bodie' (III. 6. 5). Her sojourn in the temple prepares her for the ensuing combat by strengthening her resolve. Like the House of Holiness, the temple stands firm as a centre of moral and spiritual energy affording Apocalyptic visions of ultimate reality. The House of Busirane vanishes to nothing as Amoret and Britomart emerge to continue the temporal quest. Yet theirs is merely one quest of many and it too is eventually subsumed into the cosmic patterns of decline and renewal which pervade the poem. The episode in Isis Church vindicates the belief that the axis about which all such experiences revolve is that of divine justice. It represents the ultimate expression of the historical sense informing all of the poem's Briton chronicles.

CHAPTER FOUR

Perpetuity

All be he subiect to mortalitie,
Yet is eterne in mutabilitie,
And by succession made perpetuall,
Transformed oft, and chaunged diuerslie. (III. 6. 47)

I. *Secular Typology*

Spenser was increasingly fascinated by the unity of history and the perpetuation of life, and such interests led him to re-assess the limitations of mortality in the light of a greater scheme. No character, action, or age has its meaning alone, but must find its place in the continually unfolding pattern. From the viewpoint of the individual, time's creative powers seem preferable to its powers of destruction although, rightly considered, these are merely the twin facets of one dynamic force. The more sophisticated become the methods of interpretation, the more complex the resulting view of history, the events of one age anticipating those of another not merely as cause and effect but as type and antitype. Furthermore, amid the flux of life certain things are perceived to endure. Certain elements of human society, as also of the biological forces sustaining it, prove impervious to the passage of time, achieving the condition of perpetual duration. A bedrock of permanence underlies the currents of change and Spenser's poem attempts to reflect this situation in its profusion of images of continuity and return.

The 'Letter to Raleigh' together with the proems to the various books establish for the reader a dual frame of reference in time by exploiting the popular legend of the 'once and *future* king', the implication being that the spirit of Arthur is restored in his Tudor descendants.[1] As we have seen, Polydore Vergil's attack upon Arthur's historicity had proven premature, and the king continued to enjoy the support even of those who, like Leland and Selden, deplored the romantic fictions attaching to his name.[2] Despite his

1 Edwin Greenlaw, *Studies in Spenser's Historical Allegory* (Baltimore, 1932), pp. 2-57; Henry Ansgar Kelly, *Divine Providence in the England of Shakespeare's Histories* (Cambridge, Mass., 1970), pp. 72-5.

2 John Leland, *The Assertion of King Arthure*, translated by Richard Robinson with the Latin Original in Christopher Middleton, *The Famous History of Chinon of England*,

acceptance of Arthur's historicity, however, Spenser employs similar fictions with the result that few, if any, of the events described in *The Faerie Queene* correspond to those chronicled by Geoffrey of Monmouth.

In adopting this course, Spenser was following in the footsteps of Virgil. Aeneas, too, was a national hero the outlines of whose story were well-known and broadly accepted as historical, but his descent to the underworld, his dealings with gods and goddesses, his private hopes and fears, were recognised as products of the imagination. Furthermore, as a result of commentaries by Donatus and Servius, it was generally agreed that the activities of the fictionalized Aeneas made covert allusion to those of Virgil's patron Augustus.[3] It was not a question of continued allegory in Spenser's sense of the term but of scattered, and sometimes obscure, anticipations of later Roman history in the heroic narrative. The most striking instance is Anchises's prophecy of the future glories of 'empire', a prophecy made to culminate in the family of Augustus as Merlin's culminates in that of Elizabeth. This is not to say that such interpretations preoccupied Virgilian critics, but rather that a new level of interpretation had been added to the critical approach. Hereafter, it was recognised that narrative time was uniquely related to the time of composition.

Such modes of critical thought were greatly strengthened by the insistence of biblical exegetes upon typological interpretations of the Old Testament, interpretations in which characters and events were held to prefigure crucial incidents in the ministry of Christ.[4] The method was distinct from allegory in that it cast no doubt on the historicity of the Old Testament itself: Moses could prefigure Christ and still remain Moses. It was acknowledged that some books of the Old Testament, such as the Book of Daniel, were primarily prophetic and typology was reserved for the interpretation of the historical books alone. However, the adoption of a providential outlook made possible the extension of typological interpretations from the written word to the living word. Contemporary kings and popes could then be regarded as antitypes of Old Testament figures — 'antitypes' in the sense that, living within the Christian dispensation, they fulfil or complete the actions of those who lived prior to the incarnation. Elizabeth I might be seen as the antitype of Judith

edited by William Edward Mead, Early English Text Society, Original Series, 165 (London, 1925), pp. 57-8, 125; For Selden's views see Michael Drayton, *Complete Works*, edited by W.J. Hebel, 5 vols (Oxford, 1961), IV, 46-7, 66-7.

3 Domenico Comparetti, *Vergil in the Middle Ages*, translated by E.F.M. Benecke (London, 1895), pp. 56-63; Michael O'Connell, *Mirror and Veil: The Historical Dimension of Spenser's 'Faerie Queen'* (Chapel Hill, 1977), pp. 23-31.

4 Erich Auerbach, *Scenes from the Drama of European Literature*, translated by Ralph Manheim (New York, 1959), pp. 28-60; Northrop Frye, *The Great Code* (London, 1982), pp. 78-138; Marie Axton, *The Queen's Two Bodies* (London, 1977), pp. 36-7.

and the Reformation itself as the antitype of Israel's escape from Babylon.[5] In order to be strictly typological such interpretations had to involve appropriate biblical reference.[6] Interpreting contemporary events in the light of Revelation was a different matter. To identify, say, Mary Queen of Scots with the Whore of Babylon or the papacy with the Beast from the Sea was not, strictly speaking, to engage in typological interpretation. The same is true of the various attempts to decipher the Galfridian prophecies attributed to Merlin, a sort of pagan equivalent to Revelation.[7] The one thing that all such interpretations had in common, irrespective of whether the prophecy were pagan or Christian, was the interpreters' assumption that the relevant material held a particular significance for their own time, an illusion maintained despite generations of disappointment.[8]

Amongst Spenser's most influential predecessors a splendid example of the extension of typology from biblical to national history is to be found in John Bale's *King Johan.* At the close of the first act the king is cast as the antitype of Moses, leading his people to the borders of the promised land but unable to effect its conquest. The allusion is highly appropriate since Bale presents John as the first royal reformer, beginning the work destined to be completed by Henry VIII. According to this view, Henry emerges as the antitype of Joshua.[9] Furthermore, although John remains an historical character, he is surrounded throughout the play by such *personae* as Sedicyon, Dissymulacyon, Usurpid Powr, and Privat Welth. In approaching the king, however, Sedicyon takes upon him the form of Stephen Langton, the individual who, in Bale's opinion, embodied sedition most perfectly at that time. In order to underline the point, Sedicyon is made to remark that in former ages he has worn other shapes and in the future will wear many more. Thus typology and allegory support one another and the resolution of the play is placed, significantly, outside the time of dramatic action. A passage of years brings forth the figure of Truth who uncovers the crime and inspires Imperial Majesty (in the early versions Henry VIII, in the later Elizabeth) to take retributive action. Even though the historical Langton is long dead, Sedicyon is apprehended.[10] The important thing is that the Papacy is still very much

5 Frances A. Yates, *Astraea: The Imperial Theme in the Sixteenth Century* (Harmondsworth, 1977), pp. 77, 118.

6 Harry Berger, *The Allegorical Temper: Vision and Reality in Book II of Spenser's 'Faerie Queene'* (New Haven, 1957), p. 179.

7 Angus Fletcher, *The Prophetic Moment: An Essay on Spenser* (Chicago, 1971), pp. 106-21. See also *The Prophetia Merlini of Geoffrey of Monmouth: A Fifteenth-Century English Commentary*, edited by Caroline D. Eckhardt (Cambridge, Mass., 1982).

8 Frank Kermode, *The Sense of an Ending* (Oxford, 1966), pp. 67-89.

9 *King Johan* (1007-1120) in *Four Morality Plays*, edited by Peter Happé (Harmondsworth, 1979), p. 364.

10 *Ibid.* (2451-2592), pp. 420-6. For a full account of Bale's views see Leslie P. Fairfield,

alive though working through other agents. Bale, therefore, displays a remarkably ordered sense of history. Born centuries after John, Henry effectively fulfils his work, just as Elizabeth fulfils the work of Arthur. Typology tends to collapse the philosophical distinction between individuals and universals by lending the former timeless significance.

Here, however, we encounter the obvious objection that the 'historical' Arthur bears little resemblance to his fictional counterpart, an argument which applies equally to Bale's King John. Whereas Arthur's 'historic' defeat of the Emperor Lucius and subsequent establishment of the British empire may find their fulfilment in the victories of the Tudor family, can the same be said of Spenser's fictional hero? Can his deeds be said to 'prefigure' those of Elizabeth? I use the term 'prefigure' with extreme caution. Strictly speaking only something that has actually happened can be said to prefigure anything else and in any case strict typology requires reference to the historical books of the bible. It is clear, however, that within a fictional work one event can be made to prefigure another if the author so chooses. The bible itself presents the perfect model for all such literary devices.[11] The question is whether an event of fictionalized history or romance can be said to prefigure an event in the real world, and it leads us into a very difficult theoretical area concerning the nature of poetic truth and the source of aesthetic inspiration.[12]

Taking his cue from continental critics, Sir Philip Sidney preferred poetry to history on the grounds that poets deal in universal truths whereas historians are tied to particular facts. Renaissance scholars commonly faulted poets such as Lucan and Silvius Italicus for their over-reliance upon the details of history.[13] Accordingly Tasso can hold what at first appear to be two contradictory opinions. In the first place he demands that an epic should be founded upon fact whereas in the second he regards fiction or 'feigning' as the very essence of poetry.[14] Spenser, too, adopted this dual viewpoint. For him, Arthur is an historical character, yet the events of the poem constitute an 'historicall fiction'.[15] The complex structure of romance literature led Northrop Frye to dub it 'secular scripture', a designation particularly suited to a Christian romance such as *The Faerie Queene*. Its various 'legends' are

John Bale, Mythmaker for the English Reformation (West Lafayette, Indiana, 1976), p. 124; Thora Balslev Blatt, *The Plays of John Bale* (Copenhagen, 1968), pp. 99-129.

11 Jewish interpretations of the Old Testament involved such a technique. See Northrop Frye, *The Great Code*, p. 83.

12 Auerbach, pp. 11-76. See below p. 192.

13 Herschel Baker, *The Race of Time* (Toronto, 1967), p. 83.

14 *Discourses on the Heroic Poem*, translated by Mariella Cavalchini and Irene Samuel (Oxford, 1973), pp. 25-7, 34, 58-62.

15 For an alternative reading of 'historicall' see S.K. Heninger, 'The Aesthetic Experience of Reading Spenser', in *Contemporary Thought on Edmund Spenser*, edited by Richard C. Frushell and Bernard J. Vondersmith (Carbondale, 1975), p. 92.

presented as scripture of a sort in so far as Spenser regards his inspiration as proceeding from divine grace. Developing Frye's insight towards its logical conclusion, I wish to suggest that a secular scripture may admit of a secular typology, an idea implicit in my treatment of both Briton and Fairy chronicles in the preceding chapter. Spenser's choice of Arthur was a masterstroke of invention, gaining for the poem a hero central to a complex matrix of religious and chivalric legend, intimately associated with the quest of the Holy Grail, 'a tale chronicled', according to Malory, 'for one of the truest and one of the holiest that is in this world'.[16] By proceeding in this manner, Spenser afforded himself a wide range of allegorical and typological devices exploiting to the full the many resemblances between sacred and secular exegesis.

The Orgoglio episode, for example, though composed from hints in Dante and the Book of Revelation, is placed squarely in the time of the historic Arthur.[17] In other words, Spenser has attributed to an historical character an action which, had it really happened in the way he describes it, would certainly have been taken by a commentator such as Bale to prefigure Henry VIII's conflict with the papacy. But Orgoglio is not an historical character, even by the standards of Geoffrey of Monmouth, and Duessa rides straight out of the vision of St John. The historical fiction has Arthur battling for the freedom of St George against an improbable giant and an Apocalyptic witch. The etymology of the giant's name and the iconographic description of his partner alert us to their allegorical significance.[18] The basis for Arthur's defeat of Rome lies in the chronicles of the historic king, but Spenser has chosen to present this defeat symbolically. His 'historical' fiction is informed by Geoffrey of Monmouth's historical fact.

The literary reason for this procedure is the youth of Spenser's hero and his presence in Fairyland, the place or state in which the young prince will develop into the mature king. The projected second half of *The Faerie Queene*, the 'other part of polliticke vertues', would presumably have dealt with the chronicle material. The deeds of Spenser's prince prefigure the deeds of his 'historical' maturity, and the echoes of Revelation are there to ensure that the point is taken. Prince Arthur defeats Orgoglio and Duessa just as King Arthur defeats the forces of the Roman Empire and Henry VIII, brother of a second Arthur, defeats those of the papacy and its allies. Within the historical fiction, the 'secular scripture', we have a series of prefigurations. Ultimately all three prefigure the final destruction of the forces of darkness. Past, present, and future are thus drawn together in a manner to which the modern mind accommodates itself only with the greatest difficulty. But just how seriously

16 Malory, *Works*, edited by Eugene Vinaver, second edition (Oxford, 1977), p. 513.

17 John Erskine Hankins, *Source and Meaning in Spenser's Allegory* (Oxford, 1971), pp. 221-2.

18 Geoffrey of Monmouth (IX. 15 — X. 13).

the Tudors took such matters is indicated by the reliance of the Henrician 'Act of Restraint of Appeal to Rome' upon 'divers old Chronicles' (like those of Geoffrey of Monmouth) which declared England to have been anciently an 'empire' independent of Roman or papal power. In this view of history there are no isolated events or characters since no age can 'trammel up its consequence'. Providential historians could read national chronicles, as they read the bible, in the belief that one story is being told not many.

For reasons such as these Spenser's 'Legend of Ivstice' has given offence to those who object to Elizabeth's foreign policy, and particularly to her treatment of Ireland. In fact, the book is generally judged an artistic failure even by those who specialize in interpreting historical allegory.[19] Its proem is explicit in drawing the link between Artegall and the Queen. The virtue of justice is the 'most sacred' of all 'resembling God in his imperiall might':

> That powre he also doth to Princes lend,
> And makes them like himselfe in glorious sight,
> To sit in his owne seate, his cause to end,
> And rule his people right, as he doth recommend. (5 Proem, 10)

Hence the heavy emphasis on Mercilla's imperial seat. Presented there is an image of the queen *vice dei*. This notion of the monarch as an image of absolute justice or equity stretches back to the time of John of Salisbury and was developed by the lawyers of Frederick II who credited their sovereign with a share in immortality as the hypostasis of an immortal idea.[20] Allegorical accounts of this theory were common, and it was widely accepted in sixteenth-century England. William Baldwin's introduction to the *Mirror for Magistrates* asserts that,

> as Justice is the chief vertue, so is the ministracion thereof, the chiefest office: and therefore hath God established it with the chiefest name, honoring and calling Kinges, and all officers under them by his owne name, Gods. Ye be all Gods, as many as have in your charge any ministracion of Iustice.[21]

Spenser upholds the same theory in the proem by addressing Elizabeth as 'Dread Souerayne Goddesse, that doest highest sit/ In seate of iudgement, in th'Almighties stead'. Artegall is introduced as an instrument of Elizabethan justice — the first time any knight is associated so expressly with con-

19 O'Connell, p. 156.
20 Ernst H. Kantorowicz, *The King's Two Bodies: A Study in Medieval Political Theology* (Princeton, 1957), pp. 94, 112-4, 143.
21 *The Mirror for Magistrates*, edited by Lily B. Campbell (Cambridge, 1938), p. 65.

temporary policy. Here it is not just a matter of the broad implications of sixteenth-century history but of the minute details of Tudor policy particularly as this effected Belgium, Ireland, and France. On the surface the giants and dragons are much as before but they possess a more immediate and contemporary reference. Indeed a desperate urgency characterizes much of book five. Readers who have little difficulty accepting Arthur's conflict with Orgoglio as an allusion to the English Reformation seen in providential perspective, balk at finding the apparently less savoury details of Elizabeth's foreign policy represented in the same manner, as if possessed of the same universal significance. Moreover, book five concludes on a very sour note. Although George leaves Una at the end of book one, the sense of achievement, of having brought a period of history to a close, remains intact. Una will not reappear but 'enioyes sure peace *for euermore*' (II. 1. 2). By contrast, as Artegall leaves the Land of Irena pursued by Envy, Slander and the Blatant Beast, the sense of frustration and incompleteness is unmistakable. The force of 'necessity' used to justify military solutions in *A View of the Present State of Ireland* is invoked in the poem to justify their failure:

> But ere he could reforme it thoroughly,
> He through occasion called was away,
> To Faerie Court, that of necessity
> His course of Iustice he was forst to stay,
> And *Talus* to reuoke from the right way,
> In which he was that Realme for to redresse. (V. 12. 27)

The state of the deserted Irena invites comparison with that of Una. Spenser is treating of events virtually contemporary with the composition of the poem and once again (as in Merlin's cave) we have reached the point at which 'prophecy' gives way to speculation. Irena's fate is as dark to the author as it is to his readers: his personal blueprint for that future was destined to be consigned, like 'Artegall' himself, to the sidelines of history. In writing his 'Legend of Ivstice' he faced problems similar to those which confronted Foxe and Bale in their attempts to detect a spiritual rationale beneath the welter of political and military history. With the example of the *Acts and Monuments* before him, he must also have anticipated how the business of detection gradually transforms itself into that of imposition. In describing the chaos of the supposedly immutable and timeless heavens in his proem, he illustrates the difficulty of the undertaking in vivid terms since nature proves as intractable as history and man's search for a pattern is doubly frustrated. The very choice of a 'savage' knight to patronise justice confirms such suspicions. To argue for reason in a jungle is to risk collapsing into absurdity. Yet such is the world in which Elizabeth *must* represent divine justice since both a moral and a personal imperative are involved. Complicit as he is in his sovereign's policy, Spenser must justify her to defend himself. To this extent his earlier detachment from his material is seriously impaired. Theoretically, following the logic of providential history, it should have been possible to discover the hand of God in the politics of the queen. But since the aim of the book is itself overtly political such 'discovery' relies increasingly upon 'invention', just as propaganda informs 'vision'. In the world of real politics the doctrine of Providence becomes a formidable polemic weapon equally available to the cynical and the devout. If anything, Ireland's violent history would seem to demonstrate that the weapon is sharpest in the hands of those who believe in it. Spenser's problem is that he both believes and manipulates without necessarily being able to reconcile the two. Where divine authority is most needed there is only self-conscious poetic fiction.

Arthur's championship of Belge, defeat of Geryoneo, and destruction of the monster recall his progress in book one. Belge makes a plea for the delivery of her homeland to Mercilla just as Una approaches Gloriana in similar circumstances. The champions dispatched are St George, England's patron saint, and Prince Arthur, its national hero. The Chapelle of the Inquisition with its hecatombs of human sacrifice displays a marked similarity to the Dungeon of Orgoglio with its altar of martyrs drawn from Revelation. Duessa's giant and many-headed beast are complemented by a triple-headed giant, a 'huge great beast' and an Idol. The latter recalls the adoration of Duessa's beast by the kings of the earth in St John's account of the last days. In each book the slaying of a giant leads to a conflict with a dragon the destruction of which occasions scenes of public rejoicing. In each case, too, there occurs 'a great feast with joyous merriment' before the knight takes his leave of a people reluctant to see him go. In other words, Spenser has imposed upon contemporary events exactly the same sort of Apocalyptic pattern previously imposed upon distant history. Like scripture, the poem 'quotes' its own structure and offers such quotation as vindication of its politics. Within the system in which Spenser is working such development was both logically and emotionally predictable. As Mircea Eliade argues,

> The more religious man is, the more paradigmatic models does he possess to guide his attitudes and actions. In other words, the more religious he is, the more does he enter into the *real* and the less is he in danger of becoming lost in actions that being nonparadigmatic, 'subjective', are finally aberrant.[22]

22 *The Sacred and the Profane*, translated by Willard R. Trask (New York, 1959), p. 96. On this aspect of Spenser's treatment of contemporary history see M. Pauline Parker, *The Allegory of 'The Faerie Queene'* (Oxford, 1960), p. 317.

But poetry is 'subjective'. The ground-plan of book five eloquently bespeaks a conscious refusal to enter 'aberrant time', but the tone and texture of the verse bespeak aberrant experience. Thus Elizabeth's temporal policies declare, rather than reveal, themselves to be repetitions of the eternal paradigm of Christ's victory over evil. Spenser had an advantage over Foxe in that, functioning as poet rather than chronicler, he was not obliged to record every minute and murky detail of the events which formed his theme. Ideally, he should have succeeded in precisely those areas where Foxe failed, abstracting 'universal' truth from a multiplicity of particular occurrences. In the event he has the worst of both worlds since the incidents chosen to illustrate the pattern are often ambiguous or, at best, ambivalent. Historical hindsight supplies the reader with a better perception of reality than a providential theory wrenched towards the defence of questionable policies. But Spenser could not have known that even the Book of Daniel, that most 'vatic' of scriptural texts, postdates the events it prophesies.[23] Attempting to interpret time even as it passed, he could not rid himself of its inherent uncertainties. His presentation of spiritual truth reads like a distortion of political fact, his interpretation of particular incidents reads like suppression of moral evidence. Theory and practice never quite meet.

The dramatic conclusion to book five, as the 'paradigm' appears to collapse in ruins mirrors the frustration of a man trapped in his own recalcitrant time. Paradoxically, the only hope seems to lie in the continuation of the historical romance and the history it 'shadows', in the assurance that Artegall's story is yet unfinished: he rides to the Fairy Court 'where what him fell shall else be told'. By the time this line was published, however, Arthur Grey was already three years dead. For Artegall's story to continue, his spirit must be reborn in another agent. Book five ends, as does *A View of the Present State of Ireland*, anticipating such an event, possibly in the person of the Earl of Essex. Thus in life, as in romance narrative, the identification of a central theme imposes a continuity across the abrupt closures of death. Ideally, literary skills ally themselves to religious attitudes. And yet, despite all its gestures towards Apocalypse the most fascinating feature of book five remains its fidelity to *human* truth — or human confusion. A persistent undertone of disquiet murmurs beneath the epic diction, almost as though two poems were being written simultaneously. As his treatment of the Duessa episode demonstrates, none knew better than Spenser the deliberately distorting methods of the polemic historian, and after such knowledge there can be no true innocence.[24] He has reached the point in book five at which fidelity

23 S.G.F. Brandon, *History, Time and Deity* (Manchester, 1965), p. 137.

24 Richard A. McCabe, 'The Masks of Duessa: Spenser, Mary Queen of Scots, and James VI', *ELR*, 17 (1987), 224-42.

to creed entails fidelity to deception, at which vision entails blindness. Such single-mindedness was beyond him at least as poet, if not as man. He qualifies where epic demands assertion, apologises where it demands praise. Altogether there is too much blood and too much circumspection. At times the very vehemence of the defence proves counter-productive and the heroic ideals dwarf their supposed exemplars both fictional and real. The conclusion is honest, if sour. Unexpectedly, typological verse exacerbates the unresolved tensions detectable in Spenser's discursive prose. The poetry of experience overcomes the poetry of wish-fulfilment.

II. *Time and Majesty*

The attribution of 'divinity' to any character puts them, or some aspect of them, outside the normal influence of time. It is the poetic equivalent of painting a halo around a figure's head, and one such visual depiction of Elizabeth herself has actually survived. The halo was designed to remove its bearer 'from *tempus* to *aevum*, from Time to Sempiternity . . . the haloed person, or rather the person *qua* halo his *ordo, never died*'.[25] The practice is best understood in the light of the medieval confrontation between imperial and papal power. As the latter arrogated to itself the trappings of temporal monarchy, the former began to encroach upon the priestly office. Dante insisted upon the centrality of imperial power to the struggle for spiritual salvation, exalting Roman emperors such as Trajan and Justinian at the expense of figures such as Brutus and Cassius who appear in Hell along with Boniface VIII who in 1302 issued the bull 'Unam Sanctam' asserting the supremacy of the papacy over all secular authorities.[26] As a result, for English writers such as John Foxe, Dante seemed a prophet of Apocalyptic imperialism.[27] Such trends of thought developed rapidly after the Reformation. Once Henry VIII had rejected the universal authority of the papacy with all its spiritual and temporal associations, it became necessary for the state to substitute some equivalent symbol. So powerful had been the claims of the papacy to act as the sole agent of human redemption (after Christ) that 'any secular commonwealth or kingdom desiring to assert its autonomy was almost obliged to assert that it possessed redemptive significance'.[28] Apocalyptic historiography developed not merely as the pastime of fanatics, but as a valuable tool in effectively establishing the independence of the secular

25 Kantorowicz, p. 84.

26 J.G.A. Pocock, *The Machiavellian Moment: Florentine Political Thought and the Atlantic Republican Tradition* (Princeton, 1975), p. 50.

27 Yates, *Astraea*, pp. 45-6.

28 Pocock, p. 45.

authority.[29] Imperial iconography replaces religious iconography: the 'cult' of the Virgin Queen, for instance, is closely related to the discredited 'cult' of the Virgin Mary.[30] Sir Roy Strong remarks that 'the Tudor cult of royalist symbols offers a striking parallel with the Byzantine Empire under the iconoclastic emperors' where imperial art was often substituted for offensive religious icons.[31]

The portrait of Elizabeth to which I referred above depicts her as the woman of Apocalypse wearing a halo of stars and about to accept a cosmic crown from the hands of an angel. We are witnessing an imperial apotheosis. Although the portrait dates from the Stuart period (1617-19) its claims are no greater than those put forward in Spenser's 'Legende of Holinesse' where the conflict between Una and Duessa is consciously suggestive of that between Elizabeth and Mary Queen of Scots.[32] Una is the daughter of time but so, in the eyes of her contemporaries, was Elizabeth. The final sections of Foxe's *Acts and Monuments* chronicle the slow emergence of the good prince through the various complexities of Tudor politics to the glorious moment she ascends the throne and renews the work of her father and brother.[33]

By the 1590's Queen Elizabeth was already an old woman yet the official portraits of her last years continued to present a countenance of sustained maturity. The suggestion of encroaching age in the Ditchley and Buccleuch portraits gave way to what Sir Roy Strong has called a 'mask of youth'. By this time portraits of the queen have become icons of sovereignty. Under the influence of Renaissance Neoplatonism, the 'idea' of kingship has displaced the individual monarch. Paintings such as the famous 'Rainbow' portrait are full of symbols and emblematic props designed to endow the central figure with an other-worldly, timeless significance.[34] It was merely the culmination of a trend that had been developing steadily since the beginning of the reign but the ever-widening gap between the image and the reality rendered it all the more remarkable. One recalls Ben Jonson's cruel insinuation to Drummond of Hawthornden that 'Queen Elizabeth never saw herself after she became old in a true glass; they painted her, and sometimes would vermilion her nose'.[35]

29 The best study is William Lamont, *Godly Rule: Politics and Religion 1603-60* (London, 1967).

30 Yates, *Astraea*, pp. 76-80.

31 *Portraits of Queen Elizabeth I* (Oxford, 1963), p. 39.

32 *Ibid.*, p. 154-5.

33 See especially *The Acts and Monuments of the Church*, edited by M. Hobart Seymour (London, 1838), pp. 534, 989. On Elizabeth's own attitude towards time see Christopher Morris, *The Tudors*, revised edition (London, 1976), pp. 154-6.

34 Strong, *Portraits*, pp. 19-21, 34-8.

35 *Complete Poems*, edited by George Parfitt (Harmondsworth, 1975), p. 470.

One early depiction showed Elizabeth reversing the judgement of Paris. In this version of the legend the goddesses of wisdom, beauty, and love concur in awarding the prize to the English goddess who combines within her person the virtues of all three.[36] Similarly the dazzling wardrobe of sophisticated costumes which appear in successive portraits create the impression of personified splendour of which Spenser's Gloriana is the verbal equivalent. His 'mirrour of grace and maiestie diuine' was a familiar image of the 1590's. Indeed the whole cult of courtly panegyric associated with the Land of Faerie was drawn from the pageantry of the Accession Day tilts. The various elements of fairy legend lay close to hand; it was Spenser's task to weave them into the unifying pattern of romance, an aesthetic goal of which Elizabeth approved.[37] Years later James Harrington was to remark upon how she converted her reign 'through the perpetual love tricks that passed between her and her people into a kind of romance'.[38]

The style of romance Elizabeth cultivated served a highly pragmatic political purpose. Behind the conventions of courtly compliment lay the notion of the monarch's 'two bodies', a theory born of the contrast between the perpetuity of sovereignty and the transience of individual sovereigns. Thus legal fiction precedes and inspires poetic fiction. As in the celebrated case of Henry IV's attempt to separate the Duchy of Lancaster from the royal lands, a crucial distinction is drawn between the monarch's private and public *personae*.[39] As Ernst Kantorowicz explains,

> The king, at least with regard to Time, had obviously 'two natures' — one which was temporal and by which he conformed with the conditions of other men, and another which was perpetual and by which he outlasted and defeated all other beings.[40]

This distinction between the king's two bodies, central as it is to Renaissance concepts of time, is clearly drawn in Spenser's prefatory remarks to Raleigh. Having asserted that Gloriana's 'particular' significance is 'the most excellent and glorious person of our soueraine the Queene', he immediately adds that 'she beareth two persons, the one of a most royall Queene or Empresse, the other of a most vertuous and beautifull Lady, this latter part in some places I doe expresse in Belphoebe'.[41] The distinction is observed

36 Edgar Wind, *Pagan Mysteries in the Renaissance*, revised edition (London, 1967), pp. 82-3.

37 Yates, *Astraea*, pp. 97-101, 104-8.

38 *The Political Works of James Harrington*, edited by J.G.A. Pocock (Cambridge, 1977), p. 198.

39 Kantorowicz, pp. 7-13.

40 *Ibid.*, p. 171.

41 *The Faerie Queene*, edited by A.C. Hamilton (London 1977), p. 737; Compare Plowden's view quoted in Kantorowicz, p. 13.

throughout the poem. Gloriana is the 'Glorious Queene of *Faerie* lond' (I. 1. 3) but Belphoebe, as a recent critic has noted, appears to have no comparable social role.[42] Gloriana's eventual death may be inferred from the succession of fairy monarchs but her sovereign vitality subsumes her personal fate into the perpetuity of her office. By contrast, Belphoebe asserts her own transience in the plainnest possible terms. She represents that aspect of Elizabeth rapidly deteriorating before the eyes of the court. Although it has become quite common to identify her with the 'idea' of virtuous beauty, she functions merely as one fleeting embodiment of that idea.[43] Spenser encourages his female readers to follow her 'ensample dead' (III. 5. 43) thereby emphasising the element of mortality involved. When Timias first sees Belphoebe he takes her for an angel or a goddess, but she quickly repudiates both terms:

> Thereat she blushing said, Ah gentle Squire,
> Nor Goddesse I, nor Angell, but the Mayd,
> And daughter of a woody Nymphe . . .
> We mortall wights, whose liues and fortunes bee
> To commun accidents still open layd,
> Are bound with commun bond of frailtee,
> To succour wretched wights, whom we captiued see.
>
> (III. 5. 36)

'We mortall wights' — the words capture the very essence of Belphoebe's situation and serve to set her apart from the Fairy Queen. Beauty constitutes no claim on sovereignty. Of Elizabeth's two bodies one is fated to degenerate and die, the other to defy the passage of time by surviving the onset of death in the continuing life of the monarchy.[44] According to the old legal adage, 'Imperium semper est': imperial power never dies.[45] Evoking this theme, Spenser allies himself with the Virgilian vision of unending empire presented here through the prophecies of Merlin and the dream vision of the Temple of Isis.[46] Through the concept of perpetual empire human society partakes in the greater cosmic forces of renewal whereby the universe itself continues to subsist from age to age. The ultimate effect of Spenser's preoccupation with time is to heighten his awareness of Elizabeth's mortality. The ultimate effect of his fascination with perpetuity is to make it seem less significant.

Crediting great families with fairy genealogies was a common device of

42 Berger, p. 125.

43 Isabel G. MacCaffrey, *Spenser's Allegory: The Anatomy of Imagination* (Princeton, 1976), p. 275.

44 Kantorowicz, pp. 409-19.

45 Kantorowicz, pp. 192, 291-302.

46 Fletcher, *Prophetic Moment*, pp. 205-7.

Renaissance compliment much popularised by the revival of interest in the euhemeristic tradition of mythological interpretation.[47] By translating 'gods' into 'heroes' it became acceptable, within a broadly Christian tradition which was also a witty Christian game, to discover the ancestors of various noble houses amongst the protagonists of classical myth. Spenser may, perhaps, have known how Arthur Kelton ingeniously traced the Tudor line back to Osiris when he introduced their ancestor Britomart to Isis Church.[48] In any case, he asserts the humanity of both Hercules and Bacchus — outstanding 'ensamples' of 'Heroicke heat' (V. 1. 1-2) — and handles Isis and Osiris in much the same fashion. Thus ancient gods are demoted to heroes so that contemporary heroes may be elevated (within certain agreed conventions) to the status of gods. Elizabeth benefits accordingly, but her position remains problematic. Many critics have regarded her as the pivot about which the romance turns but this is to simplify the position unduly. A series of conflicting themes and moods play about a myriad of contrasting *personae* each of which 'shadows' some aspect of the queen. She is as much a source of anxiety as a source of inspiration. Necessarily so, since a virgin queen is a sterile queen automatically excluded from the vibrant cycles of sexual perpetuity upon which the poem so often insists.

Spenser was intrigued by Elizabeth's paradoxical fusion of strength and weakness, wisdom and petulance. In folklore's unpredictably benign or sinister fairy queen he found a perfect 'type' for the monarch tellingly described in the *Amoretti* as his 'dear dred' (33), a phrase which perfectly encapsulates the ambivalence of his attitude. All of his sovereign female figures, both good and bad, reflect aspects of a personality that by turns attracted and repelled him. When he invites his queen to view herself within his work 'in mirrours more than one', it is as though she has been stationed before a set of diversely angled, distorting 'glasses' no two of which reflect the same image of their subject. By fragmenting the complex unity of the individual they help us to appreciate the relationship between the various elements comprising that unity. Fragmentation is the tool of imaginative analysis. So well does the technique work, that one tends to forget that Gloriana herself makes not a single appearance in the extant poem. Her presence is apprehended through a variety of surrogates, some like Belphoebe jealous, unreasonable, and cruel, others like Mercilla elevated beyond worldly desire. Whether Spenser could ever have synthesised such diversity within the person of his fairy monarch must forever remain in doubt. Only the most symbolic technique could hope to encompass such multiplicity. The

47 On euhemerism see Jean Seznec, *The Survival of the Pagan Gods*, translated by Barbara F. Sessions (Princeton, 1953), pp. 11-36. Isabel E. Rathborne, *The Meaning of Spenser's Fairyland* (New York, 1937), pp. 167-80.

48 Rathborne, p. 69.

more prolific the reflections, the more elusive the reality. In its present unfinished state, *The Faerie Queene* disintegrates the source of its inspiration. For Spenser, as for his hero Prince Arthur, Gloriana remains an unrealised dream. The fairy queen eludes *The Faerie Queene*.

The April eclogue of *The Shepheardes Calender* celebrates 'fayre *Elisa*, Queene of shepheardes all' by asserting her claims to divinity:

> So sprong her grace,
> Of heauenly race,
> No mortall blemishe may her blotte. (52-4)

In so far as majesty was ordained by providence and monarchs might legitimately be referred to as gods, the allegory is justified. As queen, Elisa is of 'heauenly race' and her father 'Pan' is Christ. However, as E.K. points out, 'the redde rose medled with the white yfere' locates this goddess in a very precise historical setting. In this context 'Pan' is Henry VIII and Elisa serves to perpetuate the 'firste vnion' of York and Lancaster achieved in his person. Despite the pastoral tone of the passage, it is Calliope, muse of heroic poetry, who hastens to applaud her, as if Spenser were already promising a future epic. Thenot's emblem, 'O quam te memorem virgo' (*Aeneid* I, 327-8) associates Elizabeth with Venus while that of Hobbinol confirms the matter, 'O dea certa': truly a goddess. The allusion to the *Aeneid* is most apposite. Aeneas addresses a beautiful young woman whose divine identity is revealed only by her dazzling disappearance. Although he is her acknowledged son, their relationship has been lived through a sequence of delusive charades ('falsis/ ludis imaginibus'). He is doomed never to know her, never take her by the hand nor enjoy her confidence ('veras . . . voces'). He may only glimpse her true nature through a series of mortal masks. From Spenser's viewpoint the episode encapsulates the frustrating evasiveness of sovereign 'divinity', the insoluble enigma of human guile and spiritual truth. Speaking on his behalf, his *alter ego* Colin Clout responds to the goddess beneath Elisa's mortal disguise yet his eulogy remains firmly rooted in time, in the cyclical mutability of the passing years. The accompanying woodcut shows Elisa and her ladies-in-waiting enjoying the spring beneath the astrological sign of Taurus. The cosmos dwarfs them. At this stage Elisa's sphere is still the earth and Colin shrinks from the impropriety of comparing her to Cynthia — a comparison for which Raleigh is liberally praised in *The Faerie Queene*. Thus the eclogue represents an early stage in Spenser's approach to the perplexities of the queens's 'two bodies', with their respective relationships to time and perpetuity. The distinction between Gloriana and Belphoebe is the final result:

> But either *Gloriana* let her chuse,
> Or in *Belphoebe* fashioned to bee:
> In th'one her rule, in th'other her rare chastitee. (3 Proem, 5)

The choice is courteously offered yet it involves a potentially schizophrenic endeavour. In the eclogue the queen cuts a more unified figure, 'goddess' Elisa and 'dame' Elisa are one and the same. What Spenser cannot afford to declare openly is that the distinction between the queen's two bodies is less a poetic or legal fiction than a fundamental necessity of monarchical government. The poem is full of corrupt and corrupting potentates of whom Mary Queen of Scots (Duessa) is merely the most notorious. Somehow, the ideal of monarchy had to be rendered immune from contamination by its transient embodiments. In times of disillusionment there must remain something to believe in beyond the individual to hand. Thus the device allows of a strange development: loyalty to Elizabeth may dispense with Elizabeth. The mortal Belphoebe may be set astray amongst the tangled contradictions of romance narrative while Gloriana never moves. The separation of roles ensures that the royal icon can never be embarrassed by the wayward idiosyncrasies of the jealous, demanding spinster. To become Gloriana all Elizabeth need do is die. This is, perhaps, the final irony of an epic which cultivates the ideal of achievement. Constantly the poem looks beyond Elizabeth towards England's heroic future. In one sense at least Gloriana is Elizabeth in premature retrospect, what she might someday be perceived to have stood for rather than what she was. In time the compliments were intended to serve as an epitaph, but an epitaph to an office rather than an individual, to a 'Magnificent *Empresse* Renowmed for Pietie, Vertue, and all Gratiovs Government'. In the *Mutabilitie Cantos* even Raleigh's Cynthia suffers the insults of time.

III. *Gods and Mortal Men*

During the twelfth and thirteenth centuries the received Augustinian duality of time and eternity was upset by the revival amongst the Averroists of the Aristotelian notion that the world was itself without beginning or end.[49] According to this view time became a limitless duration of successive cycles of birth, growth, and decay.[50] As mentioned in chapter one, the new theories made a momentous contribution to the scholastic outlook by elucidating the problem of angelic existence thereby providing 'an otherworldly equivalent of the changing and infinite Time which the Averroists claimed for this present world'.[51] Partaking neither of God's eternity nor man's time, angels

49 Kantorowicz, p. 277.

50 F.C. Copleston, *Aquinas* (Harmondsworth, 1955), p. 143.

51 Kantorowicz, p. 281.

needed a third category of existence, that of the *aevum*, to explain their unique intermediary position 'midway between time and eternity participating in both'.[52] Strictly speaking, it allows of no past and no future, so although angels may experience succession their nature remains unaffected. In other words, angelic 'moments', like those of mystical vision, are discontinuous.[53] Such is the being which descends to aid Guyon on his emergence from the cave of Mammon:

> Beside his head there sate a faire young man,
> Of wondrous beautie, and of freshest yeares,
> Whose tender bud to blossome new began,
> And flourish faire aboue his equall peares;
> His snowy front curled with golden heares,
> Like *Phoebus* face adornd with sunny rayes,
> Diuinely shone, and two sharpe winged sheares,
> Decked with diuerse plumes, like painted Iayes,
> Were fixed at his backe, to cut his ayerie wayes. (II. 8. 5)

As the ensuing comparison with '*Cupido* on *Idaean* hill' makes clear, the allusion to the 'bud' beginning to 'blossome' does not imply that the angel may one day grow old. Like Cupid, he will appear 'of freshest yeares' forever, and this particular manifestation of his spiritual being captures his very essence. The message of the 'Song of the Rose' in the Bower of Bliss is of the inevitable cycle of bud, blossom, and decay, of beauty locked into the relentless succession of temporal decline. But this flower cannot fade. Its mode of existence is perfectly described in Spenser's *Hymne of Heavenly Love*:

> Both day and night is vnto them all one,
> For he his beames doth still to them extend,
> That darknesse there appeareth neuer none,
> Ne hath their day, ne hath their blisse an end,
> But there their termelesse time in pleasure spend. (71-7)

Angelic time is 'termeless' in the sense that it continues indefinitely but since the passage of time is invariably associated with the computation of various 'terms' of duration, the phrase 'termelesse time' also constitutes an effective oxymoron designed to capture the peculiarly paradoxical nature of

52 Frank Herbert Brabant, *Time and Eternity in Christian Thought* (London, 1937), pp. 75-6.

53 *Ibid.*, pp. 78, 82. See also Richard Hooker, *Works*, edited by John Keble, seventh edition, 3 vols (Oxford, 1888), II, 381-2.

such creatures' existence. Similarly, the angel's intuitive knowledge of Guyon's situation bespeaks an intelligence neither successive nor discursive but instantaneous. What men discover, angels perceive. From a human perspective the Palmer and his enemies encounter Guyon by accident and come to terms with their discovery gradually. The angel's apprehension is total and atemporal. Moments of illumination elevate their recipients to the angelic plain and the narrative time-scheme is accordingly distorted.

Fascinating as such speculations were, however, Spenser's real interest centred in man: the angel withdraws so that providence may operate through the human agency of Prince Arthur. But human agency had been shown to have its own share in the concept of *aevum* since the fate of the species differs so markedly from that of its individual members, a contrast adumbrated in the fairy chronicles. Extreme Averroists exploited this contrast to insist upon creation from eternity but, as we saw in chapter one, various modifications could easily be made within the constraints of revealed truth. Facilitating such developments was the widespread belief that all angels were unique, each one a species unto itself.[54] As far as man was concerned, the continued existence of the species in cyclical change, despite the deaths of its individual members, raised questions about the nature of time which the theory of *aevum* seemed designed to answer. Man's soul was generally held to be immortal, but now, through succession and generation, his mortal part could also be regarded as perpetuating itself indefinitely. Human life was hereby endowed with a sempiternity of its own as indeed was all mortal life. Understandably, 'nature' emerged as a key element in these speculations.

The goddess Venus appears several times throughout *The Faerie Queene* — as the erotic goddess in the House of Malecasta, as the Lucretian Venus in the Gardens of Adonis, and the goddess of love and concord in the Temple of Venus, an hermaphroditic figure resembling the goddess Nature of the *Mutabilitie Cantos*. Essentially Venus is as we see her and her image alters to suit the needs of the fiction. Yet it is misleading to speak in terms of three distinct divinities. What we have are three different manifestations of a single force sustaining human life.[55] It is not that the Venus of Malecasta presides over a house of debauchery, but that the house defines the Venus. The poem's classical deities are of far less importance than its human protagonists. Except in the case of the Marinell episodes where special circumstances obtain, the two seldom meet. Britomart sees the 'erotic' Venus depicted on an arras, encounters Cupid in an illusory masque, and prays before a statue of Isis. Similarly it is a statue of Venus, not Venus herself, that Scudamour sees in book four. Most of the poem's gods confront the protagonists as artistic

54 Kantorowicz, pp. 273-91 (p. 282); Brabant, pp. 74-84.
55 Wind, pp. 141-151.

artifacts fashioned to symbolise perpetual aspects of human nature. In the *Fowre Hymnes*, for example, Venus is merely an 'idole' of 'fayning thought' invented by pagan artists and poets (IV. 211-24), what Lord Bacon would call an 'idol of the mind'. Similarly, Malecasta's Venus is the ultimate symbol of erotic sexuality appropriately depicted in a scene of suffering and loss, whereas the hermaphroditic Venus of book four is the supreme symbol of creative sexuality suggesting in her own dual nature the fulfilment of married love. One notes, however, that on Mt Acidale the goddess is replaced by Colin's mistress since the source of even the most elevated romantic inspiration is personal desire. Even Platonic love must begin its ascent in 'the foul rag-and-bone shop of the heart'. On Arlo Hill, despite the pervasive echoes of Lucretius, Nature takes Venus's place.

All three modes of mythological interpretation — euhemeristic, moral, and cosmological — centre upon analysis of the human condition. Broadly speaking, euhemerism converts the gods into heroes, moralization into personifications of virtue and vice, and cosmology into planetary influences. As one might expect, many of the resulting interpretations do scant justice to the syncretic nature of their source material — despite Plutarch's timely warnings, in his account of Isis and Osiris, of the dangers of facile explication.[56] Various forms of systematic analysis proved irresistible to a poetic which identified universal truth as its proper subject. Though doubtless familiar with Plutarch's misgivings, Spenser made frequent use of such popular handbooks as Natalis Comes's *Mythologiae* (1551) and Lilio Giraldi's *De Deis Gentium* (1548).[57] As many of these were expressly compiled for the use of writers they emphasise and often exaggerate the general applicability of classical myth, lavishly converting deities into abstract equivalents. Spenser frequently follows their example. Discussing the fertility of 'the flouds in generation', for instance, he remarks on how,

> the antique wisards well inuented,
> That *Venus* of the fomy sea was bred;
> For that the seas by her are most augmented.
> Witnesse th'exceeding fry, which there are fed,
> And wondrous sholes, which may of none be red. (IV. 12. 2)

Passages such as these prosaicly disembody the figures concerned but for purely localized effects. The totality of Spenser's 'darke conceit' runs counter to such methods. Seldom are the interpretations supplied adequate to the allegory in which they occur. The poet in Spenser resists the rationalisations

56 *Isis and Osiris*, 22.
57 Seznec, pp. 279-323.

of the scholar. He approaches mythology as he does the Bible, finding in its arcane intricacy rather than its coherence adequate analogies for human life. The birth of Venus was a human 'invention' but its inventors were 'wisards', philosophers or even seers. No single interpretation nor mode of interpretation can hope to encompass more than a fraction of such a figure's significance. The baffling complexity of myth, of which Mutabilitie so eloquently complains (VII. 7. 53-4), 'shadows' the mutable turbulence of the consciousness from which it springs, a consciousness as prolific as the 'fomy sea' and equally responsive to the perpetual rhythms of time.

Spenser's gods have no share in the eternity of the *nunc stans* but inhabit the *aevum*, their forces persisting from generation to generation. In this sense man confers immortality upon his gods and the outlook of the poem is staunchly humanist. In kneeling before such deities man worships idealized aspects of himself. But the qualities concerned are also aspects of the Christian deity and Spenser's humanism is fraught with the anxieties of the Reformation with the result that his 'gods' must constantly be distinguished (as in the *Mutabilitie Cantos*) from his 'God'. It is as though he has conflated Virgil and Calvin. The theology of grace qualifies, and is qualified by, ideals of classical heroism. For individual human characters to aspire to any form of personally achieved immortality, even that of 'fame', is repeatedly shown to be the highest possible vanity.[58] Only through damnation may such desires be effected. Such is the *aevum* of Dante's *Inferno* and the hell to which Duessa descends in the fifth canto of book one. Representative of that state is the monster Echidna, mother of the Blatant Beast, which dwells, 'in hideous horrour and obscurity,/Wasting the strength of her immortall age' (VI. 6. 11). She is a monster of the mind perpetuating moral decay. So too with such figures as Despair and Jealousy. In the latter case we witness the transformation of man into demon. Although Malbecco's 'soule' is transfixed with

58 The matter is clarified in the case of the damned physician, Aesculapius, consulted in Hell on behalf of Sansfoy by Duessa and Night (I. 5. 36-44). His crime is having opposed himself to fate by restoring life to the dead Hippolytus, and critics have often regarded him as a false Christ, healing the body but not the soul. It should be noticed, however, that the exact details of the myth as Spenser records them — the gathering together and reconstitution of Hippolytus's 'dismembred' limbs 'scattered on euery mountaine' — make Aesculapius an infernal equivalent of the goddess Isis who performed exactly the same office for Osiris. As he cannot be deprived of 'endlesse life', Aesculapius is cast 'aliue' into Hell,

> Where long remaining, he did alwaies striue
> Himselfe with salues to health for to restore,
> And slake the heauenly fire, that raged euermore. (40)

What he has effected is endless misery, limitless time to experience limitless pain. This is the very essence of Hell, and a parody of the eternal justice and concord established by Isis.

'deathes eternall dart',

> Yet can he neuer dye, but dying liues,
> And doth himselfe with sorrow new sustaine,
> That death and life attonce vnto him giues.
> And paineful pleasure turnes to pleasing paine.
> There dwels he euer, miserable swaine,
> Hatefull both to him selfe, and euery wight;
> Where he through priuy griefe, and horrour vaine,
> Is woxen so deform'd, that he has quight
> Forgot he was a man, and *Gealosie* is hight. (III. 10. 60)

Depicted here is a travesty of the mutable 'eternity' presented in the Gardens of Adonis, the limitless *aevum* of human corruption.

IV. *'Eterne in Mutabilitie'*

Spenser's presentation of the Gardens of Adonis marks his most subtle and imaginative exploration of the *aevum* enjoyed by the race but denied the individual. At the centre of the garden, 'in the middest of that Paradise', lies the arbour in which Adonis is perpetually preserved, 'transformed oft, and chaunged diuerslie' (III. 6. 47). John Hankins has convincingly demonstrated the significance of the episode to the physical allegory as representing both 'the immortality of the species in the world of perishable forms' and 'the god of reviving vegetation that had seemed to perish with the onset of winter', but I wish to concentrate upon its relationship to the themes of time and providence.[59] The spontaneous generation of Belphoebe and Amoret in the womb of Chrysogone through the influence of the sun ('great father of generation') foreshadows the Adonis passage (6-7) and Spenser expressly relates it to the universal process of vegetative growth: 'the fruitfull seades/ Of all things liuing, through impression/ Of the sunbeames in moyst complexion,/ Doe life conceiue and quickned are by kynd' (8). Thus, after the inundations of the Nile, 'infinite shapes of creatures' are discovered in the mud, just as 'infinite shapes of creatures' are bred in the garden (35). Womb images pervade the canto, but since the womb is controlled by the phases of the moon the process of birth remains meticulously responsive to the cyclical changes of time (9).

Venus in a sense initiates the main action of the canto in her pursuit of the errant Cupid: Adonis's bower is no less than her '*earthly* abode' (29). The emphasis is important since she is represented as forsaking her celestial home

59 Hankins, pp. 246-55 (p. 250). See also James Nohrnberg, *The Analogy of 'The Faerie Queene'* (Princeton, 1976), pp. 519-68.

('her blisfull bowre of ioy aboue') to seek her son as he wanders the globe 'disguiz'd in thousand shapes' (11). This detail, combined with that of Venus's descent, serves to establish her allegorical significance in the present context. According to Ficino the world soul is possessed of three distinct powers: 'one whereby it always adheres to the good itself, the first principle of things; another whereby it gazes upon the beauty of the divine intelligence; a third whereby it extends the forms of things into matter. The first power is called *Jupiter*, the second *celestial Venus*, the third *inferior Venus*'.[60] With the celestial Venus is associated the contemplative worship of God producing 'supernal joy and true pleasure' ('supernum gaudium veraque voluptas'). But whereas this Venus contemplates the 'beauty of the divine species' ('pulchritudinem divinarum specierum'), the inferior Venus 'turns to the exemplar of higher things in order to bring forth the beauty of corporeal forms . . . its drive to procreate is "love", its peace in the fulfilment of procreation is "pleasure". So you have twin Venuses, twin loves and twin pleasures'.[61]

Venus's pursuit of Cupid through a thousand earthly shapes until his eventual discovery in the earthly bower, sporting with Adonis, 'the Father of all Forms', defines the goddess as 'inferior'. In the Neoplatonic system, 'form' is the material expression of soul — hence the paramount importance of form in literature and the plastic arts.[62] Regarded from the viewpoint of successive generations, form is also the expression of the durability of the species. Whereas the senses perceive only a multiplicity of bodies or 'shapes', the intellect apprehends the underlying unity of form provided by the concept of species even though 'forms' inevitably tend to lose their perfection in matter.[63] It is the soul that corrects delusive visible impressions and 'approves or condemns every structure made by art and the measures of music, and decides about the goodness and badness of natural things . . . The soul possesses the truer forms and with them it judges concerning corporeal things. For the judge is more perfect than what is being judged'.[64] The 'inferior' Venus is inferior only in the sense that the world-soul must realise the concepts of the species in matter so that the present world may subsist. The enlightened soul duly rises from a sensual apprehension of this activity to its guiding and informing spirit, from the 'infinite shapes' of creatures to the 'father of all forms'. Thus the pursuit of Cupid through a thousand adopted 'shapes' and environments leads inevitably to Adonis. As Plotinus puts it, 'when living things . . . produce, it is the rational principles within which

60 *The 'Philebus' Commentary*, edited and translated by Michael J.B. Allen (Berkeley, 1975), p. 136. Hereafter *Philebus.*

61 *Philebus*, p. 136.

62 *Ibid.*, pp. 178-80; Plotinus, *Enneads* III. 4. 1.

63 *Philebus*, pp. 192, 248.

64 *Ibid.*, p. 196.

move them, and this is an activity of contemplation . . . for creating is bringing a form into being, and this is filling all things with contemplation . . . lovers, too, are among those who see and press on eagerly towards a form'.[65]

In his commentary upon Plato's *Philebus*, Ficino was much concerned with the problems occasioned by the concept of species as it affects man's knowledge of being and existence. In effect, the species exist in three quite separate though interrelated modes. In the first place, as conceptions in the mind of God 'before they are drawn out into matter' ('antequam in materiam educantur'), they constitute the rational principle informing the common nature of all individual members of any given species.[66] As such, they may be identified with the Ideas which provide the plan for all creation.[67] In the second place they exist in an imaginary way ('imaginario modo') in human intelligence as the mind ascends from imperfect material 'forms' to their perfect exemplars, to the 'reasons' and 'ideas' ('rationes ideasque') of various defective forms apprehended by the senses.[68] Significantly, these two modes of existence are related through the resemblance between divine and human creativity: 'the species for creating things are in God's intelligence exactly as the models for products are in an artificer's mind, or the reasons for all the members and parts are in the seed ('in semine') of an animal or tree'.[69] The allusion to 'seed' indicates a third mode of existence since the concept of species, formed in the divine intelligence and apprehended by its human counterparts, must also be manifest in the world of nature. At this point Ficino argues from the process of orderly generation, from the exact reproduction of kind by kind.[70] Indeed, it is the very function of reproduction to propagate the species: 'intentio quoque genitivae est ad speciem cuius propagandae gratia est inserta'.[71] Thus the species constitute the very essence of the material universe ('ergo essentia universi constat ex speciebus') and central to all forms of propagation — vegetative, animal and human — is the 'seed'.[72] Spenser can, therefore, refer to the Gardens of Adonis as, 'the first seminarie/ Of all things, that are borne to liue and die,/ According to their kindes' (30).

This much is clear, but confusion arises from the interrelationship of the various elements which constitute Spenser's subsequent descriptions. These would seem to be four in number: 1. The 'seeds' of generation just referred to; 2. The 'naked babes' whom Genius 'clothes with sinfull mire,/ And

65 *Enneads* (III. 8. 7), translated by A.H. Armstrong, Loeb Classical Library, 6 vols (London, 1965-), III (1967), 383-5.
66 *Philebus*, pp. 208-9.
67 *Ibid.*, p. 206.
68 *Ibid.*, pp. 195, 199.
69 *Ibid.*, p. 178.
70 *Ibid.*, pp. 182, 204.
71 *Ibid.*, p. 201.
72 *Ibid.*, p. 201.

sendeth forth to liue in mortall state', most of whom return to the garden to 'grow afresh' and re-embark upon life's journey after a lapse of one thousand years; 3. The 'infinite shapes of creatures' (apparently distinct from the 'babes') which grow in the garden, providing bodies for rational and irrational souls; 4. The 'huge eternall *Chaos*, which supplyes/The substances of natures fruitfull progenyes'. One must ask whether these elements are presented in any specific order and in particular whether Spenser is attempting to analyse the entire process of generation from the planting of the seed to the birth of the individual being.

The nature of the 'seed', much discussed by Renaissance embryologists, has given rise to a number of conflicting hypotheses. Robert Ellrodt, for example, finds an allusion to the Augustinian doctrine of seminal principles brought into being at the moment of creation but developing at allotted times as the course of history unfolds in accordance with the providential plan. Thus the 'seeds' of all species exist from the outset but mature at different times: the various biological mechanisms of nature are 'timed' to operate to a predetermined schedule.[73] Yet 'seminarie' need have no such implications and Ellrodt admits that the 'return' of the seeds (which for this purpose he identifies with the 'naked babes') can have no place in Augustine's theory.[74] Coming much closer to Spenser's image, Ficino explains how the idea of the species exist in nature 'like a nursery garden in matter' ('idea quae in natura est quam seminarium quod est in materia'), focussing attention upon the unfailing generation of reproductive seeds: 'Each mature plant also generates itself in itself from the integral creativeness of its nature, that is, it generates the seed. In the seed is the plant's total power, its total reason. Similarly in animals the seed is the whole animal being produced in itself.'[75] This explanation was common amongst Renaissance authorities and seems to offer a more satisfactory insight into Spenser's intention since what he actually depicts in the garden is not the gradual pre-timed emergence of 'seminal principles' but the process of generation.[76] In *The City of God* (XV. 16) Augustine refers to sexual intercourse as the seedbed ('seminarium') of society. Considered from this viewpoint, as John Donne reminds us, the process itself may be regarded as the 'seminarie' of creation:

> In the Creation of the World, when God stocked the Earth, and the Sea, with those creatures, which were to be the seminary, and foundation,

73 *Neoplatonism in the Poetry of Spenser*, Travaux D'Humanisme et Renaissance, 35 (Geneva, 1960), pp. 78-86. For Augustinian seminal principles see *Ruines of Rome*, 22.

74 *Ibid.*, p. 81.

75 *Philebus*, pp. 202-3.

76 Audrey Eccles, *Obstetrics and Gynaecology in Tudor and Stuart England* (London, 1982), pp. 33-42.

> and roote of all that should ever be propagated in either of those elements, and when he had made man, to rule over them, he spoke to man, and to other creatures, in one and the same phrase, and forme of speech, *Crescite, et multiplicamini*, Be fruitfull and multiply; and thereby imprinted in man, and in other creatures, a *naturall* desire to conserve, and propagate their kinde by way of *Generation.*[77]

So Spenser concerns himself with the 'endless progenie' of all that is born, generates, and dies, exploiting the common association between the earth and the womb. At one point he conflates the two referring to 'the wide wombe of the world' which contains chaos (36). Discussing the same subject, no less an authority than Galen had asserted that in the matter of planting seed there is no effective difference between earth and womb for the simple reason that, in their initial stages, all living things share a vegetative life just as man possesses a vegetative soul before acquiring a sensitive or a rational one.[78] Spenser's 'garden' image is, therefore, equally well adapted to all facets of the generative process. Thus John Hankins has argued that the bower may be interpreted, in part at least, as the female body, and the cycle of generation, poetically symbolised in the Pythagorean doctrine of metempsychosis, as the perpetual return of the generative seeds to their place of origin in the male and female genitals.[79] On this reading the rational soul takes no part in the process of renewal, nor indeed could it. According to Ficino, it was not until the forty-fifth day that the embryo received its rational soul through the direct intervention of God, and other Renaissance authorities were in broad agreement.[80] Galen himself put the act of ensoulment sometime in the second month.[81]

The iconography of the 'naked babes' together with the figure of Genius is drawn from illustrations to Cebes's *Table*, a Neoplatonic work of the first century A.D. which purports to expound an allegorical painting dedicated to Chronos, 'a patriarch of the Greek theogony who was later identified with Saturn and whose name means *time*'.[82] Spenser's employment of this highly popular work constitutes the greatest stumbling-block to the interpretation of the entire episode since it does not always appear to be fully integrated with the other material. Cebes's 'Genius' is the power which offers moral and spiritual advice to those entering upon the journey of life and is, therefore,

77 *Complete Sermons*, edited by G.R. Potter and E.M. Simpson, 10 vols (Berkeley, 1953-62), II (1955), 335.

78 Joseph Needham, *A History of Embryology*, second edition, revised by Arthur Hughes (Cambridge, 1959), p. 71.

79 Hankins, pp. 271-6.

80 Ficino, *Opera*, 2 vols (Basle, 1576), I, 406; See also Eccles, p. 45.

81 Needham, p. 75.

82 S.K. Heninger, *The Cosmographical Glass* (San Marino, 1977), p. 180.

equivalent to the true Genius or Agdistes discussed in the Bower of Bliss (II. 12. 47-8). Metempsychosis, in any form, is not mentioned but as the 'table' is attributed to 'a true follower of Pythagoras and Parmenides' this may have been sufficient to suggest the association to a poet easily attracted by its imaginative potential.[83] In Spenser's fable Genius is directed by 'eternall fate' — obviously a power beyond himself — and his two gates are clearly equivalent to birth (gold) and death (iron). The problem is that the 'naked babes' (souls of some sort) appear to exist before birth and in some cases to undergo successive births, 'so like a wheele around they runne from old to new' (33). If this were a passage from one of Giordano Bruno's dialogues few would doubt that metempsychosis was in question, but such a belief is alien to the entire outlook of *The Faerie Queene* as indeed to all of Spenser's major philosophical sources.[84] Like most Christian authors with the exception of Origen, Ficino, for example, categorically denies the prior existence of souls arguing instead that God creates new souls daily.[85] But this refers specifically to the rational soul. It was the agreed belief that the others were produced automatically within the process itself whereas the rational soul required the direct intervention of God.[86] One notes also that when the 'naked babes' return they are 'planted' in the garden like seeds: the very vocabulary seems to proclaim their vegetative nature.

There need be no objection to the pre-existence of vegetative souls which were often loosely identified with the life force of generative 'seeds'.[87] As we have seen, Ficino closely associates the concept of species with the transmission of 'rational principles' ('rationes') through the seed — rational, that is, not in the sense of conscious thought but of informing new life with the pattern or 'idea' of the species from which it takes its origin. One detects faint anticipations here of modern genetic theory although the context is dissimilar since Ficino is arguing for the existence of the ideas of the species within the divine intelligence. Nevertheless the 'seed' is more than just a useful analogy since it actually enforces the deterministic power of the species in the world of nature. As Ficino puts it, soul endues matter with form: 'In any element or compound body the forms are present. It is by their power that similar forms are generated in matter. In trees and animals there are seeds; in the seeds there are reasons that can be kindled'.[88] Since body is comprised of matter and quantity — both passive qualities — it must act through an

83 *The Tablet of Cebes the Theban Philosopher or A True Emblem of Human Life*, translated by Robert Warren (Cambridge, 1699), p. 3.

84 Frances Yates, *Giordano Bruno and the Hermetic Tradition* (London, 1964), p. 249.

85 *Opera* (1576), I, 401-4.

86 Needham, p. 91.

87 *Ibid.*, p. 80.

88 *Philebus*, p. 180.

incorporeal species or power ('incorporalis itaque speciei atque virtutis proprium est ut agant').[89] The logical conclusion is that,

> From the nature which is impressed in the world all the forms of things arise in matter. The forms are made by the power of the nature. So the seeds of the forms are present in the nature. And because the nature acts through the power of the higher essence, the reasons for all the seeds which are in it are also in the essence. We call them the Ideas. Therefore from the creativeness of the divine substance the nature is also made creative; and from the nature various offspring are drawn into matter.[90]

The same concept pervades Medieval and Renaissance embryology. The received view was that both males and females produced 'seed' but that only the male seed was endowed with a certain active power or principle. In *Purgatorio* XXV, Dante has Statius declare that once this active principle begins to operate it becomes a vegetative soul ('Anima fatta la virtute attiva/ Qual d'una pianta', 52-3) and begins to shape the organs as the body develops from the vegetative to the sensitive state. At the infusion of the rational soul the other two are subsumed into it (73-5).[91] As Donne explains, 'the reasonable soul of man, when it enters, becomes all the soul of man, and he hath no longer a vegetative, and a sensitive soul, but all is that one reasonable soul'.[92] Given the function of the vegetative soul within the seeds, their replanting, whether in the earth or the womb, is only to be expected and the figure of one thousand years may merely be poetic diction for 'a long time': If 'a thousand thousand naked babes' attend Genius desiring 'fleshly weedes' it may well be centuries before the same vegetative soul re-enters the process. Not until three stanzas later does Spenser specifically mention 'reasonable soules' and only then in a context which clearly implies the Ficinian theory of infusion. During the great debate on Arlo-Hill the subject of metempsychosis is a notable omission from Mutability's list of cyclical transformations. Had it been in any sense central to the poem's world-view it could scarcely have been excluded.

One must not be misled by the anthropomorphism implicit in the image of 'naked babes'. As the beings in question have no body, they are 'babes' only potentially. We seem, therefore, to be progressing from seeds to vegetal souls towards the development of bodies ('shapes of creatures'), 'some fit for

89 *Ibid.*, p. 184-5.

90 *Ibid.*, p. 186.

91 'Che cio che trova attivo quivi tira/ In sua sustanzia, e fassi un'alma sola,/ Che vive e sente, é se in sé rigira'. See *La Divina Commedia*, edited by C.H. Grandgent (London, 1914), pp. 212-4.

92 *Sermons*, VIII (1956), 221.

reasonable soules t'indew,/ Some made for beasts, some made for birds to weare' (35). Since the matter from which these 'bodies' are composed is 'eternall', their number is 'infinite'. This is directly in keeping with Neoplatonic philosophy which argues for a finite number of species with a potentially infinite number of constituent members within each one.[93] The substance which the garden draws from 'Chaos' is 'eterne' but changeable, as is the moisture which keeps everything alive (34). According to Bacon, this 'eternity of matter' was compatible with Hebrew cosmology 'for that represents matter without form as existing before the six days' works'.[94] Yet even here Spenser is careful to maintain an orthodox stance. His 'stock' of matter, 'remaines in euerlasting store,/ As it at first *created* was of yore' (36). The Christian God hovers in the background — though not strictly required.

Because matter exists in a state of perpetual change the 'formes' imposed upon it 'are variable and decay' (38). As Ficino explained, 'all bodies are in time and space and consist of matter and form. Because they're in time they are measured by time, so each body's condition corresponds to the condition of time'.[95] Once he has introduced the concept of variable forms Spenser's next subject must logically be that of time. To lend dramatic intensity to the point, he sets it to operate, in the very next stanza, within the garden itself: 'wicked *Time*, who with his scyth addrest,/ Does mow the flowring herbes and goodly things' (39).[96] This is time as it appears in the *Complaints*, inimical to life and happiness. The irony is that in the present context it may be seen to serve the force to which it appears hostile. The garden breeds mortality. For the process to be 'eternall', the products must be transitory: 'for one thing doesn't destroy another, except to impart its own form to the other's matter; for nature doesn't aim at the bad'.[97]

Yet time is 'wicked'. Until now, despite the similarities between the garden and Eden, Spenser has not broached the subjects of sin or fall. The relationship of the generative process to time now introduces it obliquely. In the *Mutabilitie Cantos* the curse of mutable time is directly associated with the judgment pronounced in Genesis. Time's 'wicked' aspect originates there. The lamentations of 'great mother *Venus*' as she walks through the garden (40) may well be intended to recall God's discovery of the fall in Eden. Hence the abundant 'pittie' of the passage, 'for all that liues, is subiect to that law:/ All things decay in time, and to their end do draw'. As Spenser is not primarily

93 *Philebus*, pp. 248-61.

94 Bacon, *Works*, VI, 723.

95 *Philebus*, p. 192.

96 On the controversy concerning the place of time in the garden see Ellrodt, p. 81; C.S. Lewis, *Studies in Medieval and Renaissance Literature* (Cambridge, 1966), pp. 153-4; Humphrey Tonkin, 'Spenser's Garden of Adonis and Britomart's Quest', *PMLA* 88 (1973), 408-17 (p. 411).

97 *Philebus*, p. 210.

interested in theology, however, the consolation offered is that of the continuity of the species (41). As the primary source of biological life the garden is credited with simultaneous seasons, a feature which at first appears to distance it from ordinary human experience, since it defeats time. But the ultimate effect is to make of the garden a microcosm of the globe itself, the spring of one hemisphere coinciding with the autumn of another. By observing a striking unity of place (as the earth is one place), Spenser merely focusses the imagination upon the paradoxical qualities of our global environment: 'There is continuall spring, and haruest there/ Continuall, both meeting at one time' (42).

Read in this context — and Spenser is careful to work towards such a climax — the description of the arbour (43-9) reinterprets the process of generation in the light of its motive force, the sexual transmission of the seed which propagates the species. The physical description of the place is suggestive of the Mons Veneris (43) but even more noteworthy is the mythological setting since the inner sanctum is surrounded by 'euery sort of flowre,/ To which sad louers were transformd of yore' (45). The specific allusions (Hyacinthus, Narcissus, Amaranthus, and Amitas) are to those who died without issue, those who continue only in a vegetative state. Earlier in the same book, in the House of Malecasta, Adonis too, 'deadly engored of a great wild Bore', is numbered amongst their company, transformed into a flower 'which in that cloth was wrought, as if it liuely grew' (III. 1. 38). Since Malecasta deals in illusion, 'as if' bears a heavy weight. Adonis's appearance in the arbour, in direct contrast to the state of his former fellows, enforces the significance of the passage very effectively. He has become the god of vegetation, the 'Father of all formes', guardian of the species as the universal source of seed. He thus 'defeats' time by becoming 'eterne in mutabilitie,/ And by succession made perpetuall' (47). Because the species exist ultimately in the divine mind he 'liues in euerlasting ioy,/ With many of the Gods in company' (49). The imagery of time's all-consuming scythe mowing the products of the garden is nicely reversed when we read how Venus comes to 'reape sweet pleasure of the wanton boy' (46). Perpetual mowing *is* perpetual harvest and both are implied in the imagery of 'seed'. Hence the boar is imprisoned but not destroyed (48).

Whereas the initial stages of the canto describe the descent of Venus from a celestial to an earthly habitat, the final stages are marked by patterns of reascent culminating in the fable of Cupid and Psyche. Neoplatonic doctrines of emanation and return have doubtless played their part in determining this structure. As with the episode of the House of Holiness, spiritual ascent is symbolised by its physical counterpart. The 'bowre' is situated upon the 'round top' of a 'stately Mount' where Adonis enjoys the company of 'gods' including Cupid whose flight had motivated Venus's descent. The pursuit

(12-16) is designed to illustrate his tyranny over the world of man. As there described, he resembles the sadistic Cupid of the House of Busirane whom Amoret is destined to meet by the end of book three. Only in the bower, 'laying his sad darts/Aside' (49), does he assume a more benign aspect to consort with Psyche, 'after long troubles and vnmeet vpbrayes' (50). The primary source of the myth is Apuleius's *Golden Ass* which received its standard explication in Boccaccio's *Genealogia Deorum Gentilium*.[98] Spenser follows the details quite closely emphasising the hostility between Venus and Psyche as well as the 'exyle' imposed by Cupid. However, he also uses the reconciliation of Cupid and Psyche to suggest a corresponding reconciliation between Venus and Cupid since Amoret is entrusted to her granddaughter Pleasure — the 'voluptas' of the Neoplatonic system — to be 'trained vp in true feminitee' (51). It is, therefore, in the bower that Venus 'finds' the errant Cupid.

Two factors operate here. In Apuleius the marriage of Cupid and Psyche, sanctioned by Jove, is regarded as constituting a reformation of Cupid's wanton adulterous nature: 'tollenda est omnis occasio et luxuria puerilis nuptialibus pedicis alliganda' (VI. 23). The emphasis on lawful marriage — Jove sees that all customary forms are scrupulously observed — is obviously appropriate to Spenser's intentions since Amoret is 'yfostered' to 'perfect ripenesse' (52) only to become the spouse of Scudamour who wins her from the Temple of Venus (53). Thus the sexual activity of the garden culminates in an image of divinely hallowed marriage. But something more is also implied. Psyche was traditionally interpreted as the human soul and her various trials (including her sojourn in the underworld, the world of matter) as those of the spiritual or contemplative life. Depending upon the emphasis one places upon various details of the story she may be seen as gaining illumination in this life or overcoming the perils of mortality to be reunited with her creator in the next.[99] However, Boccaccio's interpretation is the most specific and seems best to accord with Spenser's intentions.

In describing the transmigrations of the 'naked babes' Spenser excludes the rational soul which enters the 'shape' of the body at a later stage. Commenting upon Apuleius's narrative, however, Boccaccio specifically identifies Psyche with the rational soul, expressly distinguishing her from the other two. According to this account, borrowed from Martianus Capella, Psyche is the daughter of Apollo and Endelichia (Entelechy) because only the sun (symbolising God, the father of life) may create and infuse the rational

98 *Genealogie Deorum Gentilium Libri*, edited by Vincenzo Romano, 2 vols (Bari, 1951), I, 259-61.

99 Don Cameron Allen, *Image and Meaning: Metaphoric Traditions in Renaissance Poetry* (Baltimore, 1960), pp. 26-31.

soul, the operations of which become manifest only in the perfection of time ('perfecta etas'/'perfect ripeness').[100] That is to say, although we receive the rational soul in the womb the full use of our rational faculties comes with maturity. Boccaccio's acknowledged source for the notion of entelechy is Calcidius's commentary upon Plato's *Timaeus* where the term is more precisely defined as the species or perfect form through which individual things come into being, through which mere potentiality gains actual effect.[101] To all intents and purposes it may be identified with soul, 'anima'. Thus the 'late' or recent arrival of Psyche in Spenser's garden and her 'late' reconciliation with Venus and Cupid at the close of the process. In the Apuleian account, as also in Boccaccio, Psyche's beauty arouses the jealousy of Venus for whom she is mistaken and whose temples consequently lie deserted. The 'inferior' Venus, operating through the world of nature, must somehow be reconciled to the higher aspirations of the soul. According to the myth, Cupid is dispatched to punish Psyche but becomes enamoured of her himself until she violates the prohibition of looking upon his true form. Boccaccio interprets this aspect of the story as representing too great a curiosity on the part of the rational soul into the affairs of God, amounting to a desire to see the ultimate form hidden from all.[102] Only by suppressing all its lower instincts may the soul expiate this crime and regain true contemplative pleasure (voluptas). In the manner of the Church Fathers, he makes little attempt to reconcile this interpretation with the letter of the narrative but proceeds unimpeded by the inconsistencies involved. The result was to establish the standard interpretation of the myth as representing a victory for the rational soul over its baser instincts both sensual and vegetative. Thus, by concluding his canto with so celebrated an episode, Spenser combines an allusion to the human institution of marriage with a vision of the soul's ascent from the cruel, tyrannous Cupid of carnal desire to the divine Cupid who offers celestial union. Contemplation of material beauty leads to contemplation of the species or ideas and these in turn lead to the deity. Venus's 'late' acceptance of Psyche represents a reconciliation between the 'inferior' Venus and the rational soul. No longer is the soul tormented by desire for the material products of the divine plan. The initial descent of Venus effects a new raising of the spirit.

To be 'eterne in mutabilitie' is possible for man only vicariously through the lives of his descendants. In effect, as the fable of Psyche adumbrates and as Ficino believed, his desire for generation bespeaks a desire for a more

100 *Genealogie* I, 259-60; *The Marriage of Philology and Mercury*, translated by William Harris Stahl, Richard Johnson, and E.L. Burge in *Martianus Capella and the Seven Liberal Arts*, 2 vols (New York, 1971-7), II, 6-7.

101 *Timaeus a Calcidio Translatus Commentarioque Instructus*, edited by J.H. Waszink (London, 1962), pp. 235-6.

102 *Genealogie*, I, 260.

personal eternity: 'In what consists the love of men, you ask, and what end does it serve? The desire of generation in the beautiful so that everlasting life may be preserved in mortal things; this is the love of men living on the earth and this is the goal of our love'.[103] In the *Hymne in Honovr of Love* Spenser distinguishes man from the animals on the grounds that, bearing 'a more immortall mynd', he 'seekes to enlarge his lasting progenie' for the sake of 'eternitie' rather than 'lust' (103-5). Nevertheless, the 'pittie' of the garden posits the need for individual men to break free of the generative cycle, to exchange eternal flux for eternal rest. In the *Mutabilitie Cantos* the successive cycles of the material world, however vividly imagined, depress the poet locked within them. Ironically Nature herself is chosen to supply a vision of hope.

V. *Perpetuation and Decay*

In the *Physics* Aristotle explained how the cyclical view of creation could be regarded as rising directly from men's experience of the passage of time:

> we say that human affairs and those of all other things that have natural movement and become and perish seem to be in a way circular, because all these come to pass in time and have their beginning and end as it were 'periodically'; for time itself is conceived as 'coming round'; and this again because time and such a standard rotation mutually determine each other. Hence, to call the happenings of a thing a circle is saying that there is a sort of circle of time; and that is because it is measured by a complete revolution, and the whole measurement of a thing is nought else but a defined number of units of its measurement.[104]

Ideas such as these were extremely topical throughout the Renaissance and are detectable in Spenser's work as early as *The Shepheardes Calender*, but problems arise the moment we attempt to relate them to the equally prevalent theme of the world's progressive decline. His description of the Gardens of Adonis demonstrates the potentially limitless perpetuation of the natural order, necessitating neither creation nor destruction, whereas in the proem to book five he depicts an aging debilitated world growing daily 'wourse and wourse'.

103 'Quid hominum amor sit postulatis; ad quid conducat? Cupido generationis in pulchro observandam vitam mortalibus in rebus perpetuam; hic hominum in terra viventium amor est, hic nostri finis amoris.' *Marsilio Ficino's Commentary on Plato's Symposium*, edited and tranlated by Sears R. Jayne, University of Missouri Studies, 19, no. 1 (Columbia, 1944), pp. 93, 203.

104 *The Physics* (223b), translated by Philip H. Wicksteed and Francis M. Cornford, Loeb Classical Library, 2 vols (London, 1929-34), I, 425.

The general view of the leading sixteenth-century authorities, including Bodin, was against Aristotle. The six thousand years allotted to creation were almost spent and the present bore no comparison with the past.[105] Logically speaking, of course, the belief that the world would end, as it began, by an act of divine will necessitated no theory of *progressive* decay prior to the fated destruction. It was enough that the bible had predicted the degeneracy of the last days. There were a few divergent opinions. As we have seen, Bodin rejected the idea of the Golden Age, and in a work entitled *La Vicissitude des Choses* (1577) Louis Le Roy argued that change should be regarded optimistically as a sign of progress, a sign that the present world has developed into a better place. In 1594 Le Roy's work was translated into English by Robert Ashley and seems to have made a considerable impact.[106] The forces that were to crystallise in the great confrontation between Godfrey Goodman and George Hakewill were already beginning to take shape in the Elizabethan period.[107] Spenser's reception of such ideas is unusual in that he appears to have anticipated both sides of the debate.

In *The Fall of Man* (1616) Goodman rested much of his case upon the theory that, since man could be regarded as a microcosm of the universe, the curse pronounced in Genesis took effect upon nature.[108] Spenser adopts a similar attitude in the *Mutabilitie Cantos* where he expressly associates Mutability with the Fall, and again in book five where the correspondence between fallen men and fallen creation is worked out in some detail. The difficulty, however, is that Mutability's witnesses attest to orderly, cyclical change and Nature identifies this continuing process as vital to the perpetuation and development of life — a point made repeatedly by Goodman's opponents. Spenser seems unaware of any contradiction. Furthermore, until Goodman's day it was quite unusual to assert the mutability of the heavens, despite the growing astronomical evidence. Yet Spenser uses much of the available information to create a vision of celestial chaos in the proem to book five and again in Mutability's reply to Jove.[109] When this material is com-

105 Don Cameron Allen, 'The Degeneration of Man and Renaissance Pessimism', *Studies in Philology* 35 (1938), 202-227 (pp. 209-12). As Rosalind puts it in *As You Like It*, 'the poor world is almost six thousand years old' (IV. 1. 91-2). Jean Bodin concurred. See his *Method for the Easy Comprehension of History*, translated by Beatrice Reynolds (New York, 1945), pp. 319-24.

106 Kathrine Koller, 'Two Elizabethan Expressions of the Idea of Mutability', *Studies in Philology*, 35 (1938), 228-37. See also Herschel Baker, *The Wars of Truth* (Gloucester, Mass., 1969 — first published 1952), pp. 70-1. Le Roy did, however, share the common expectation of eventual Apocalypse. See Peter Burke, *The Renaissance Sense of the Past* (London, 1969), p. 88.

107 Victor Harris, *All Coherence Gone* (London, 1949), pp. 87-129.

108 *Ibid.*, pp. 36-46, 197-204. For a summary of Goodman's arguments against the eternity of the world see *The Fall of Man* (1616), pp. 408-15.

109 Harris, pp. 92, 106-107, 147-8. See below Chapter Five.

bined with that handled in the Gardens of Adonis we arrive at the perplexing conclusion that Spenser was arguing on both sides of the debate simultaneously, both for creative cyclical change and progressive natural decay. The dichotomy, however, is more apparent than real.

In his celebrated reply to Goodman, *An Apologie or Declaration of the Power and Providence of God in the Government of the World* (1627), George Hakewill advanced the view that change perpetuates the species although it sacrifices the individual. In a passage which may well have been influenced by Spenser, he asserts that man 'because a *species*, by succession becomes eternall'.[110] Hakewill sees this as God's way of reconciling the potential eternity of creation with the mortality of the individuals who comprise it. The circular cycle of life and death merely reflect, albeit in an imperfect way, the perfection of their creator. As the title of his work suggests, Hakewill was concerned with upholding the doctrine of divine providence, and to his way of thinking a self-sustaining world-order seemed more in keeping with the dignity of the creator than a world in irreversible decline. The apparent inequalities of nature, deplored by Spenser's 'egalitarian' Giant, Hakewill explains by a theory of 'reciprocall compensation' virtually identical to that employed by Artegall, an examination of which I have reserved for my final chapter.[111] The key to both Spenser's and Hakewill's attitudes is the respect for Providence which informs both lines of thought.

The factor that distinguishes Spenser most clearly from Hakewill, however, is his insistence upon common human experience. The bland abstractions of the seventeenth-century debate are often achieved at the expense of human truth, dispensing with individuals as though they were purely disposable 'matter'. Spenser duly retreats from Nature's summary of the debate on Arlo Hill into the consolation of private meditation and prayer. Similarly in his description of the Gardens of Adonis he stresses the 'pity' of the individual's fate and represents time at its most destructive for the individual while engaged in its most supposedly beneficial operations for the race. Elements of discord and dissolution are regarded as essential to the continuation of the life process, but are also recognised as sources of perpetual disappointment and disillusion. The figure who most obviously personifies the forces of discord in *The Faerie Queene* is Ate and in describing her abode Spenser creates a grim parody of his magnificent description of the Gardens of Adonis:

> Such was her house within; but all without,
> The barren ground was full of wicked weedes,
> Which she her selfe had sowen all about,

110 Harris, p. 77.

Now growen great, at first of little seedes,
The seedes of euill wordes, and factious deedes;
Which when to ripenesse due they growen arre,
Bring foorth an infinite increase, that breedes
Tumultuous trouble and contentious iarre,
The which most often end in bloudshed and in warre.
(IV. 1. 25)

In its present fallen state the world is both the Garden of Adonis and the Garden of Ate. Spenser asserts God's Providence in sustaining the cycles of birth, decay, and death, but he also perceives the intense alienation of the individual trapped within them. At times Hakewill poses the notable paradox of fallen man in an unfallen universe — he will allow of no decay beyond the Moon, for example. Spenser is at once more pessimistic and more common-sensical. The miracle of the biological process has its due praise, but is never mistaken for a lost perfection — had not St Augustine maintained in his treatise *On Marriage and Concupiscence* that evil 'germinated' in Adam's seed to corrupt the entire biological process?[112] Once this is allowed, biological regeneration becomes compatible with accelerating moral decay. Disease is perpetual within the process. Such a dual view was not without precedent.

Lucretius, for example, asserted the eternal mutability of atomic matter while at the same time maintaining that the constant erosion of the world's constituent elements necessitated its eventual disintegration.[113] In the final analysis the potential eternity of the Garden is unfulfilled, and this, perhaps, is the ultimate significance of the imprisoned but still living boar. Yet Spenser did not subscribe to the view that inexorable decline would of itself occasion the world's annihilation — the logical conclusion to Goodman's arguments — but looked to a moment of divine intervention, a cataclysm such as awaits Lucifera in book one.[114] Furthermore, the theory of cyclical generation and decline could easily be accommodated to that of providential history.[115] One had merely to regard the cycles as forming part of an overall plan, or better still, like the goddess Nature, regard the entire history of creation as forming a perfect circle by finally returning upon itself. This notion, strongly influenced by Stoic and Platonic concepts of the Great Year, proved particularly

111 *Apologie*, second edition (1630), pp. 108-116 (p. 113); Harris, p. 77.
112 *Apologie* (1630), pp. 73-5, 103-8; Augustine, *On Marriage and Concupiscence* (II. 20. 48).
113 George Williamson, 'Mutability, Decay, and Seventeenth-Century Melancholy', *ELH*, 2 (1935), 121-50 (p. 132).
114 *Fall of Man*, p. 383.
115 Herschel Baker, *The Race of Time* (Toronto, 1967), pp. 60-2.

useful since it could also be employed to validate the impression that the world grows daily worse. Measuring his journey along the circumference from the point at which the motion begins, the traveller wanders ever further from his point of origin even as he closes upon it from the opposite direction. Paradoxically the distance traversed is greatest in the seconds prior to his sudden return to the point of departure. This provides us with a convenient figure for Spenser's poem as originally planned, since only circular motion can afford the experience of nearing one's destination by apparently travelling away from it.

CHAPTER FIVE

Providence

O soueraigne Lord that sit'st on hye,
And raignst in blis emongst thy blessed Saintes,
How suffrest thou such shamefull cruelty,
So long vnwreaked of thine enimy?
Or hast thou, Lord, of good mens cause no heed?
Or doth thy iustice sleepe, and silent ly?

(III. 11. 9)

I. *Providence, Fortune and Fate*

The patterns of renewal and return which permeate *The Faerie Queene* could easily degenerate into the 'giddying' cycles of time of which Bacon warns in his essay 'Of the Vicissitude of Things' were it not for Spenser's insistence upon the guiding element of providence in the dual sense of benign control and divine foresight.[1] As he passes rapidly from one set of characters to another, Spenser is fascinated by the way in which a pattern of coincidences 'exceeding thought' may at last be made to suggest a deliberate plan, by the way in which different time-sequences are eventually synchronised. When this works well the poem's structure becomes analogous to life, its aesthetic form reflecting the providential plan. This intention is underscored by the elements of prophecy and vision introduced at moments of strategic narrative importance. By forestalling the offices of time, prophecy bespeaks a controlling intelligence above contingency. In literary terms it suggests the poet's grasp of the entire scope of his narrative, the existence of an aesthetic 'idea' to which the structure must conform. In other words it suggests a resemblance between the poet and his God, the God who created man 'according to an heauenly patterne wrought,/ Which he had fashiond in his wise foresight' (*Hymne of Heavenly Love*, 108-9). Spenser, one recalls, had so 'fashioned' *The Faerie Queene* that a single 'general intention and meaning' underlay all its 'particular purposes or by-accidents'. The association is doubly enforced when the subject matter itself requires a providential interpretation of human life. Spenser's problem is that he must interpret specific segments of British

1 Bacon, *Works*, VI, 512-7 (p. 517). See above pp. 72, 149.

history providentially within the context of his fictional romance while at the same time 'fashioning' that romance as a vast analogue to the great scheme. For the analogy to be exact, the characters must remain to a large extent ignorant of the pattern.

In the hands of providential exegetes such as Augustine, allegory is primarily a tool of historical analysis, an instrument of enlightened perception designed to translate the coded messages of time into the language of eternity. However, since the transience of Augustinian time defeats apprehension, all that may actually be interpreted are the literary texts which purport to record its passage. Regarded from this perspective the historian's 'bare was' is wholly inadequate to the material it attempts to chronicle; it represents a distortion of 'reality'. Accordingly Augustinian interpreters blithely dispense with the letter of the text in pursuit of the spirit. The Augustinian 'poet historicall' proceeds one step further in attempting to rewrite the chronicles themselves in the light of the allegorical readings already abstracted from them. Spenser proceeds further still by relocating such reconstructed chronicles within the context of a fictional narrative aiming to prove analogous both to the actual experience of life (in the romance) and to its providential significance (through the allegory). To all but the most complacently simplistic of minds this is to enter a multi-dimensional maze of impenetrable complexity. Hence the poem's many unresolved dichotomies: history is both fact and 'fiction'; romance is both 'historicall' and feigned; allegory is both illuminating and 'darke'; the author is both omniscient and 'amazed'. As in metaphysical poetry the 'darkness' of the 'conceit' is a necessity of the subject-matter. Both for poet and protagonists the central quest underlying all others is that of human providence for its divine counterpart.

Spenser's enterprise is fraught with difficulties. To rewrite history from a providential perspective is to risk hostile reassertions of the chroniclers' 'bare was' potentially damaging to the concept of providence itself. Furthermore, once poetry becomes a medium of providential insight, the poet, unlike the exegete, cannot afford to dispense with the letter of the text since the letter itself has become providentially significant. As a result the reconstruction of providential history demands a reconstruction of historiographical complexity involving an acknowledgement within time of all of the recalcitrant details providential exegesis obscures in order to 'explain'. In particular it necessitates exploration of the relationship between foresight, free will, and grace. The thematic difficulties of Spenser's poem may thus be regarded as the inevitable consequence of his aesthetic vision while the vision itself develops and distorts under pressure of an increasingly convoluted theme. If the world constitutes a 'divine allegory' providential history can be 'written' only by God from the perspective of the *nunc-stans*. Spenser endeavours to find a human equivalent by converting 'history' into 'prophecy' thereby confounding past and future in the perpetual present of the angelic intelligence enjoyed by the Magus.

The problem of providence, though incalculably ancient, retains the force of perpetual novelty because each generation casts the central issues in terminology precisely appropriate to its own intellectual preoccupations. For example, Plato's interest in spiritual evolution led him to argue for individual moral responsibility within a divinely ordered universe whereas the logical implications of Aristotle's more academic arguments upon the nature of causation, necessity, and time would appear to be deterministic.[2] Stoic philosophy with its severely ethical attitudes focussed attention upon the conflict between wisdom and fortune while at the same time maintaining a belief in the overriding control of providence or fate.[3] Attempting to reconcile the existence of evil with that of the supreme intellect, Plotinus struggled with the paradoxes of Platonic philosophy in a series of poetic analogies designed to demonstrate the operations of free choice within an entirely ordered world-system.[4] But the undeniable brilliance of his imagery cannot disguise the logical flaws undermining his arguments, and St Augustine duly rejected his notion of retributive metempsychosis for that of original sin.[5] So earnestly did Augustine argue for personal moral responsibility in his early works, and particularly in *De Libero Arbitrio*, that, to his considerable embarrassment, the Pelagians were later to regard them as validating their own position. By way of refutation Augustine was forced to shift his emphasis towards Pauline doctrines of predestination and grace. The implications of this development were to trouble the Christian world for the next fourteen centuries.[6] While Boethius endeavoured to reconcile apparent contradictions between providence and free will by placing God beyond human time, the influence of semi-Pelagianism continued strong and a further outbreak of the controversy centring upon Gottschalk disturbed the ninth-century church and remained dangerously latent in all subsequent theological speculation.[7]

Throughout the Middle Ages Calcidius's commentary upon Plato's *Timaeus* ensured the continued association of Platonism with Christian providence, and Aquinas unhesitatingly endorsed Boethius's outlook ar-

2 Plato, *Laws*, 904B-C. For Aristotle see, Richard Sorabji, *Necessity, Cause and Blame: Perspectives on Aristotle's Theory* (London, 1980), pp. 91-140.

3 Cicero, *De Fato*; Seneca, *De Providentia* (*Dialogues* I).

4 *Enneads*, III. 2-3.

5 *On the Grace of Christ and Original Sin*, II. 36.

6 *A Companion to the Study of St Augustine*, edited by Roy W. Battenhouse (New York, 1955), p. 115-24, 203-29.

7 The essential texts were republished by Archbishop James Ussher in *Gotteschalci et Praedestinatianae Controversiae ab eo Motae, Historia: Una cum duplice ejusdem Confessione, nunc primum in lucem edita* (Dublin, 1631), pp. 211-37.

guing that, 'human providence is included under the Providence of God, as a particular under a universal cause'.[8] However, by distinguishing predestination to glory from predestination to grace (Spenser's George would seem to be predestined to glory) he made an important contribution to the development of the debate concerning the relationship of free will to reprobation. 'Providence', he argued, 'of which Predestination is a part, does not do away with secondary cause, but so provides for effects, that the order of secondary causes falls also under Providence'.[9] Thus the stage was set for the great Renaissance debate between Luther and Erasmus on the nature of the will. In effect, Erasmus jealously maintained individual autonomy in the humanist tradition of Lorenzo Valla while Luther, and later Calvin, developed towards their logical conclusion the implications of Augustine's Anti-Pelagian tracts.[10]

Calvin's *Institutes* dominated Reformation theology but without ever providing an entirely cogent explanation of what their author regarded as genuine Augustinian, or Pauline, doctrine. In England the reaction was confused. Whereas the *Thirty-Nine Articles* trod a cautious middle path between Rome and Geneva and were officially endorsed, the less cautious Lambeth Articles, championed by Puritan factions towards the end of the sixteenth century, proved abortive.[11] The appearance about the same time of Hooker's *Ecclesiastical Polity* (1594-7) bore eloquent testimony to an opposed outlook. The powerful impact of the Counter-Reformation necessitated constant re-assessment of the Protestant position and finally resulted in the Arminian controversy which divided the Dutch Church and dominated the Synod of Dort (1618-9). Not surprisingly, the debate defied theoretical resolution particularly since the challenge to Rome had developed such intricate political ramifications. A poet of an intensely intellectual cast of mind, acutely responsive to topical concerns, writing towards the end of the Tudor Age, would inevitably be led to explore such problems in the light of the contemporary debate, however inconclusive. Indeed the very inconclusiveness would contribute to its imaginative attraction. A sense of mystery haunts the world of *The Faerie Queene* and intrigues its readers. Arthur well articulates this feeling when attempting to explain his presence in fairyland:

8 *Summa Theologica*, Part One, Q. XXII, art 1, 2 ad. 4. *The 'Summa Theologica' of St. Thomas Aquinas*, Part One, No. I, translated by Fathers of the English Dominican Province (London, 1911), pp. 305, 309. Hereafter *Summa.*

9 *Summa Theologica*, Part One, QQ. XXII-XXIV. *Summa*, pp. 333, 337.

10 *Luther and Erasmus: Free Will and Salvation*, edited by E. Gordon Rupp and Philip S. Watson, The Library of Christian Classics (Philadelphia, 1969). See especially pp. 89-91 (Erasmus) and pp. 291, 319-27 (Luther).

11 M. M. Knappen, *Tudor Puritanism: A Chapter in the History of Idealism* (Chicago, 1939), pp. 369-70.

Full hard it is (quoth he) to read aright
The course of heauenly cause, or vnderstand
The secret meaning of th'eternall might
That rules mens wayes, and rules the thoughts of liuing wight.
(I. 9. 6)

While the immediate cause of his coming, his love for the Fairy Queen, is clear, the ultimate cause remains hidden. The 'secret meaning' which directs not merely man's 'wayes' but even his 'thoughts' admits of no easy explanation but resembles the 'darke conceit' of Spenser's poem, its perplexities apparently contrived to some remote moral or spiritual effect. The certainty that some dark purpose informs the fable renders the situation equally problematic for reader and character alike. Most of the poem's heroes undergo periods of uncertainty and confusion similar to Arthur's. It is by carefully contrived structuring that George's encounter with Despair occurs shortly after the Prince has finished speaking.

The connection between despair and predestination was quite traditional. The seventeenth article of the Established Church, 'De Praedestinatione et Electione', concludes its doctrinal formulations with a warning against desperation.[12] Views such as Arthur puts forward are vital to the interpretation of *The Faerie Queene* since he, the poem's foremost instrument of providence, no less than the knights he assists, is caught in the toils of contingency and chance, in the baffling sequence of successes, failures, and apparent non-sequiturs resulting from Spenser's intricate narrative technique. Because of its inherent difficulties, polyphonic narrative provides the perfect medium for reflecting the cross-currents and coincidences of human life. Its order emerges gradually and in many cases the overall structure can be appreciated only on re-reading. The irony in the present case is that Arthur seems to have met Una by chance, although the encounter is vital to the salvation of George later identified as one of the elect. It had to happen. Arthur suggests several possible explanations for the sequence of events that has just occurred, but without committing himself to any:

For whither he through fatall deepe foresight
Me hither sent, for cause to me vnghest,
Or that fresh bleeding wound, which day and night
Whilome doth rancle in my riuen brest,
With forced fury following his behest,
Me hither brought by wayes yet neuer found,
You to haue helpt I hold my selfe yet blest. (I. 9. 7)

12 E. J. Bicknell, *A Theological Introduction to the Thirty-Nine Articles of the Church of England*, (London, 1933), pp. 277-8.

'Fatall deepe foresight' suggests the foreknowledge and providence of the Christian God, but the terms thus associated are by no means synonymous. Providence or 'foresight' is distinct from fate. As Boethius was at pains to explain, 'Providence is the divine reason itself which belongs to the most high ruler of all things and which governs all things; Fate, however, belongs to all mutable things and is the disposition by which Providence joins all things in their own order'.[13] Chaucer translated 'fatum' as 'destyne', and this distinction, upheld by Richard Hooker amongst others, between fate (or 'destyne') on the one hand and providence on the other, is something we should constantly bear in mind while reading *The Faerie Queene*: many of the poem's moral paragons eloquently complain of the injustice of fate, but seldom, if ever, of God.[14] One is reminded of Ficino's assertion, based upon a reading of Plato's *Theaetetus* (176a-b), that whereas the soul is guided by the 'laws of providence' the body is enslaved to the 'forces of fate, as a single particle is dragged by the total mass of which it is a part'. Only when the mind allows itself to become 'submerged' in the body does it too become a prisoner of fate.[15]

Boethius also developed a further distinction relating to the passage of time when he wrote that, 'Providence is the unfolding of temporal events as this is present to the vision of the divine mind; but this same unfolding of events as it is worked out in time is called Fate'. Furthermore, 'Providence is the immovable and simple form of all things which come into being, while Fate is the moving connection and temporal order of all things which the divine simplicity has decided to bring into being'. As this recalls Plato's assertion that time is the moving image of eternity, Boethius proceeds to remark that 'the changing course of Fate is to the simple stability of Providence as reasoning is to intellect, as that which is generated is to that which *is*, as time is to eternity, as a circle to its centre'.[16] Fate is implicated in time and motion, but providence is of God's unmoved tranquillity. Fate is the moving, temporal image of 'foresight'. By persistently emphasising the 'eternal', and therefore timeless, nature of providence, Spenser attempts to avoid the crippling fatalism of Night (I. 5. 25) and Despair (I. 9. 42) whose combined insistence upon the force of 'necessitie' within human time serves to drain life of all

13 *The Consolation of Philosophy* (Book 4, Prose 6), translated by Richard Green (Indianapolis, 1962), p. 91. All further references are to this edition. For Boethius's views see J.G.A. Pocock, *The Machiavellian Moment* (Princeton, 1975), pp. 37-40.

14 *Complete Works*, edited by F.N. Robinson (Boston, 1933), p. 368. Richard Hooker, *Works*, edited by John Keble, 3 vols (Oxford, 1888) I, 210.

15 *The Letters of Marsilio Ficino*, translated by Members of the Language Department of the School of Economic Science, London with a preface by Paul Oskar Kristeller (London, 1975-), I, 94-5.

16 Boethius (Book 4, Prose 6), pp. 91-2.

positive meaning. By emphasising the benign effects of providential guidance he attempts to contradict Night's virtual identification of the eternal with the necessary (I. 5. 25). Semantic confusions of this nature mislead many of the poem's principal characters but all explicit statements of the providential outlook are assigned either to the author or to characters who, for the time being, enjoy similar authority. On no occasion does any of the evil characters ever acknowledge true 'providence'.

Arthur qualifies his mention of 'fatall deepe foresight' with the phrase 'for cause to me unghest' since the major problem of life is that man cannot recognise the unity and simplicity of the providential plan in the disorganised multiplicity of 'fate'.[17] His own multiple explanations bear this out. The second begins as if it were in some sense detachable from the first: 'or' implies an alternative view. Perhaps it is not some secret plan but the 'fury' of love that has 'brought' Arthur to Fairyland 'by wayes yet neuer found'. His attitude towards the 'bleeding wound' that rankles 'day and night' is still uncertain. If it has led him like a faithful guide through trackless countryside he could never otherwise have hoped to penetrate, its nature is clearly benign, but if he finds himself astray in a world of danger and illusion the opposite is true. At this stage of his adventures he cannot decide between the two. What is more, he makes no direct attempt to relate the 'foresight' of the first explanation to the uncontrollable passion or 'fury' of the second — the fifth line of the stanza is ambiguous on this point. In its treatment of love, however, the poem works gradually towards their reconciliation, towards the recognition of God as the supreme Cupid.

Though unaware of the solution implicit in his own language, Arthur concludes that whichever of his explanations is correct 'you to haue helpt I hold my selfe yet blest' — a crucial insight since a 'blessing' cannot but hallow either explanation. Although not yet in a position — or a 'iust' time — to realise it, he is closer to the truth than he thinks. For the present, however, the problem remains. In book two Arthur is still searching for the elusive Gloriana, 'yet no where can her find: such happinesse/Heauen doth to me enuy, and fortune fauourlesse' (II. 9. 7). The new element here is that of fortune.

Fate and fortune are classical concepts. The former suggests supernatural determinism, the latter the irresistible force of contingency, good or bad depending upon the recipient's point of view. As he sees it, Arthur encounters

17 For Arthur's role in the poem, both providential and otherwise, see Merritt Y. Hughes, 'The Arthurs of *The Faerie Queene*', *Études Anglaises*, (1953), 193-213; Sherry L. Reames, 'Prince Arthur and Spenser's Changing Design', in Kenneth John Atchity, ed., *Eterne in Mutabilitie: The Unity of 'The Faerie Queene'* (Hamden, Connecticut, 1972), pp. 180-206; Ronald Arthur Horton, *The Unity of 'The Faerie Queene'* (Athens, Georgia, 1978), pp. 19-24.

Guyon and the Palmer entirely by chance, but they, and the reader, think otherwise. As Guyon collapses and lies defenceless on the ground outside the cave of Mammon, Spenser pauses to consider the mystery of divine involvement in mortal affairs:

> And is there care in heauen? and is there loue
>   In heauenly spirits to these creatures bace,
>   That may compassion of their euils moue?
>   There is: else much more wretched were the cace
>   Of men, then beasts. But O th'exceeding grace
>   Of highest God, that loues his creatures so,
>   And all his workes with mercy doth embrace,
>   That blessed Angels, he sends to and fro,
> To serue to wicked man, to serue his wicked foe. (II. 8. 1)

Providence, fate and love are hereby linked indissolubly. The angel remains until the Palmer arrives, led by a mysterious voice 'that called loud and cleare'. Can it then be chance that Arthur arrives so unexpectedly to succour the Palmer when the angel has withdrawn? Aided by the structure of the poem the reader concludes that it cannot. In canto eight of book one Arthur delivers George, in canto eight of book two he delivers Guyon. Aesthetic order insinuates providential order, and the power of contingency is effectively denied by the poem's construction. Such a denial was common amongst Elizabethan divines. As Thomas Cooper put it, 'that which we call fortune, is nothing but the hand of God, working by causes, and for causes, that we knowe not'.[18] Even more germane to a poem in which Christian knights battle continually against 'paynims' or pagans — Pyrochles and Cymochles are referred to as paynims (10), pagans (45), and sarazins (19) throughout the episode under discussion — is John Knox's assertion that 'fortune and adventure are the wordes of Paynims, the signification whereof oght in no wise to enter into the heart of the faithfull'.[19] Knox was merely echoing his mentor, Calvin, who was careful to distinguish Christian providence from Stoic fate:

We do not, with the Stoics, contrive a necessity out of the perpetual

18 *Certaine Sermons* (London, 1580), p. 164.

19 Knox is quoting from St Basil the Great whose views would entirely eliminate the idea of fortune: 'For if all prosperitie be the benediction of God, and adversitie his malediction, there remaineth no place to fortune in such things as come to men'. *The Works of John Knox*, edited by D. Laing, 6 vols (Edinburgh, 1846-64), V (1856), p. 32. See Keith Thomas, *Religion and the Decline of Magic*, second edition (Harmondsworth 1973), pp. 90-132.

> connection and intimately related series of causes, which is contained in nature; but we make God the ruler and governor of all things, who in accordance with his wisdom has from the farthest limit of eternity decreed what he was going to do, and now by his might carries out what he has decreed.[20]

Calvin proceeds to recognise the problem of identifying the hand of God in the apparently confused state of temporal affairs. The 'sluggishness' of the human mind is responsible for this failure:

> However all things may be ordained by God's plan, according to a sure dispensation, for us they are fortuitous. Not that we think that fortune rules the world and men, tumbling all things at random up and down, for it is fitting that this folly be absent from the Christian's breast! But since the order, reason, end, and necessity of those things which happen for the most part lie hidden in God's purpose, and are not apprehended by human opinion, those things, which it is certain take place by God's will, are in a sense fortuitous. For they bear on the face of them no other appearance, whether they are considered in their own nature or weighed according to our knowledge and judgment. Let us imagine, for example, a merchant who, entering a wood with a company of faithful men, unwisely wanders away from his companions, and in his wandering comes upon a robbers' den, falls among thieves, and is slain. His death was not only foreseen by God's eye, but also determined by his decree. For it is not said that he foresaw how long the life of each man would extend, but that he determined and fixed the bounds that men cannot pass (Job 14:5). Yet as far as the capacity of our mind is concerned, all things therein seem fortuitous. What will a Christian think at this point? Just this: whatever happened in a death of this sort he will regard as fortuitous by nature, as it is; yet he will not doubt that God's providence exercised authority over fortune in directing its end. The same reckoning applies to the contingency of future events.[21]

This is a perfect description of the wanderings and accidental calamities

20 *Institutes of the Christian Religion*, translated by Ford Lewis Battles, edited by John T. McNeill, The Library of Christian Classics, 2 vols (Philadelphia, 1960), I, 207. For Calvin's contribution to the theory of providence see G.F. Waller, 'Transition in Renaissance Ideas of Time and the Place of Giordano Bruno', *Neophilologus*, 55 (1971), 3-15 (pp. 5-6).

21 *Institutes*, I, 208-9. For the same view as propounded by Holinshed and Fleming see R. Mark Benbow, 'The Providential Theory of Historical Causation in *Holinshed's Chronicles* 1577 and 1587', *Texas Studies in Language and Literature*, I (1959-60), 264-76 (p. 266).

of Spenser's romance. As we proceed to books three and four the pattern becomes even more difficult to determine as the narrative technique grows increasingly polyphonic in imitation of Ariosto. Arthur does not intervene in the expected canto of book three, but early on issues a long and weary complaint against the powers of evil and misfortune (symbolised by Night, 'foule Mother of annoyance sad') which appear to be at odds with the plan of 'th'eternall Maker'. The numerologically-minded reader is tricked into identifying 'significant sequences' only to see them dashed. There is no simple 'key' to providence, not in numbers, not in planets, not in dates. The whole point is that chance is not dispensable, but integral to the grand design. Like Milton's angels, Spenser's heroes are 'regular/ Then most, when most irregular they seem'. Even Calvin could not exclude contingency 'in regard to human understanding'.[22]

Book six is, perhaps, the most episodic and frustrating of the entire work for readers and protagonists alike. Indeed the structural paradigm established in book one seems entirely lost. Yet even here, re-echoing the imagery of the first book at precisely the same point of development (I. 12. 1), Spenser assures us that,

> Like as a ship, that through the Ocean wyde
> Directs her course vnto one certaine cost,
> Is met of many a counter winde and tyde,
> With which her winged speed is let and crost,
> And she her selfe in stormie surges tost;
> Yet making many a borde, and many a bay,
> Still winneth way, ne hath her compasse lost:
> Right so it fares with me in this long way,
> Whose course is often stayd, yet neuer is astray. (VI. 12. 1)

The perplexities of the narrative mirror those of life. Poet and reader stray as far off course as the 'errant' knights, but the implication is that both the fictional and the real world remain firmly under control. Romance enforces the isolation of the hero in a chaotic world of contingency and flux, a world which 'to the eye of the human understanding is framed like a labyrinth; presenting as it does on every side so many ambiguities of way, such deceitful resemblances of objects and signs, natures so irregular in their lines, and so knotted and entangled. And then the way is still to be made by the uncertain light of the sense, sometimes shining out, sometimes clouded over, through the woods of experience and particulars'.[23] The words are those of Francis

22 *Paradise Lost*, V. 623-4; *Concerning the Eternal Predestination of God*, translated by J.K.S. Reid (Cambridge, 1961), p. 170.

23 Bacon, *Works*, IV, 18. On providence and romance conventions see John Arthos, *On*

Bacon, describing not the universe of romance narrative but of common experience. Their striking applicability to the world of *The Faerie Queene* illustrates the function of Spenser's narrative technique.

In Medieval literature the archetypal romance hero Ulysses, wandering frustratedly from port to port, was commonly regarded as the plaything of fortune. This was to be expected since the sea itself, in its fickleness and unpredictability, traditionally served as an emblem of the same power, hence its far from accidental prevalence in books three and four. Britomart's complaint prior to her combat with Marinell consciously evokes the same conceit (III. 4. 8-10). There is even a reference in book six to 'the tempests of these worldly seas' (VI. 9. 19). Yet the fact remains that Ulysses did not wander aimlessly. He came home. The same is true of Aeneas whose tortuous journeyings after the fall of Troy eventually led to the founding of Rome and the establishment of world empire.[24] At the beginning of the *Aeneid* the hero is described as the man 'qui primus ab oris/ Italiam *fato* profugus Lavinaque venit/ litora'. This is precisely how Paridell explains it to Britomart in book three when he describes the 'fatall errour' (fated wandering) that led Aeneas to the shores of Latium, and the circumstances of his marriage to Latinus's daughter as 'the fates ordained'. In the *Disputationes Camaldulenses* (1474) Cristoforo Landino interpreted the poem as an allegory of spiritual trial and development. The great patterns of epic upon which Spenser was drawing move towards the suggestion of a 'divinity that shapes our ends', a divinity Christianized in Ariosto and Tasso under the influence of the bible: the archetypal pattern of providential wandering, with all the frustrations and anxieties it entails, was that of the Jews on their forty-year trek to the promised land. Seen from this perspective all coincidence is pre-ordained, all fortune beneficial, and time, however tedious its passage, the instrument of a providentially ordered fate.[25] Boethius concluded that 'everything which is subject to Fate is also subject to Providence, and that Fate itself is also subject to Providence'.[26] There are few accidents in Spenser's world. For him, the

the Poetry of Spenser and the Form of Romances (London, 1956), pp. 65-91. In *The Wisdom of the Ancients* Bacon makes his providential outlook even more explicit: 'All the works of Divine Providence in the world are wrought by winding and roundabout ways — where one thing seems to be doing and another is doing really — as in the selling of Joseph into Egypt and the like'. *Works*, VI, 711. See also Jerome S. Dees, 'The Ship Conceit in *The Faerie Queene*: ''conspicuous allusion'' and poetic structure', *SP*, 72 (1975), 208-25.

24 H.R. Patch, *The Goddess Fortuna in Medieval Literature* (Cambridge, Mass., 1927), pp. 101-7; Northrop Frye, *The Secular Scripture* (Harvard, 1976), pp. 148-9.

25 Merritt Y. Hughes, 'Virgilian Allegory and *The Faerie Queene*', *PMLA*, 44 (1929), 696-705 (pp. 700-701); 'Romance . . . is not only central to literature as a whole, but the area where we can see most clearly that the maze without a plan and the maze not without a plan are two aspects of the same thing'. Frye, *Secular Scripture*, p. 31.

26 Boethius (Book 4, Prose 6), p. 92.

startling oxymoron of 'fatall errour' (in the sense of predestined accident) merely serves to express the apparently impossible synthesis that Providence achieves and narrative endeavours to attain.

It was the nature of the goddess Fortuna to be fickle. Should her wheel cease to turn, she would cease to be herself.[27] As a result, her gifts are distributed without regard to the moral character of their recipients. To Arthur's complaint in book two, Guyon replies that,

> Fortune, the foe of famous cheuisaunce
> Seldome . . . yields to vertue aide,
> But in her way throwes mischiefe and mischaunce,
> Whereby her course is stopt, and passage staid.
> But you, faire Sir, be not herewith dismaid,
> But constant keepe the way, in which ye stand. (II. 9. 8)

This is fortune as man is condemned to experience it, but the 'good hap' that brings Arthur to the aid of George and Guyon is simply a manifestation of the same power seen from a different point of view. When George falls for the first time during his combat with the dragon, 'it fortuned' that the well of life lay directly behind him. When he falls a second time, 'it chaunst' that the tree of life lay in his way, in fact 'eternall God that chaunce did guide' (I. 11. 45). This is one of Spenser's most explicit pronouncements on the connection between prouidence and fortune marking the direct intervention of a timeless power into the world of contingency. It now emerges that, in some cases at least, 'chance' is 'guided' by an external force. Similarly, it is by 'providence' that Belphoebe encounters and saves the wounded Timias just after the poet has prayed, 'Now God thee keepe, thou gentlest Squire alive'. The distinction between grace and fortune tends to collapse:

> Prouidence heauenly passeth liuing thought,
> And doth for wretched mens reliefe make way;
> For loe great grace or fortune thither brought
> Comfort to him, that comfortlesse now lay. (III. 5. 27)

The notion that providence surpasses 'living thought' is one Spenser often stresses. 'Eternall prouidence exceeding thought' secures the release of Una from Sansloy (I. 6. 7), while the sudden rescue of Calepine and Serena is effected by 'wondrous chaunce . . . such chaunces oft exceed all humaine thought' (VI. 3. 51). When elect knights seem doomed, when their own

27 Boethius (Book 2, Prose 1), p. 22. See Chaucer *The Knight's Tale*, ll. 1663-72; *Troilus and Criseyde*, V. 1541-7; 'Fortune'. On the iconography of Fortuna and her relationship to time see Samuel C. Chew, 'Time and Fortune', *ELH*, (1939), 83-113.

resources have completely failed, help 'exceeding thought' appears as if from nowhere, yet except in the case of Guyon's angel the agency is invariably human. The point is emphasised in Arthur's case when Timias, by no means his equal in valour or nobility, unexpectedly comes to his rescue:

So greatest and most glorious thing on ground
May often need the helpe of weaker hand;
So feeble is mans state, and life vnsound,
That in assurance it may neuer stand,
Till it dissolued be from earthly band.
Proofe be thou Prince, the prowest man aliue,
And noblest borne of all in *Britayne* land;
Yet thee fierce Fortune did so nearely driue,
That had not grace thee blest, thou shouldest not suruiue.

(II. 11. 30)

This belies the aggressive Machiavellian view that man must struggle to fashion fortune to his own requirements since the outcome depends entirely upon the strength and cunning of the fashioner. The concept of 'grace' — a term used persistently throughout the poem — displaces such notions. For Spenser, virtue is not synonymous with *virtú*, at least in theory.[28] The Machiavellian outlook emphasises strength, adaptability, and the trick of recognising the critical moment and acting accordingly.[29] Spenser deals with this too, as we have seen, but from a spiritual and other-worldly point of view. In discussions of this sort Fortuna is usually depicted as Occasion, her long forelock blowing in the breeze.[30] In *The Faerie Queene*, however, Occasion appears only as the companion of Furor and Pyrochles, the perpetual occasion of strife. When finally defeated by Arthur, Pyrochles 'wilfully refused grace' thereby condemning himself to death, a nice comment on the Machiavellian viewpoint since grace is shown to function when self-help is impossible. Even Satyrane, an apparently self-reliant product of 'savage' nature, arrives to aid Una by 'iust *occasion*' through 'wondrous grace' (I. 6. 26).

The idea that providence, of its very nature, exceeds the grasp of prudence goes far towards explaining the problem of despair. An intellectual creature, man is increasingly frustrated by his own weakness of comprehension. The reason for God's failure to intervene in human affairs on behalf of the elect exceeds his thought even more than the most miraculous of such rare

28 Quentin Skinner, *The Foundations of Modern Political Thought*, 2 vols (Cambridge, 1978), I, 186-9. For the limitations of theory see above pp. 123-7.

29 *The Prince* (XXV), translated by George Bull (Harmondsworth, 1961), pp. 131-2.

30 Patch, p. 45; Chew, 'Time and Fortune', pp. 103-4.

interventions. The answer lies in faith, and faith presumes ignorance. Scudamour's complaint against the apparent injustice of God (based on the notion that grace is a right not a privilege) is typical of all such outbursts in the poem:

> If good find grace, and righteousnesse reward,
> Why then is *Amoret* in caytiue band,
> Sith that more bounteous creature neuer far'd
> On foot, vpon the face of liuing land?
> Or if that heauenly iustice may withstand
> The wrongfull outrage of vnrighteous men,
> Why then is *Busirane* with wicked hand
> Suffred, these seuen monethes day in secret den
> My Lady and my loue so cruelly to pen? (III. 11. 10)

The theological fallacy of his argument is underlined by the later assertion that no 'worldly price' can 'redeeme' Amoret 'out of her thraldome and continuall feare'. Redemption is what Christianity offers but of an exclusively spiritual kind. While acknowledging the human aspect of the problem, Britomart's reply to Scudamour shifts the emphasis elsewhere:

> submit you to high prouidence,
> And euer in your noble hart prepense,
> That all the sorrow in the world is lesse,
> Then vertues might, and values confidence,
> For who nill bide the burden of distresse,
> Must not here thinke to liue: for life is wretchednesse.
> (III. 11. 14)

The 1590 ending to book three enforces the providential element of the story in the union of Scudamour and Amoret, but that of 1596 marks Scudamour as one of those who will not wait on providence. Very much in the realm of human thought, 'his expectation to despaire did turne'. The former note of exaltation changes to one of grim irony as Amoret emerges to find her lover gone through lack of patience. Once again despair is shown to be unfounded. Thus, amongst other advantages, the revised ending serves to highlight one of the poem's central themes. The redemptive pattern is preserved but none of those involved recognise it for what it is.

Boethius's idea that the fortune allotted to each man is uniquely suited to his spiritual needs and that no-one is tempted beyond his power to resist was one to which Spenser obviously assented. Indeed the very fickleness of fortune means that it cannot continue indefinitely malign:

> So when as fortune all her spight hath showne,
> Some blisfull houres at last must needes appeare;
> Else should afflicted wights oftimes despeire.
> So comes it now to *Florimell* by tourne,
> After long sorrowes suffered whyleare. (V. 3. 1)

'Tourne' makes an effective pun on Fortuna's ever-mobile wheel to enforce Spenser's point most succinctly. As in Dante, fortune emerges as the instrument of providence, a creature of God:

> Quest' è colei ch'è tanto posta in croce
> pur da color che le dovrian dar lode,
> dandole biasmo a torto e mala voce;
> ma ella s' è beata e ciò non ode:
> con l'altre prime creature lieta
> volve sua spera, e beata si gode.[31]

So it is with the 'fortune' of the various combats that pervade the poem. Fortuna was often seen as presiding over war, but Spenser so orders it that the outcome is always morally significant, not accidental.[32] In this way the allegory enforces the providential theme. Fortune, whether it brings success or failure, always works on the side of God. Radigund, for example, rides out against Artegall 'to try her Fortune, and his force assay' (V. 4. 47), and Calidore declares that no knight has reason to grow proud, however 'strong and fortunate in fight', for,

> All flesh is frayle, and full of ficklenesse,
> Subiect to fortunes chance, still chaunging new;
> What haps to day to me, to morrow may to you. (VI. 1. 41)

This is indeed how it seems to the mortal combatants, but even in Calidore's summary there remains the suggestion that misfortune serves the moral purpose of curbing arrogance. One notices that the 'ficklenesse' traditionally attributed to Fortuna is here transferred to human 'flesh', to the

31 Lo! this is she that hath so curst a name
Even from those that should give praise to her —
Luck, whom men senselessly revile and blame;
But she is blissful and she does not hear;
She, with the other primal creatures gay,
Tastes her own blessedness, and turns her sphere.

Inferno VII. 91-6. See *The Divine Comedy*, translated by Dorothy L. Sayers and Barbara Reynolds, 3 vols (Harmondsworth, 1949 1962), I, 112.

32 Patch, pp. 107-110.

condition of our own mortality. For the good to enjoy perpetual worldly success would be spiritually inappropriate. The price of winning the war is countless lost battles, but the final outcome is seldom in doubt. As Cambell stands in mortal danger, we read that '*Cambels* fate that fortune did preuent' (IV. 3. 18). 'Prevent' has something of the force it possesses in the prayer-book: 'Prevent us O Lord in all our doings'. Fate 'goes before' fortune. It is not Cambell's time to die. During the combat between Britomart and Artegall matters go so badly 'that seemed nought but death mote be her destinie' (IV. 6. 18). The important element here is that of 'seeming'. 'The wicked stroke vpon her helmet chaunst' and in so 'chancing' saves her life. In one instance 'fate' prevents 'fortune', in the other 'chance' prevents 'destiny' and we are very close to the implication that fate and chance work in the same direction. Destiny is the name man gives to something that is apparently inevitable, fortune to the sudden and unexpected; he is frequently deceived in the nature of both.[33] One recalls the confidence of Malory's King Pellynour who tells Merlin that 'God may well fordo desteny'.[34] Too much depends on the union of Britomart and Artegall for her to die in a senseless skirmish at the hands of the man she loves. A 'chance' blow preserves a life that has already been foretold. On other occasions, however, 'who can shun the chaunce, that dest'ny doth ordaine?' (III. 1. 37). Determining what constitutes destiny is usually impossible unless the future has been miraculously revealed. No divine intervention, working through 'chance' or otherwise, will deliver Artegall from the hands of his murderers (III. 3. 28).

II. *Grace, Will and Love*

The question now arises as to whether the powerful element of providence in the poem strips the characters of free will and free agency, a problem which perplexed Christian thought from the time of Augustine to that of Spenser's contemporaries. The poem makes it clear, however, that man cannot attribute his personal failings to a supposedly unalterable destiny. In his disgrace Sir Terpine poses the question, 'who can scape, what his owne fate hath wrought?/ The worke of heauens will surpasseth humaine thought' (V. 4. 27). This echoes frequent authorial pronouncements and comes in response to Artegall's suggestion that 'heauens hard direction' is somehow involved.

33 'For it seems there are two kinds of harmony and music; one of divine providence, the other of human reason; and to the human judgment, and the ears as it were of mortals, the government of the world and nature, and the more secret judgments of God, sound somewhat harsh and untunable; and though this be ignorance, such as deserves to be distinguished with the ears of an ass, yet those ears are worn secretly and not in the face of the world — for it is not a thing observed or noted as a deformity by the vulgar.' Bacon, *Works*, VI, 713.

34 *Works*, edited by Eugene Vinaver (Oxford, 1971), p. 75.

What Terpine has chosen to ignore is the strong implication that he has 'wrought' his own fate and must suffer the consequences. Accepting the justice of the remark on fate and providence, Artegall wittily replies by returning the discussion to the point of departure:

> Right true: but faulty men vse oftentimes
> To attribute their folly vnto fate,
> And lay on heauen the guilt of their owne crimes. (V. 4. 28)

This recalls the passage in *A View of the Present State of Ireland* where Eudoxus contends that 'it is the manner of men that when they are fallen into anye Absurditye or theire accions succede not as they woulde they are readye allwaies to impute the blame theareof vnto the heavens, soe to excuse theire owne follies and imperfeccions'.[35] It is true, of course, that Sir Terpine is a very minor character, but the real importance of his debate with Artegall is that it immediately precedes his own shameful submission to Radigund. He has effectively condemned himself, and his misfortune teaches him a very salutary lesson.

Spenser preserves the traditional Christian view that God is not responsible for the evil in the world and that misfortune, as is particularly clear in the case of Arthur, is usually the occasion for spiritual trial. An amount of moral determinism remains, however, since some characters are clearly elect and others are not. There is a marked division in the poem between the 'Sons of Day' and the 'Sons of Night'. According to Arthur, for example, 'Dayes dearest children be the blessed seed,/Which darknesse shall subdew, and heauen win' (III. 4. 59). This is acknowledged on the opposing side also, and accounts for the pathos the evil sometimes evoke. Duessa's appeal to 'griesly Night' convinces the old woman that God is against her and inspires one of the most resonant lines in the poem: 'the sonnes of Day he fauoureth, I see' (I. 5. 25). It is not merely that, in the fullest sense of the term, Night cannot 'see', but that all subsequent action on her behalf is doomed to failure. From her point of view existence is meaningless. Her sole consolation is that 'some shall pay the price of others guilt' (26). This sort of crazed logic — a deliberate parody of the redemption — is the hallmark of the non-elect. All share the same warped mode of thought and their genealogies are, therefore, traced back to Chaos, Titan, or Night herself.

Whereas reprobation is invariably associated with sin, election would seem to operate without any reference to moral merit as a cause. Una's assertion

35 *Prose*, p. 44. Emphasising the same point, Belphoebe tells Timias that 'he whose daies in wilfull woe are worne,/ The grace of his Creator doth despise./ That will not vse his gifts for thanklesse nigardise' (IV. 8. 15). See above p. 41.

of her champion's election distinguishes him from all less favoured sinners: 'Why shouldst *thou* then despeire that chosen art' (I. 9. 53). By contrast, Malbecco hurls himself off a precipice 'all desperate of his *fore-damned* spright' (III. 10. 56). As Una asserts, only the 'greater grace' of God can cancel the 'accurst hand-writing' of reprobation and save those elected to life. In order to put the point beyond dispute, the following canto opens with a remarkably forthright statement of Spenser's theological outlook. If George has indeed 'withstood' despair, as the epigraph to canto nine suggests, the victory is not his own:

> Ne let the man ascribe it to his skill,
> That thorough grace hath gained victory.
> If any strength we haue, it is to ill,
> But all the good is Gods, both power and eke will. (1)

Contemporary readers would recognise the point as topical since the last three words appear to exclude, or at least limit, the operation of free will. Calvin's doctrine of the relationship between grace and will was one of the most contentious tenets of reformed theology. Perhaps no other issue distinguishes the Calvinist outlook so clearly from that of its Anglican and Catholic opponents. In the second book of the *Institutes* Calvin discusses the sense in which the will may be said to be 'free' and draws the conclusion that, owing to its bondage to sin, its original state has grown corrupt.[36] Accordingly it is 'enslaved' and 'free' at one and the same time, enslaved by sin and free to commit sin (p. 296). Of itself, it remains entirely incapable of choosing what is right. The very term 'free will' is, therefore, a misnomer, an 'empty name' which 'cannot be retained without great peril' and which should best be abolished (p. 266). Thus the key-word in Hooker's justification of providence, as described in the fifth book of the *Ecclesiastical Polity*, is completely expunged in the *Institutes.* Instead Calvin insists upon the total efficacy (and irresistibility) of election, rejecting all distinctions between 'operating' and 'co-operating' grace (p. 305). 'Simply to will', he asserts, 'is of man; to will ill, of a corrupt nature; to will well, of grace' (p. 295). Furthermore, 'free will is not sufficient to enable man to do good works, unless he be helped by grace, indeed by special grace, which only the elect receive through regeneration' (p. 262). By 'regeneration' Calvin means that election recreates the will: 'Because of the bondage of sin by which the will

36 *Institutes*, edited by McNeill, I, 255-70. All further references given in the text are to the same volume of this edition. Spenser enjoys a joke at the expense of free will when at the sound of Timias's horn outside Orgoglio's castle, 'euery dore of freewill open flew' (I. 8. 5). Inside, George's will has succumbed to despair.

is held bound, it cannot move towards good, much less apply itself thereto; for a movement of this sort is the beginning of conversion to God, which in Scripture is ascribed entirely to God's grace' (p. 294). To put the matter succinctly: 'The first part of a good work is will; the other, a strong effort to accomplish it; the author of both is God . . . He does not move the will in such a manner as has been taught and believed for many ages — that it is afterward in our choice either to obey or resist the motion — but by disposing it efficaciously' (pp. 302-3).

Many statements in *The Faerie Queene* seem to indicate Spenser's sympathy with such an outlook. It is entirely through the grace of God that George withstands despair even though his will seems bent on self destruction: 'all the good is God's, both power *and eke will*'. He enters the house of Holiness through the gateway of Humility, the attitude Calvin described as the 'foundation' of his theology (p. 268). There he gains the three 'infused' virtues of faith, hope and charity, 'infused' because they lie entirely in God's gift.[37] It would appear, therefore, that the faith and hope ascribed to George at the outset of the book are of themselves insufficient. Certain people are chosen to enter the House of Holiness and others are not. What this means, in effect, is that certain people are chosen to be saved while others are left to perish in their sin (I. 10. 57). Even in the *Institutes*, however, the matter is hardly cut and dried and one would scarcely expect it to be so here. In the House of Holiness, Fidelia teaches George doctrines, 'that weaker wit of man could neuer reach,/Of God, of grace, of iustice, of free will' (19). We never hear what she has to say concerning 'free will' but presumably it cannot conflict with the attitudes adopted by Spenser himself at the opening of the canto. Nevertheless, Spenser seems far less reluctant than Calvin to use the term in theological debate, and in his *Hymne of Heavenly Love* he urges the reader 'through meditation' of God's 'endlesse merit' to 'giue thy selfe vnto him full and free,/ That full and freely gaue himselfe to thee' (255-66). One must, of course, make sufficient allowance for the difference of context and genre while noting that even here the sole 'merit' acknowledged is God's.

Replying to the Palmer's praise in book two, George ascribes his victory over the dragon entirely to God:

> His be the praise, that this atchieu'ment wrought,
> Who made my hand the organ of his might;
> More then goodwill to me attribute nought:
> For all I did, I did but as I ought. (II. 1. 33)

If this statement is consistent with the doctrine of will asserted in book one,

37 Rosemond Tuve, *Allegorical Imagery* (Princeton, 1966), pp. 69, 81, 113-4.

we must ask in what sense 'goodwill' is here to be 'attributed' to George. Calvin held that man may be said to possess 'goodwill' only in the sense that a gift becomes the possession of the receiver (p. 306). If this is what George intends — and the tone of humility might well suggest that it is — there is no contradiction. Moreover, it is clear from the preceding stanza that the Palmer now regards George as incapable of falling from grace. However, if George implies that some measure of 'goodwill' must be attributed to him absolutely, the assertion is more in line with the cautious wording of the Thirty-Nine Articles than with the *Institutes*: 'Ea est hominis post lapsum Adae conditio, ut sese naturalibus suis viribus, et bonis operibus, ad fidem et invocationem Dei convertere ac praeparare non possit. Quare absque gratia Dei (quae per Christum est) nos praeveniente, ut velimus, et cooperante, dum volumus, ad pietatis opera facienda, quae Deo grata sunt et accepta, nihil valemus'.[38] Aptly entitled 'De Libero Arbitrio', this article is particularly notable for its employment of the twin formulations, 'praeveniente, ut velimus' (preceding so that we should will) and 'cooperante, dum volumus' (working with us while we will). While not contradicting Calvin outright, this form of words allows of a wider interpretation than the *Institutes* which effectively abolish any need to speak of 'co-operating' grace.

In the *Ecclesiastical Polity*, Hooker acknowledges the corruption of the will subsequent to the Fall while at the same time attempting to preserve as much of free will as is consistent with the doctrine of grace.[39] In the end he strikes a very delicate, not to say vulnerable, balance between the two:

> the natural aptness of man's will to take or refuse things presented before it, and the evidence which good things have for themselves, if reason were diligent to search it out, may be soundly and safely taught without contradiction to any syllable in that confession of the Church, or in those sentences of holy Scripture . . . alleged, concerning the actual disability of reason and will, through sin, whereas God's especial grace faileth. (p. 545)

But Hooker is wary of displaying an overly philosophical attitude. Calvin attributed the origin of the controversy to the misguided desire of some early Christians to facilitate the work of conversion by rendering faith compatible

38 'The condition of man after the fall of *Adam* is such that he cannot turn and prepare himself, by his own natural strength and good works, to faith and calling upon God: Wherefore we have no power to do good works, pleasant and acceptable to God, without the grace of God by Christ preventing us, that we may have a good will, and working with us, when we have that good will'. Bicknell, p. 219.

39 Hooker, II, 537-97 (pp. 537-40). All further references supplied in the text are to the same volume of this edition.

with classical philosophy (p. 259). The result was a conflict between logic and revelation. Not wishing to incur similar criticism, Hooker preserves an element of mystery. 'In grace', he declares, 'there is nothing of so great difficulty as to define after what manner and measure it worketh' (p 548). The reader of *The Faerie Queene* senses the same atmosphere of complexity despite such apparently definitive assertions as that which opens the tenth canto of book one. In the *Areopagitica*, for example, Milton cites the Cave of Mammon episode as a perfect example of the use of free will, and since then Spenser has often been regarded as leaning more to the Catholic or Arminian side of the debate than to the Calvinist.[40] Such arguments, however, tend to misrepresent Calvin's views by confounding them with those of his less subtle followers. It is true, for instance, that Guyon is asked to choose between God and Mammon, but not that such choice effects election. Guyon's temptation is modelled upon that of his 'redeemer' but the episodes diverge to demonstrate the inadequacy of 'wary wisdom' ('election' as mere human choice) to spiritual success. It is 'th'exceeding grace/ Of highest God' that sends first the angel and then Prince Arthur to his rescue. Both appear in direct response to Guyon's yearning for a form of 'angelic' life in total harmony with his 'Creatours grace' (16).

During the temptation Mammon twice offers his victim 'grace' (18, 32) but is rejected on the grounds that Guyon has in view, 'another blis . . . another happinesse, another end' (33). In the light of this assertion, the narrator invokes 'Eternall God' to preserve Guyon throughout the rest of his ordeal. The outcome implies that the prayer has been heard. Similarly the emphasis on Philotime's 'fall' seems designed to undermine all theories of self-sufficient honour (45): even confronted by 'the Lord of life' Pontius Pilate proved unable to choose salvation (62). Arthur, the 'flowre of grace', dispenses 'bounteous' and 'timely' grace to an impotent recipient (II. 9. 17-25). If Guyon withstands Mammon it is because he too is elect. Pyrochles and Cymochles are aspects of his own psyche and the 'temptation' continues through canto nine. Given the final outcome, his decision to enter the underworld seems ill-advised as he is left 'senselesse' on the ground, incapable of will, and defenceless before his enemies. Were it not for direct providential intervention his experience in the cave would have been his last. If free will is operating here — and Calvin would argue that the will of the elect is never 'free' — it is less inconsistent with the attitudes of book one than might at first be supposed.

40 *Complete Prose Works*, edited by Don M. Wolfe et al., 8 vols (New Haven, 1953-82), II (1959) 516; For a modern statement of this outlook see Virgil K. Whitaker, *The Religious Basis of Spenser's Thought* (Stanford, 1950), pp. 8, 23, 30, 54-8. The case for Spenser's Puritanism is argued forcefully (but with equal selectivity) in Anthea Hume, *Edmund Spenser: Protestant Poet* (Cambridge, 1984).

At the close of canto eight, Pyrochles 'wilfully refused grace' (52) and perishes both bodily and spiritually as a result. There is no question here but that the choice is free, the more so as Pyrochles has everything to gain by adopting the opposite course. It is one of the poem's most striking demonstrations of the will's freedom to promote its own corruption. One could argue, of course, that the offer is more important than the refusal, in that it *might* have been accepted. But no rational explanation can be given for the decision actually taken and Pyrochles would appear to be one of those whose hearts are hardened against grace. The classic example of this spiritual condition, frequently examined by Calvin and his supporters, was that of Pharaoh.[41] In the course of a long and intricate reply, in which he argues that such hardening is to be regarded as a punishment for former sin, Hooker makes the potentially damaging admission that 'we can yield no reason, why of all other wicked tyrants in Egypt, Pharaoh alone and the people under him should be made such a tragical spectacle' (p. 592). Reprobation supplies an easy answer. Viewed from a Calvinist stance, Pyrochles is one of those whose will has not been effectually moved. He lacks the grace to accept grace.

According to book one, it is grace, and grace alone, that 'vpholds' the 'righteous man' who 'falls' daily: 'Else should this *Redcrosse* knight in bands haue dyde' (I. 8. 1). This is the element which distinguishes George from Pyrochles who effectively commits suicide. Similarly, in *A View of the Present State of Ireland*, we learn that the 'generall profession . . . of the Crosse and faithe in Christe' will not be sufficient to save the Irish Catholics without 'the powerfull grace of that mightye Saviour'.[42] Theoretically, therefore, the outlook of *The Faerie Queene* is determined by the doctrine of grace, but such attitudes are tempered partly by the aesthetic demands of the narrative, and partly by a very optimistic view of the extent of election. Spenser has no doubt, for example, that 'many' Catholics will receive saving grace despite the corruptions of their Church. Admittedly, it remains unclear whether or not such election will necessitate a public conversion to the Protestant communion. It would be going beyond the evidence of the text to assert positively that Spenser envisaged the salvation of Catholics as Catholics. On this point he seems deliberately ambiguous. In *The Faerie Queene* salvation spreads its nets widely and figures such as Poeana are conspiciously 'reformed' (IV. 9. 16). 'Secular' scripture, like its sacred counterpart is 'a worke of wondrous grace, and able soules to saue' (I. 9. 19).

Throughout the poem Spenser attempts to remain true to human experience. From the viewpoint of the elect individual, certain choices remain to be made, more often than not without any obvious sign of divine inter-

41 *Institutes* I, 311-3; *Eternal Predestination*, pp. 174-6.

42 *Prose*, p. 137.

vention. However it may be explained away in retrospect, a sensation of free will is certainly present at the moment of decision just as sensations of personal creativity infuse moments of 'inspiration'. A clear indication of this is the way in which the reader's understanding of a particular episode is made to diverge from that of the protagonist. George doubts his success against the dragon, we do not. The paradox of election, as Calvin recognised but never satisfactorily explained, is that the chosen must continue to labour as if everything depended upon themselves. As a modern commentator argues, 'in the actual life of the Christian the grace of God and our own natural powers are so united that we cannot separate in our consciousness what is due to the one from what is due to the other'.[43] Hence the battle which raged about the Pauline verse, 'I laboured more abundantly than they all: yet not I, but the grace of God which was with me' (I Corinthians 15:10). Calvin understood the second half of the sentence as a qualification or correction of the first, but others, including Erasmus and Hooker, took it to mean that St Paul co-operated with divine grace.[44] For all practical purposes 'grace' and 'goodwill' are virtually indistinguishable, although humility is likely to assign the greater part to God. Many apparent inaccuracies in Spenser's treatment of grace reflect unresolved tensions in Reformed theology compounded by the artistic demands of an intricate story-line.

Spenser's narrative method varies from episode to episode. Sometimes he provides his readers with a clear authorial pronouncement designed to distance them from the action (as when he refers to the interventions of providence), while at others he allows the questing knights to speak for themselves out of their discontent and disappointment. The theological position is complicated by the fact that the service of Cleopolis involves the pursuit of personal fame even though Spenser attempts to resolve the potential inconsistencies by dwelling upon Gloriana's heavenly antecedents. Thus George sets out 'to winne him worship' and the Palmer can speak of his having 'wonne' a place in the 'heauenly Registers', of the Book of Life (II. 1. 32). It is this implication that George is at pains to reject and, as later appears, even Arthur's 'prays-desire' must ultimately be understood in the context of his combat with Maleger, his graceless self. In the Calvinist system no-one may be said to merit salvation, but under the chivalric code they can and do merit fame.[45] As a result some confusion is inevitable. Spenser frequently asserts a doctrine which, pushed to its logical conclusion, becomes highly deterministic, in Hooker's words, 'making man little more than a block'

43 Bicknell, p. 246.

44 *Institutes*, I, 306; *Hooker*, II, 548; *Luther and Erasmus: Free Will and Salvation*, edited by Gordon Rupp and Philip S. Watson, The Library of Christian Classics (Philadelphia, 1969), p. 82.

45 For possible resolutions see Tuve, *Allegorical Imagery*, p. 80.

(p. 540). The *Institutes* cite with approval the opinion of St Augustine that 'nothing is ours but sin' (p. 289). The position is notoriously difficult to argue against since any objection may be dismissed as the product of pride (p. 310). Spenser, however, greatly values human endeavour and the concept of spiritual trial which seems to inform most of the quests bespeaks a keen interest in the workings of the will. It is not that spiritual trial is incompatible with Calvin's view of grace — witness the temptation in the wilderness or the agony in Gethsemane — but that during such episodes, as in the Gospels, the interest necessarily centres, not upon the final outcome, which is assured, but upon the painful process by which it is achieved. At such moments it becomes almost impossible not to speak in terms of free will. However efficacious the grace, its recipient feels isolated. As Hooker put it, '*our experience* teacheth us, that we never do any thing well, but with deliberate advice and choice, such as painfully setteth the powers of our minds on work' (p. 540). Nevertheless, in the light of Spenser's more explicit pronouncements, it would be unwise to interpret such instances as evidence of Catholic or Arminian sympathies.

Acknowledging the difficulty of the position, Calvin describes the resulting situation in terms surprisingly close to those of Spenser, particularly for an authority usually deemed hostile to the world of romance:

> The matter stands thus: Unbelief does not hold sway within believers' hearts, but assails them from without. It does not mortally wound them with its weapons, but merely harasses them, or at most so injures them that the wound is curable. Faith, then, as Paul teaches, serves as our shield (Eph 6:16). When held up against weapons it so receives their force that it either completely turns them aside or at least weakens their thrust, so that they cannot penetrate to our vitals. When, therefore, faith is shaken it is like a strong soldier forced by the violent blow of a spear to move his foot and to give ground a little. When faith itself is wounded it is as if the soldier's shield were broken at some point from the thrust of the spear, but not in such a manner as to be pierced (p. 567).

This serves as a remarkably accurate description of the many allegorical conflicts depicted throughout *The Faerie Queene*. One notices also that the reference to the shield of faith makes direct allusion to the same Pauline passage from which Spenser borrowed the idea for the armour of St George. Elsewhere Calvin argues against the folly of those who provide man 'with his own armour' (p. 266) by trusting to human sufficiency. Life, he asserts, is a battle in which 'God arms both the devil and all the wicked for the conflict, and sits as a judge of the games to exercise our patience' (p. 221). Only by putting on 'that armour capable of sustaining so great and dangerous a contest' (p. 173) — the Pauline armour — can man hope to win. Thus Spenser's imagery and mode of allegorical narration remain consistent with an essentially Calvinist outlook despite what might at first appear to be serious differences of intention. The most that may safely be said is that Spenser pursues a cautious course between the second book of the *Institutes* and the articles of the Established Church, themselves strongly influenced by Calvinism.

The will is free to choose evil but the elect are frequently saved despite themselves. Regarding their histories in retrospect, they ascribe their victories to grace and their defeats either to themselves or to the 'wicked will' of their spiritual adversaries (I. 12. 32). Never does their sense of election occasion an abandonment of the active life. Herein lies the problem since this commitment gives every impression of conscious decision-making, of a free will moved by, but co-operating with, grace. Hooker maintained that, 'the manner of God's operation through grace is, by making heavenly mysteries plain to the dark understanding of man, and by adding motive efficacy unto that which there presenteth itself as the object of man's will' (p. 541). Even here, however, 'motive efficacy' is suspiciously close to effectual grace, but such problems apart, Spenser was interested in the workings of grace through revelation. This accounts for the numerous dreams, visions, revelations, and prophecies which pervade the poem, providing a reason for choice, a rationale for 'goodwill'. Regarding God, Merlin tells Britomart to 'submit thy wayes vnto his will,/ And do by all dew meanes thy destiny fulfill' (III. 3. 24). 'Submit' suggests a conscious act of free will to be made in the light of the national prophecy Merlin proceeds to present. Since he invokes 'eternall providence', it could be argued that, in this instance at least, grace disposes Britomart's will to its purpose through the prophecy, that Calvin's 'regeneration' becomes a rational enlightening. However, the problem of 'motive efficacy' remains since Britomart is in the grip of a predetermined but initially involuntary passion (24). First impressions to the contrary, this is not a simple act of 'free' will, nor does it directly conflict with the doctrine of grace. In assessing Spenser's attitude one must do justice to the considerable flexibility of the *Institutes*.

Spenser is closest to Calvin in his insistence upon the preservation of the elect and the efficacy of grace. However, partly for aesthetic reasons, and partly to preserve the value of human endeavour, he presents the experience of the 'chosen' from their own point of view, attempting to reproduce the uncertainties of actual life. We do not feel we are watching a puppet play. By consciously associating the reforming activities of the questing knights with the fulfilment of the divine plan, he strikes a workable balance between human achievement and sustaining grace. One cannot afford to forget that it was amongst the Calvinists, despite their insistence upon innate depravity, that the idea of creating the perfect Christian state took firmest hold: Hooker labours to undermine it in the preface to the *Ecclesiastical Polity*. The elect of Spenser's poem are frequently the children of a special revelation, yet throughout their adventures they are required to operate as if their every act contributed to their final destiny. In practice they seldom pause to distinguish between effectual grace and free will (except in retrospect) and when they do they are frequently perplexed. By contrast the non-elect would appear to be abandoned to their own folly. Relying upon physical prowess or intellectual cunning, they enjoy no special insight into the workings of providence. Rather, the gifts of Fortune are their ultimate goal and Mammon their god.

Mammon offers Guyon a travesty of the eternal, an earthly existence free from the uncertainty of contingency, a life wedded to his daughter Philotime, to the fulfilment of human ambition. Her court with its 'preace' of suitors is suggestive of the various 'courts of Fortune' depicted in Medieval and Renaissance drawings.[46] These satirize the profane desire to enjoy a sort of materialistic paradise here and now in defiance of the providential plan. Tantalus and Pilate are their ultimate representatives, the former as an example of insatiable greed, the latter of the preference for human policy over spiritual truth. Spenser locates fortune's palace in the underworld, a place of fallen time and values. Philotime is not one of Dante's joyous primal creatures but, as her name suggests, a perverted lover of temporal honour who parodies Catholic theology by rewarding 'workes and merites iust' thereby implying (contrary to the doctrine of grace) that one can prove oneself 'worthy of heauen' (II. 7. 49). She stands as a warning to Arthur and his companion: in 1593 the term 'philotimy' was approvingly associated with 'princely magnificence' by Richard Harvey while discussing the civic achievements of the legendary Brutus, Arthur's Trojan ancestor.[47] In *The Faerie Queene*, honour must be more than 'a mere scutcheon', and the cult of Philotime represents a regression to pagan values. She constitutes Spenser's comment on the classical goddess.

As one might expect from what has already been said of its form, it is in book six that the vicissitudes of fortune are most in evidence. Set off with dozens of references to fortune, hap, or chance, the narrative emerges as the most intricately polyphonic Spenser had yet constructed. Accidents, chance-meetings, and coincidences abound, yet all contribute in some way towards the final resolution thereby enforcing the point Spenser is trying to make concerning the nature of human illusions. Approaching Meliboe's farm, Calidore feels weary of the interminable quest 'which fortune on him cast' (VI. 9. 2). Amongst the 'greene fields' he discovers a pastoral life of ease and

46 Patch, pp. 143-5.

47 *Philadelphus, or A Defence of Brutes, and the Brutans History* (London, 1593), p. 24.

tranquillity shielded, as he thinks, from the vicissitudes of time and fortune, 'as if some miracle of heauenly hew/ Were downe to them descended in that earthly vew' (VI. 9. 8). It is the age-old dream of an earthly Paradise full of joy and innocence. Even for Meliboe himself the countryside is actually a place of retreat. In his youth he had aspired to 'great things', abandoning his home for the 'roiall court' in the footsteps of Colin Clout:

> Where I did sell my selfe for yearely hire,
> And in the Princes gardin daily wrought;
> There I beheld such vainenesse, as I neuer thought. (VI. 9. 24)

The notion of selling oneself recalls the ethos of Mammon's cave but for Meliboe this 'time' is long past. He now rests 'contented' (17, 22) with little, having learned to despise the 'idle hopes' of those 'ten yeares' (25). To Calidore he appears to lead,

> a life so free and fortunate,
> From all the tempests of these worldly seas,
> Which tosse the rest in daungerous disease. (19)

The irony implicit in 'fortunate' he does not pause to consider, resolving to adopt a lifestyle 'fearelesse of foes, or fortunes wrackfull yre' (27). He has 'lost himselfe' and become 'entraunced' (26) wishing that his 'fortunes' (his allotted rank and position in life) might 'transposed bee/ From pitch of higher place, vnto this low degree' (28). Meliboe's response is very much to the point since he asserts that one must accept what the heavens have decided:

> It is the mynd, that maketh good or ill,
> That maketh wretch or happie, rich or poore . . .
> For wisedome is most riches; fooles therefore
> They are, which fortunes doe by vowes deuize,
> Sith each vnto himselfe his life may fortunize. (30)

This is a psychological development of Artegall's more abstract reply to Sir Terpine, and constitutes one of the most unequivocable statements on the issue in the entire poem. Calidore perverts its intention by twisting the words to suit his present dejected humour thereby unwittingly proving their point. In particular, he interprets the highly Juvenalian conclusion — 'sith each vnto himselfe his life may fortunize' — as an invitation to 'fashion his owne lyfes estate' by abandoning the quest and seeking refuge in obscurity far from the 'stormes of fortune and tempestuous fate' (31). Since the purpose of the poem is 'to fashion a gentleman or noble person in vertuous and gentle discipline',

Calidore's 'fashioning' would unravel its heroic texture. Appropriately, it is in this anti-creative mood that he clumsily intrudes upon Colin Clout and dispels the vision of the Graces, source of all social and poetic achievement. In fact, the use of the exceedingly rare verb 'fortunize' — which may well have been invented for the purpose — epitomises Spenser's outlook: whatever his station in life, a man may render his circumstances 'fortunate' (in the best sense of that term) by adopting the correct mental attitude. In this way, not Machiavelli's, he controls his own fortune. Ironically, however, Calidore proceeds to offer Meliboe gold, an offer instantly rejected since the 'good man' is not 'tempted'. Calidore acts the part of Mammon and the sage's response echoes that of Guyon:

> Sir knight, your bounteous proffer
> Be farre fro me, to whom ye ill display
> That mucky masse, the cause of mens decay,
> That mote empaire my peace with daungers dread. (33)

Meliboe is merely being truthful. The pastoral life is not innocent but 'rude' and soon afterwards he is murdered by the brigands who overrun the countryside. The notion that Calidore's 'paradise' lies outside fortune's sphere of influence is the product of his own wish-fulfilment. The catastrophe renews his commitment to the quest and sets him once more within the progressive, linear time-scheme of the epic. Only in their destruction do the poem's apparently timeless 'paradises' prove beneficial. No matter how idyllically 'proportioned' to the rhythms of the natural cycle, human time reasserts its fallen nature. The result in the present case is the reuniting of Pastorella with her parents and her eventual marriage to Calidore. The tragedy of canto ten, so devastating in its immediate effect, serves merely as a prelude to the happiness of canto eleven. One cannot hide from fortune. By leaving their rural retreat Calidore and Pastorella find their true identities. A quest despairingly attributed to fortune proves 'fortunate' because providential.

Perhaps the best illustration of this principle is to be found in the tangled narrative of book four. In canto two Blandamour and Paridell come upon a party consisting of Cambell, Triamond, Canacee and Cambina. All four have separate, but tightly interwoven histories 'as antique stories tellen vs', and Spenser breaks the narrative to relate that history, telling a story within a story.[48] For the first time in *The Faerie Queene* the major exploits of a book's eponymous heroes are related in flashback. Flashback is to narrative what memory is to mind, an essential facet of creative 'prudence'. With prophecy it secures for romance all three dimensions of time. But the matter is more

48 For the same narrative technique see the *View* in *Prose*, p. 97.

complex still: in order to relate the conflict between Cambell and Triamond Spenser must first tell us the story of Agape's three sons breaking the narrative yet again. The corridor of memory recedes as we pace it. We now have the Chinese-box effect of story within story within story, yet the immediate narration of book four can be understood only in the light of such convoluted associations. Layers of time are pealed away as we are led straight back to the House of the Fates, to the very heart of the mystery of existence. Its location in the underworld distinguishes fate from providence:

> Downe in the bottome of the deepe *Abysse*,
> Where *Demogorgon* in dull darknesse pent,
> Farre from the view of Gods and heauens blis,
> The hideous *Chaos* keepes, their dreadfull dwelling is.
>
> (IV. 2. 47)

Here Agape discovers the 'vtmost date' of her childrens' lives 'ordained by eternall fate'. Such is the difference between things 'diuine' and 'humane' that this fate may never be 'altred', 'for what the Fates do once decree,/ Not all the gods can chaunge, nor *Iove* him self can free' (51). Her subsequent bargain with the sisters relates to her function in the allegory of concord as the element of brotherly love, it neither can nor does alter the mortality of her sons, two of whom perish during the combat.[49] The duration of their lives, symbolised by the length of their respective threads, is preordained, as Lachesis points out. However, in stark contrast to the pessimistic fatalism of Duessa and her kind, Agape returns with 'full contented mynd' since her sons will live through one another's lives (52) thereby realising the goal of the Fairy chronicles. Deliberately omitting to reveal the secret to her offspring, she warns them instead 'to tend their safeties well,/ And loue each other deare, what euer them befell' (53). So too divine love 'intreats' for the salvation of its sons with fate without altering the course of nature or disclosing the exact manner in which this salvation is to be effected.

Clotho, Lachesis, and Atropos (birth, life and death) lie at the centre of existence, as here at the centre of a labyrinthine narrative.[50] In mortal terms they remain implacable since fate cannot be altered and all men die. Only love can impose an order and meaning upon their operations, however puzzling this meaning may appear to those involved. According to Boethius,

49 Thomas P. Roche, *The Kindly Flame: A Study of the Third and Fourth Books of Spenser's 'Faerie Queene'* (Princeton, 1964), pp. 19-22.

50 'Fate is divided into three parts, *Clotho, Lachesis*, and *Atropos*: That which is one in Providence, indivisible in Eternity, when it comes into Time and Fate is divisible, into Past, Present, and Future.' Pico della Mirandola, *A Platonick Discourse upon Love* in *The Poems and Translations of Thomas Stanley*, edited by Galbraith Miller Crump (Oxford, 1962), p. 213.

'all this harmonious order of things is achieved by love which rules the earth and the seas, and commands the heavens'.[51] Not Agape (brotherly love) but Cambina who 'seemed borne of Angels brood' (IV. 3. 39) resolves the issue, functioning as a symbol of heavenly love and reconciliation, of the universal principle of concord. After the horrors of the 'doubtfull' battle with 'diuerse fortune' varying 'to and fro' her arrival prevents the 'fatall fine' predicted by all the onlookers. It is a case of God's 'fordoing' destiny. Cambina symbolises the ultimate harmony towards which all the supposed accidents of time and fortune are inexorably tending.

When Scudamour seeks entrance to the Temple of Venus later in the same book, he finds the figure of Concord holding together Hate and Love (IV. 10. 32). Hate is described as the elder brother and this has caused much critical controversy. The explanation, however, intimately connected with the passage we have just been examining, is supplied by Plutarch in his treatise on Isis and Osiris, Spenser's probable source for the central sections of book five. Plutarch asserts that in praying for the total abolition of strife Homer invokes 'a curse on the origin of all things since all things originate from strife and antagonism'.[52] So it must be while providence unfolds its plan in a world of time, flux and multiplicity. In his discussion with Una in book one, Arthur feared that the fury of his passion for the Fairy Queen might conflict with the 'secret meaning' of 'fatall deepe foresight'. Originally he had equated love with 'losse of time', one of the figures in the Masque of Cupid, and consequently regarded it as 'vertues enimy' (I. 9. 10). In this context Gloriana offers her affections in '*iust* time' since the undoubted virtue of her love justifies the years Arthur devotes to its pursuit. By book six he understands that the god of love is 'iust' (7. 23).

As the quest proceeds, therefore, it gradually emerges that the fortune of love, no less than the fortune of combat, is guided by the power which 'binds the actions and fortunes of men in an unbreakable chain of causes and, since these causes have their origins in an unchangeable Providence, they too must necessarily be unchangeable'. Boethius's conclusion that all fortune is good might be specifically directed to Spenser's suffering heroes: 'therefore, even though things may seem confused and discordant to you, because you cannot discern the order that governs them, nevertheless everything is governed by its own proper order directing all things towards the good'.[53] In the final analysis divine love distinguishes Providence from Fate. Thus, according to Ficino's interpretation of ancient 'Orphic' philosophy, 'Love rules the Three

51 Boethius (Book 2, Prose 8), p. 41.

52 *Isis and Osiris*, 370D. *Moralia*, translated by Frank Cole Babbitt, Loeb Classical Library, 15 vols (London, 1927-69), V (1936), 117.

53 Boethius (Book 4, Prose 6), p. 93.

Fates, in whom Necessity resides'.[54] Throughout *The Faerie Queene* 'love' aspires to the condition of eternity while 'lust' degenerates into the destructive patterns of malign fate.

III. *Prophecy and Providential History*

The pattern Spenser imposes upon his narrative reflects the eccentric order he believes to be detectable in history, 'eccentric' because it cannot be made to centre upon that limited species of providence available to the participants. Unlike Milton, Spenser does not attempt to 'justify the ways of God to man', but employs providential historiography as a tool of self-defence, both personal and national. Milton's God speaks volubly in his own defence because free will is absolute in the universe of *Paradise Lost*. Spenser's God is a divine ventriloquist endlessly justifying the corrupt to himself through the theology of grace. Merlin, the spokesman reserved to a climactic moment as Anchises is reserved in the *Aeneid*, functions to assert patterns merely adumbrated in the preceding narrative. Spenser is determined to meet the challenge of history however recalcitrant.[55] His decision to pursue such a course was determined by his conception of the relationship between art and life, the Land of Faerie and the land of Elizabeth. As a result, almost the entire course of British history is related at various points throughout the narrative. In the House of Malbecco, Paridell and Britomart explain how the fall of Troy led to Brutus's founding of Troynovant or London. In the House of Alma, Arthur reads the account of British history from the arrival of Brutus to his own time. In Merlin's cave, Britomart hears the story continued by way of prophecy to the time of Elizabeth. The details involved are often depressing — murders, suicides, invasions and civil wars — yet both Britomart and Arthur feel greatly uplifted by what they learn. The multiplicity of fortune and the degradations of time give way before a sense of order and control located less in history than in the minds of the observers.[56]

In keeping with his general policy of allowing patterns to emerge through complexity, Spenser has deliberately disjointed the historical narrative so that the beginning, the fall of Troy, comes after the end, an appropriate arrangement since hindsight facilitates interpretation. Moreover, the places in which the chronicles and prophecies are delivered contribute to their significance. The 'temperance' of right rule is essential to the smooth course of historical progress so Arthur reads the 'Briton Moniments' in the House of Alma. Similarly, Merlin's Welsh cave ringing with daemonic energy forms an

54 *Commentary on Plato's Symposium*, edited and translated by Sears R. Jayne, University of Missouri Studies XIX, no. I (Columbia, 1944), p. 180.

55 *Elizabethan Critical Essays*, edited by G. Gregory Smith, 2 vols (Oxford, 1904), I, 167.

56 Mircea Eliade, *The Myth of the Eternal Return* (Princeton, 1954), pp. 130-7.

effective backdrop to his inspiring vision of Tudor glory. Credited by antiquarian divines such as Bale and Leland with delivering a sort of secular Apocalypse, he was the perfect instrument for Spenser's purposes: he is expressly dubbed 'prophet' immediately prior to his address to Britomart (III. 3. 21). The anxious House of Malbecco is more problematic. The point here is that Paridell and Helenore are about to re-enact the tragic events which led to the fall of Troy. Concerned solely with themselves, they represent the destructive side of the historical cycle. As a result, Paridell recounts the circumstances of Troy's ruin while Britomart concerns herself with its survival and recovery. For Paridell, history forms a repetitive sequence of tragic falls occasioned by wild, undisciplined passion.[57] For Britomart, seeking the legitimate creative union of marriage, disaster heralds rebirth and renewal. Focussing upon an extended version of the 'matter of Troy', Spenser explores both sides of time's activity as described in Stephen Hawe's *Pastime of Pleasure*:

> In tyme Troye the cyte was edefyed
> By tyme also was the dystruccyon
> Nothynge without tyme can be fortefyed
> No erthely Ioye nor trybulacyon
> Without tyme is for to suffre passyon
> The tyme of erthe was our dystruccyon
> And the tyme of erthe was our redempcyon.[58]

The early cantos of book three describe how Britomart has chanced to fall in love with an image glimpsed in her father's magic globe. The fact that the globe in question is the handiwork of Merlin strongly suggests that Britomart's curiosity is not as fortuitous as might at first appear. The globe is an instrument of divination and it later transpires that Merlin has long anticipated Britomart's passion. He shows no surprise at her arrival, recognising her instantly despite her disguise as he recognises dynamic processes beneath the historian's 'bare was'. The disguise is emblematic of the difficulty involved. Glauce fears the outcome of the meeting but Spenser's association of the 'sacred fire' of love with his invocation to Clio, the Muse of History, puts the matter in proper perspective to resolve the problems posed by Arthur in his discussion with Una. Here it appears that love is destiny, as 'the dreadfull Mage' himself points out:

57 Michael O'Connell, *Mirror and Veil: The Historical Dimension of Spenser's 'Faerie Queene'* (Chapel Hill, 1977), pp. 84-7.

58 *The Pastime of Pleasure*, edited by William Edward Mead, Early English Text Society, Original Series, 173 (London, 1928), p. 218.

It was not, *Britomart*, thy wandring eye,
Glauncing vnwares in charmed looking glas,
But the streight course of heauenly destiny,
Led with eternall prouidence, that has
Guided thy glaunce, to bring his will to pas:
Ne is thy fate, ne is thy fortune ill,
To loue the prowest knight, that euer was.
Therefore submit thy wayes vnto his will,
And do by all dew meanes thy destiny fulfill. (III. 3. 24)

This notion was common among Spenser's contemporaries. In Bacon's opinion, the very 'blindness' of Cupid 'makes the supreme divine Providence all the more to be admired, as that which contrives out of subjects peculiarly empty and destitute of providence, and as it were blind, to educe by a fatal and necessary law all the order and beauty of the universe'.[59]

The most serious objection to Merlin's interpretation is that raised by Glauce who questions Britomart's need to undertake the rigours of the quest if the union is indeed preordained: 'what needs her to toyle, sith fates can make/ Way for themselues, their purpose to partake?' (25). The point is aptly raised in a canto dedicated to unravelling the Gordian knots of history, but the very context demonstrates its naïvety. The 'purposes' of fate are bound to the passage of time and in this sense they 'make way for themselues' as Glauce suggests. But such 'purposes' are equally bound to the employment of human agency since it is human fate that is involved. Britomart's destiny comprises not merely her union with Artegall but also her quest for him. The journey is as important as the arrival and much is to be learned along the way. Fate involves the whole of life not simply its final goal, otherwise history itself could not exist.[60] Merlin replies:

Indeed the fates are firme,
And may not shrinck, though all the world do shake:
Yet ought mens good endeuours them confirme,
And guide the heauenly causes to their constant terme. (25)

Thus a direct conflict between free will and predestination is to some extent avoided. Artegall is 'the man whom heauens haue ordaynd to bee/ The spouse of *Britomart*' yet she must actively seek him out. She is both 'guide' and 'guided'. As the quest involves danger and disappointment she must 'submit' her 'wayes' to the will of providence, a doctrine in which she vainly tries to

59 Bacon, *Works*, VI, 731.

60 See the discussion in William Haller, *Foxe's Book of Martyrs and the Elect Nation* (London, 1963), pp. 140-86.

instruct Scudamour later in the same book (III. 11. 14-16). The 'fates' are 'confirmed' in human action, the 'heauenly *causes*' drawn to their desired effect. In terms of Spenserian characterization maturity originates in the coincidence of prudence and providence. Since the guiding force of providence remains 'eternal', Britomart's moment of self-discovery lies, paradoxically, both within and without human time. Like the Virgin Mary, she is uniquely privileged in having the providential will revealed to her in such clear-cut terms, yet since God perceives not only what will happen but all possible alternatives as well, the prediction remains conditional from man's point of view.[61] As Hooker maintains,

> Whensoever we find therefore in Scripture divine predictions, the declarations of God's foreknowledge alleged, whether it be before they take effect, or after, this is perpetually true in them all, they are alleged as arguments, proofs and testimonies, only, that so it would be, but never as causes imposing a real necessity on that which is foreshewed. Prescience, as prescience, hath in itself no causing efficacy.[62]

Even here, however, Spenser preserves a delicate balance between grace and will the workings of which become inextricable once again. Whereas the act of 'submission' implies a conscious choice — even if this entails a harsh subordination of human will to divine will — there remains an entirely involuntary element in Britomart's history. Merlin argues that her love for Artegall is itself predetermined, a suggestion borne out by the manner in which it originates. Her oblique, 'unwary' glance is 'guided' by the 'streight' vision of providence. Though not necessarily to be attributed to 'prescience' supernatural 'causes' underlie human motivations. Doubtless one might distinguish here in the Aristotelian manner between efficient and final cause, but as the latter is for Spenser very much a matter of conscious design and spiritual influence, the problem of grace remains. Like Arthur, Britomart has no choice but to love, and 'all the good' is again God's, 'both power and eke will' (I. 10. 1). Merlin's prophecy may strengthen Britomart's resolve but it cannot be said to initiate her quest. That begins the moment she lays eyes upon Artegall: her visit to Merlin is the result not the cause. Significantly, therefore, his prophecy begins in the past tense:

> Most noble Virgin, that by fatall lore
> Hast learn'd to loue, let no whit thee dismay
> The hard begin, that meets thee in the dore,
> And with sharpe fits thy tender hart oppresseth sore.

61 Hooker, *Works*, II, 562.

62 *Ibid.*, p. 561. Sir Walter Raleigh expresses similar views, *The History of the World* (London, 1614), p. 15.

For so must all things excellent begin,
And eke enrooted deepe must be that Tree,
Whose big embodied braunches shall not lin,
Till they to heauens hight forth stretched bee.
For from thy wombe a famous Progenie
Shall spring, out of the auncient *Troian* blood,
Which shall reuiue the sleeping memorie
Of those same antique Peres, the heauens brood,
Which *Greeke* and *Asian* riuers stained with their blood.
(III. 3. 21-2)

Faith and perseverance are qualities essential to moral success. Inspired by her vision of the future, Britomart must endure the personal trials and tribulations of the coming years for the good of posterity. The 'tree' to be 'enrooted deepe' is the genealogical tree of the House of Tudor. As Spenser portrays her, Britomart is the pivot about which turns the history of Europe, the vital link between the 'auncient *Troian* blood' and the promised dynasty of 'renowmed kings, and sacred Emperours' destined to 'reuiue' the glory of those heroic spirits. It is important that such a summary should precede Merlin's full account of British history since it forcefully asserts the positive value of human endeavour, and pithily identifies a providential pattern sometimes obscured in the following welter of historical detail. In this epitome empire emerges as the instrument of 'vniuersall peace' and Troynovant realises the Augustan dream. A modern historian remarks: 'the footsteps of God might be in history, but history as a whole did not consist of such footsteps; eternity might be in love with the products of time, but time was a passive and inert beloved'.[63] Merlin's intuitive grasp of the structural pattern underlying the confusion sustains his listeners. By perceiving the 'footsteps' he accurately deduces the direction in which they move. In contrast to book two, the pattern is specifically applied to the chronicle through the authority of the Magus.

The account moves in several clear stages from the Arthurian age to that of Cadwallader and on through eight hundred years of subjection to the coming of Henry VII. The story of Britomart's son is typical of the chronicle as a whole. He is the 'lion' later foretold in the Temple of Isis and as a 'lyon' he issues forth to avenge his father's murder and regain the usurped throne. He is destined for success and even tranquillity: 'if he then with victorie can lin,/ He shall his dayes with peace bring to his earthly In' (30). His peace, we

63 Pocock, p. 7. For the theory of providential history see C.A. Patrides, *The Grand Design of God* (London, 1972); S.G.F. Brandon, *History, Time and Deity* (Manchester, 1965), pp. 106-47.

notice, is conditional on the curtailment of ambition. However, although the facts of mortality remain unalterable, 'in' implies a resting place not a final destination, and 'earthly' suggests the existence of a *patria* elsewhere. The picture is in no sense depressing but potentially transcendent. What is disturbing, however, is the pattern that begins to unfold in the immediate sequel: 'His sonne, hight *Vortipore*, shall him succeede/ In kingdome, but not in felicity' (31). Spenser is at pains to have the succession move as smoothly as in the Fairy chronicles: in the following stanza he improves upon Geoffrey of Monmouth's account of history by claiming Careticus as Vortipore's grandson. Yet here 'succession' is not synonymous with 'success' and the overall effect is to highlight the power of 'froward fortune' and the force of circumstance. The rightful line cannot withstand the barbaric invasion of Gormond, 'a straunger king from vnknowne soyle'. The scene turns to one of grim desolation perhaps unconsciously reminiscent of Lord Grey's Munster famine, perhaps unconsciously self-critical:

> He in his furie all shall ouerrunne,
> And holy Church with faithlesse hands deface,
> That thy sad people vtterly fordonne,
> Shall to the vtmost mountaines fly apace:
> Was neuer so great wast in any place,
> Nor so fowle outrage doen by liuing men:
> For all thy Cities they shall sacke and race,
> And the greene grasse, that groweth, they shall bren,
> That euen the wild beast shall dy in starued den. (34)

There is much point in dwelling upon the Christianity of the Britons since their enemies are still pagan. 'Faithlesse hands' deface 'holy Church' while, in one of those mysterious paradoxes of providential history, the people of God flee, like Una in book one, into the wilderness. The biblical resonance of the language recalls former tragedies of a similar kind: 'the greene grasse, that groweth, they shall bren'. No reason is given for the success of God's enemies, and the passage is followed by the even more remarkable account of how the papal emissary, Augustine, supported the Saxons against his own people and filled the River Bangor with 'massacred Martyrs'. Augustine's 'ambitious will' serves as an early manifestation of papal arrogance and the event echoes the persistent allegations of the early Reformers that the papacy planned an alliance with the Turks against recalcitrant Christian princes, an accommodation suggested by Duessa's patronage of the pagan Sansfoy in book one.[64] Spenser's contemporaries would recognise a topical analogy

64 John Erskine Hankins, *Source and Meaning in Spenser's Allegory* (Oxford, 1971), pp.

while Britomart grapples with increasingly intractable material. As the forces of Christianity turn upon themselves the racial issues inevitably become confused. Cadwallin's arch-enemy, the Saxon king Oswald, is a paragon of holiness, 'indewd/ With heauenly powre, and by Angels reskewd' (38). Once again Spenser has adapted chronicle material to poetic purpose. Geoffrey of Monmouth makes no mention of a rescue by angels — one is tempted to substitute Angles — nor of Oswald's 'bloodless' victory.[65] But Britomart is wearing Saxon armour as she listens, and St George is both Saxon knight and patron of holiness. As Cadwallin 'crownes with martyrdome' the 'sacred head' of 'godly Oswald', a distinct moral purpose begins to emerge. As Spenser so often wished to believe, even cruelty serves a divine end. Britons and Saxons are soon to have mutual saints and a common faith paves the way for a common political purpose.

In the chronicles of book two Harry Berger detected a 'lack of emphasis on moral causality', but no such reading is possible here.[66] The 'raine of Britons' perishes with Cadwallin not because his successor is too weak to restore it, but because 'the full time prefixt by destiny' has expired:

> For heauen it selfe shall their successe enuy,
> And them with plagues and murrins pestilent
> Consume, till all their warlike puissaunce be spent. (40)

Readers of the Old Testament would recognise the ancient pattern of reward and correction beginning to assert itself amongst the new 'chosen' people. Despite Holinshed's dismissal of the legend as absurd, Cadwallader is 'by vision staid from his intent', learning how,

> th'heauens haue decreed, to displace
> The *Britons*, for their sinnes dew punishment,
> And to the *Saxons* ouer-give their gouernment. (41).

At this point detachment fails and Britomart responds spontaneously to Merlin's lament prefaced by an Apocalyptic 'woe, and woe, and euerlasting woe' (Revelation 8:13). The 'empire' of the 'antique Troian blood' has collapsed — as twice before at the falls of Troy and Rome. Yet once again succession survives lost 'successe'. There is spiritual point to their not being

215-6; Edgar Wind, *Pagan Mysteries in the Renaissance*, second edition (London, 1967), p. 228.

65 *The History of the Kings of Britain* (XII. 10), translated by Lewis Thorpe (Harmondsworth, 1966), pp. 277-8.

66 Harry Berger, *The Allegorical Temper: Vision and Reality in Book II of Spenser's 'Faerie Queene'* (New Haven, 1957), p. 103.

synonymous. Miraculously the chosen race is destined to prevail since its 'terme' of 'thraldome' is 'limited' by divine decree. After the '*iust* reuolution' of 'twise foure hundreth yeares' the Briton line will reclaim the crown, just as Arthur is destined to join with Gloriana after the lapse of '*iust* time'. The implications of 'reuolution' are equally unmistakable. The pattern of cyclical renewal attributed to the physical universe in the *Mutabilitie Cantos* is here to be detected in the events of British history.[67] One might have expected the elapse of eight hundred years to effect the disappearance of the Britons as a separate race yet, 'during this their most obscuritee,/ Their beames shall oft breake forth, that men them faire may see' (44). The imagery recalls that of stanza nineteen where Britomart, despite her disguise, is no more hidden from Merlin 'then Sunne in cloudy vele'. That early recognition was predictive of this.

Stanzas 45-47 deal with the various waves of invaders which harass the country in the wake of the Briton decline, and carry us far from the circumstances of the prophecy's beginning. Suddenly, however, at this point of furthest distance, 'the terme is full accomplishid' and the providential plan for the return of the 'Briton blood' takes dramatic effect. Cadwallader, though strong, was prevented from fighting by the direct command of heaven; his Tudor ancestors, though weak, are delivered from 'exile' in a passage reminiscent of the Jews' return from Babylon. The result is 'eternall vnion ... Betweene the nations different afore' (49). In this case, the use of 'eternall' is clearly designed to associate the political outcome with the 'eternall prouidence' with which it is held to accord. As Spenser must surely have known, it was just such a prophecy that John Bale credited Merlin with delivering:

> As I was in wrytynge this matter an old Prophecy of Merline came unto my remembraunce. That after the manyfolde irrupcions of straungers, the kinges of thys realme shuld be ones agayn crowned wyth the Dyademe of Brute, and beare his auncyent name, the new name of straungers so vanishinge awaye. He that applyeth unto this a right understandinge shall fynde it very true. The Diademe of Brute is the pryncely power of thys whole region, immediatly geven of God without any other meane mastry worken [sic] to Antichristes behove. Fre was that power from the great whores domynyon (which is the Rome churche) tyll the violent conquest of the English Barons, which they had of the Brytaynes for their iniquities sake. And now (prayse be unto that Lorde) it is in good waye to that fredome agayne, and would fullye attayne therunto, were here heythnysh pokes in religion ones throwne a

67 Joanne Field Holland, 'The Cantos of Mutabilitie and the Form of *The Faerie Queene*', *ELH*, 35 (1968), pp. 21-31.

> syde, as I doubt it not but they will be within short space. As well may ye geve credence to this Merlyne whan he uttereth the verite, as unto olde Balaam the sothsayer, whiche at a tyme prophecyed the commynge of Christ. Num xxiiii. And as concernyng the returne of the name, marke in thys age the wrytynges of lerned men, and ye shall wel perceyve the change, for now commonly do they wryte us for Englyshemen, Brytaynes.[68]

The 'sacred peace' promised by Spenser's Merlin is consolidated by the accession of Elizabeth whose various victories are deemed worthy of inclusion in the providential pattern. But why not? In no sense do they differ from the other events so chronicled. Hence their Apocalyptic, if less sanguine, treatment in book five. The wheel has come full circle. A prophecy which began with the arrival of Brutus ends with the imperial vision of the 'royall virgin' spreading her influence over Europe. 'Galfridian' prophecy ends where Spenserian policy begins. The material disjointed in book two by a problematic division into separate chronicles of uncertain relationship is unified at last. A rigorously polemical interpretation of the present imposes a sequence of 'prefigurements' upon a fictionalized version of the past, fabricating genealogical fantasies designed to endow Tudor rule with dynastic authority. Until now political bias masquerades quite successfully as providential vision. More than a thousand years of history have been shown to fall into a clearly designed, predestined pattern at which point Merlin's prophetic powers fail. The witches in Shakespeare's *Macbeth* have the distinct advantage of seeing the Stuarts established on the English throne; Merlin has no such vision. All he can do is cautiously adumbrate his creator's hopes and fears:

> But yet the end is not. There *Merlin* stayd,
> As ouercomen of the spirites powre,
> Or other ghastly spectacle dismayd,
> That secretly he saw, yet note discoure:
> Which sudden fit, and halfe extatick stoure
> When the two fearefull women saw, they grew
> Greatly confused in behauioure;
> At last the fury past, to former hew
> Hee turnd againe, and chearefull looks (as earst) did shew. (50)

Form challenges content. The assertion of dynastic continuity is made in a curt half-line, all the more startling for its abrupt positioning in the stanza.

68 John Bale, *The first two partes of the Actes, or unchast examples of the Englysh votaryes* (London, 1551), fols. 40v-41r.

The rest is lost in an ecstasy which neither Britomart nor Spenser can share. Doubtless the queen was intended to ponder it deeply: only she held the key to succession, only she could envisage the future towards which Spenser gestures. In the confusion of Britomart and Glauce — perhaps modelled on the legendary collapse of Octavia at an equivalent point in Anchises's prophecy — she might well see the anxieties of her subjects. She might also note how the concluding alexandrine emerges hopefully from the uncertainty as Merlin 'turns againe' to face his listeners with his wonted 'chearefull looks' — yet another cyclical return after a period of perplexity. Though relatively less coherent, Arthur's chronicle ends more positively on the word 'succeeding'. Somehow, ascending to the level of the fairy monarchs, the 'royall *virgin*' must 'conceiue' a political heir, thereby defeating time. Spenser infers that the logic of providential history demands the nomination of a successor.[69] Predictably the canto ends by returning the reader from this extended flashback to the time of the poem's action, to the time and place from which the account began. The vision of British history is etched in the 'memory' of the narrative, as the 'form' of the Tudor 'tree' inheres in the generative 'seeds' of Britomart and Artegall. 'But yet the end is not' constitutes an appropriate epigraph both for Britain's history and Spenser's 'historical' fiction.

69 See below, p. 112, fn. 58.

CHAPTER SIX

Eternity

And all that vaunts in worldly vanitie
Shall fall through fortunes mutabilitie.
(*Virgils Gnat*, 559-60)

His throne is built vpon Eternity,
More firme and durable then steele or brasse,
Or the hard diamond, which them both doth passe.
(*Hymne of Heavenly Beavtie*, 152-4)

I. *Intimations of Eternity*

Contrasting the present with the past in the disturbing preface to book five, Spenser predicts an inevitable and swift decline into confusion. His imagination returns repeatedly to Eden, like a criminal to the scene of the crime:

So oft as I with state of present time,
The image of the antique world compare,
When as mans age was in his freshest prime,
And the first blossome of faire vertue bare,
Such oddes I finde twixt those, and these which are,
As that, through long continuance of his course,
Me seemes the world is runne quite out of square,
From the first point of his appointed sourse,
And being once amisse growes daily wourse and wourse. (1)

The contrast, one notes, is between present experience and an idealized concept or 'image' of past time. As motion is virtually identified with decay after the classical manner, such an 'image' is of necessity static and timeless. In this sense art preserves man's 'memory' of Eden and the Renaissance poet emerges as an instrument of grace labouring 'to restore the things of nature to the original state intended for them by their eternal Creator . . . to give them a perfection and a beauty unattained by themselves, creating in his mind the *perfetta forma intenzionale della natura*'.[1] In other words, the poet shares in

1 Erwin Panofsky, *Idea: A Concept in Art Theory*, translated by Joseph J.S. Peake (New York, 1968 — first pub. 1924), p. 95.

the goddess Nature's vision of a timeless, changeless state, but whereas she looks forward to its future attainment he looks back nostalgically to an era long gone. Yet the goddess forms part of the poet's vision and the poem works, as we shall see, towards the suggestion that past and future converge in a spiritual dimension beyond present comprehension. At that point the three facets of time collapse into one, transforming 'past continuous', which loses every moment it experiences, to present continuous, which preserves every moment through experience. In Augustinian terms, time passes from the mind of man to the mind of God. A more immediate implication of the proem, however, is that violence and disruption must be regarded as integral components of the order obtaining. In effect the proem establishes a *de facto* justification for the violence of book five since the state of the world as there presented merely reflects that of the heavens:

> Ne wonder; for the heauens reuolution
> Is wandred farre from where it first was pight,
> And so doe make contrarie constitution
> Of all this lower world, toward his dissolution. (4)

Astraea's child is fostered in a jungle where he learns to 'make experience' of his virtue 'vpon wyld beasts' (V. 1. 7). The 'horror of his wreakfull hand' maintains order in this vicious environment and a 'salvage' land is the ultimate goal of his quest. Spenser remains faithful to the common experience of justice in an age of iron: Talus is a man of his time. Even the heavens are presented as a cosmic jungle in which the constellations violently struggle for position in a confused state of flux: the ram has 'shouldred' the bull out of place, the bull has 'butted' the twins, the twins have 'crusht' the crab (5-6). As experience replaces theory the 'learned Ptolomaee's' image of order and degree is increasingly discredited. 'Who so list' to examine the supposedly immutable sky and 'search' the revolutions of the 'rowling spheares' will find that the ideal diverges as widely from the reality as do ideal patterns of virtue from actual human habits. Owing to the precession of the equinoxes the positions of the stars relative to the earth are constantly changing with the result that the signs of the zodiac no longer coincide with the constellations from which they originally took their names.[2] Correspondingly, in the world of the poem, Astraea, though '*sixt* in her degree', is assigned to the fifth book. By contrast the reader of the *Fowre Hymnes*, published the same year, is urged to 'looke . . . no further' than the sky for reflections of divine beauty (IV. 50). It is a measure of the epic's greater fidelity to human truth that it dispenses with such attitudes. Beauty is its contention not its premise.

2 Alastair Fowler, *Spenser and the Numbers of Time* (London, 1964), pp. 192-3.

But Spenser is less interested in the new science *per se* than in its human application. His poetic vocabulary — 'wandred', 'range', 'random', 'astray' — associates the planets with the wandering, ranging knights of his romance narrative and the analogy is enforced by the perplexingly erratic motion of Saturn, ascendant planet of the Golden Age 'that was wont be best' (8). During that period 'peace vniuersall rayn'd mongst men and beasts' (9) but now Saturn is second only to Mars, the patron of conflict, in its degree of variance from the expected norm. Contemporary readers might well recall the baleful effects attributed to its influence in Chaucer's *Knight's Tale*.[3] Ironically, therefore, the Ptolemaic model which served literature so long as a metaphor for moral harmony and cohesion now functions by negative analogy.[4] By raising theoretical expectations which direct observation is bound to disappoint, it becomes the touchstone of anxiety and doubt. What matters now is the remarkable divergence between image and experience. This is reflected in *The Faerie Queene* by the persistent failure of the later books, notably books five to six, to fulfil the expectations of the image supplied to the reader in the 'Letter to Raleigh' or even in their own proems. In such a universe — both real and fictional — the legend of justice can have no satisfactory conclusion nor can the Blatant Beast ever be mured up. Like the erratic planets and knights, evil 'raungeth through the world' (VI. 12. 40).

Set in this context, the concluding compliment to Queen Elizabeth is peculiarly fragile despite the popularity of her cult as Astraea. *A Theatre for Voluptuous Worldlings*, for example, opens with a dedication to the queen announcing that, 'the kingdome of *Saturne*, and the Golden worlde is come againe, and the Virgin *Astraea* is desscended from heaven to builde hir a seate in this your moste happie countrey of *England*'.[5] A similar effect is intended here but since the preceding nine stanzas have excluded any consideration of God 'in his imperiall might', the sudden re-establishment of order seems very abrupt. The laboured contrast between Golden Age and present *mores* cannot be pushed aside so easily. At best, Elizabeth may be said to uphold ancient ideals in fallen times, but like Mercilla she is beset by enemies. Her passion for justice bespeaks an heroic spirit, but the age itself is no longer heroic. As if to emphasise this, book five begins by insisting upon the increasing prevalence of evil even in Arthurian days (V. 1. 1).

If an order does indeed exist, it is of a far more complex nature than had hitherto been imagined. This is to assess experience in the light of faith. Not all are prepared to make such *a priori* assumptions: the Giant of canto two interprets the phenomena of the proem to mean that the cosmic order is radically unjust. Not surprisingly the keynote of his moral character is

3 Helena Shire, *A Preface to Spenser* (London, 1978), pp. 67-8.
4 Victor Harris, *All Coherence Gone* (London, 1949), pp. 86-148.
5 *A Theatre* (1569), sig. Avi^r.

identified as 'surquedrie' or pride. Proposing to 'weigh' the four elements, restoring each surplus to its original position, he implies that the universe is out of control, that 'all vnequall were,/ And had encroched vppon others share' (32). For him, 'unequal' is synonymous with 'unjust'. Therefore, since the inequality of the elements is necessarily reflected in the world of man, he proceeds to announce a social revolution designed to restore human affairs to the state in which 'they were formed auncienlty' (32). He will restore the 'image of the antique world' against which Spenser contrasts the 'state of present time' in the proem. The social implications of such a doctrine threaten the hierarchical structure of Elizabethan society attracting the 'vulgar' who 'cluster thicke vnto his leasings vaine' (33) in the hope of material 'benefit' and 'vncontrolled freedome'. Contemporary readers might well associate the episode with events such as the Peasants' Revolt and the notorious affair of the Anabaptist seizure of Münster (1533) so recently, and so vividly, recalled in Nashe's *Unfortunate Traveller* (1594). In fact, Nashe compared the presumption of the Anabaptists to that of the classical giants warning that all who seek 'by headlong meanes to enter into Heaven and disanull God's ordinance shall, with the Gyaunts that thought to scale heauen in contempt of *Iupiter*, be ouerwhelmed with Mount *Ossa* and *Pelion*, and dwell with the divell in eternall desolation'.[6] Similar contempt figures prominently in the *Mutabilitie Cantos.*

Artegall's response to the giant emphasises not merely his trust in divine providence but also his unyielding commitment to Elizabethan notions of social hierarchy, the implication being that the two are inextricable.[7] He speaks both philosophically and politically when he concludes that, 'all change is perillous, and all chaunce vnsound' (36). This may seem somewhat ironic in the light of the proem, but the effect is quite intentional. Ostensibly Artegall is dealing with one of the great paradoxes of Christian life, the problem of contingency within providence. More practically, he defends the providential 'inequality' in which his creator's sovereign has a vested interest. His theme is that of the Tudor *Homilies*. To disturb the order that obtains, no matter how apparently 'vnequall', is to oppose oneself, as St Paul maintained, to the will of God (Romans 13:1). From this viewpoint the great flaw in the giant's argument is that while concentrating upon appearance he mistakes the reality:

6 *Works*, edited by Ronald B. McKerrow, revised edition, 5 vols (Oxford, 1958), II, 235-6. See also Norman Cohn, *The Pursuit of the Millennium* (London, 1970 — first pub. 1957), pp. 252-80.

7 There are parallels between the Giant's outlook and the apparent, but deceptive, 'justice' of the Irish Brehon law as described in *A View of the Present State of Ireland*, *Prose*, p. 47.

Thou foolishe Elfe (said then the Gyant wroth)
Seest not, how badly all things present bee,
And each estate quite out of order goth?
The sea it selfe doest thou not plainely see
Encroch vppon the land there vnder thee;
And th'earth it selfe how daily its increast,
By all that dying to it turned be?
Were it not good that wrong were then surceast,
And from the most, that some were giuen to the least? (37)

Rather disarmingly, the emphasis falls upon actual experience and the conclusion follows as if by irrefutable logic. The tone is that of a 'practical' man. The argument glides almost imperceptibly from natural history to social comment. Upon reflection, however, it appears that the giant is offering no less than an end to mortality and, presumably, generation — points to be recalled in the *Mutabilitie Cantos*. At no time does he suggest the need for personal reform, believing providence not man to be at fault. Artegall replies by insisting upon the complementary nature of creation and destruction particularly as evidenced in the equity of death.[8] 'The earth', for example,

is not augmented more,
By all that dying into it doe fade.
For of the earth they formed were of yore . . .
What wrong then is it, if that when they die,
They turne to that, whereof they first were made? (40)

Artegall's distinctive use of the verb 'turn' is instructive. According to his antagonist human bodies are 'turned' to alien matter through the terrible metamorphosis of death, whereas for him, as for the goddess Nature, 'turn' has the connotations of 'return' both in the sense of homecoming and the just repayment of a debt. Thus the process of cyclical change imposes order upon a fallen world. Taken as a whole, Artegall's contribution to the debate constitutes the single most important statement of the providential outlook in the poem (41-2), yet the picture it presents is not substantially different from that presented by the giant himself. The distinguishing factor is trust in the inscrutable will of God: 'Ne any may his mighty will withstand;/ Ne any may his soueraine power shonne' (42). In the manner of Calvin, Artegall confronts his opponent with a divine will which cannot be reduced to the narrow confines of human reason. In any case the giant remains entirely ignorant of the central lesson of book four that both hatred and love, concord and discord, are essential to maintaining the fragile harmony whereby creation continues

8 S.K. Heninger, *The Cosmographical Glass* (San Marino, 1977), pp. 102-7.

to subsist, 'else would the waters ouerflow the lands,/ And fire deuoure the ayre, and hell them quight' (IV. 10. 35).[9] What Spenser is struggling towards is a reappraisal of experience — including the scientific and astronomical experience of the proem — in the light of older values. Ironically the violent destruction of the giant must also be regarded as a necessity of the providential order: 'so was the *high aspyring* with huge ruine humbled' (my emphasis). True balance has been restored. One is reminded of the sonnet, originally published in *A Theatre for Voluptuous Worldlings* but reproduced in the *Visions of Bellay*, which tells of the fall of the sister of Typhaeus, a Titaness whose impossible aspirations towards universal domination (she 'did seeme to match the Gods in Maiestie') ends in cataclysmic disaster. Throughout the poem giants and Titans represent presumptuous challenges to the proper order.[10]

Recalling the arguments of the 'egalitarian' giant (a suitable if anachronistic epithet), the *Mutabilitie Cantos* begin and end with an appeal to common experience. Therefore, although the exact formal relationship between this fragment of the poem and the six completed books may forever elude us, it would seem that the cantos were specifically intended to confront the problems of time and providence pervading the entire work. Nowhere are such themes handled more explicitly. Accordingly Mutability, Time, and Nature are personified in order to play their various parts in the allegorical debate enacted atop Arlo Hill. The challenge to the received order is made not by an agent of change but by change itself, and the reply is delivered in the name of the 'God of Nature'. Here then, if anywhere, all of the poems philosophical and theological attitudes converge in an intense exploration of the value of fortune, flux and time. The choice of setting is also significant. The Irish dimension lends the episode an unexpectedly personal tone, deepening the emotional resonance of the authorial voice as it comments, grieves, and prays. In *A View of the Present State of Ireland* the curse of political mutability leads many of Spenser's contemporaries, after 'the manner . . . of desperate men . . . to wishe the vtter rvine of that which they Cannot redresse' (*Prose*, p. 44). Despair of order breeds nihilism and Spenser is writing from the heart of darkness. Seen in the perspective of its Golden Age, Tudor Ireland emerges as a turbulent microcosm of the fallen world: 'which too-too true that lands in-dwellers since haue found' (VII. 6. 55).

Mutability's 'euer whirling wheele/ Of Change' virtually identifies her

9 Heninger, p. 102; Edgar Wind, *Pagan Mysteries in the Renaissance*, second edition (London, 1967), pp. 85-96.

10 *A Theatre* conflates the battles of the Titans with those of the Giants (fol. 10r) and Spenser finds it convenient to do likewise. Mutability claims to be descended from the Titans but is referred to as a 'Giantesse' (VII. 6. 13). For a clear statement of the classical distinction see Bacon, *Works*, VI, 723.

with Fortuna, and the account of 'how she at first her selfe began to reare,/Gainst all the Gods, and th'empire sought from them to beare', is strikingly similar to Natalis Comes's account of Fortuna's attempt to usurp the throne of Jove. In contemporary iconography the wheel of fortune was often identified with the wheel of life.[11] As time is the normal medium of change, Mutability's arguments depend heavily upon their relationship. Furthermore, her genealogy directly associates her with the Christian myth of the Fall, a fall into criminal time and contingency — she is lineally descended from the Titans 'that did whylome striue/ With *Saturnes* sonne for heauens regiment'. Two such figures, Hecate and 'drad' Bellona, continue to exercise power under Jove, presumably representing the forces of controlled dissension and flux which pervade the present world. Such is the context in which Mutability herself is introduced:

> So likewise did this *Titanesse* aspire,
> Rule and dominion to her selfe to gaine;
> That as a Goddesse, men might her admire,
> And heauenly honours yield, as to them twaine. (4)

Mutability's aspirations associate her with the 'high aspyring' giant of book five and the 'sad examples' of her baleful influence are such as followed the curse pronounced in Genesis (5-6). In particular, by 'making all accurst/ That God had blest' she spoils the work of creation itself. However, Nature's association with God in the creative act is highly significant in view of her role during the debate.[12] At the very outset Mutability infringes the 'lawes' of the power to which she later resigns the final judgement — an irony of which her intellectual outlook renders her entirely unaware. The moral implications of that outlook are spelt out in stanza six which reiterates the essential tenets of the proem to book five. Both passages insist upon the vital analogy between natural and moral order (the latter theoretically inclusive of 'policie'):

> Ne shee the lawes of Nature onely brake,
> But eke of Iustice, and of Policie;
> And wrong of right, and bad of good did make,
> And death for life exchanged foolishlie:
> Since which, all liuing wights haue learn'd to die,
> And all this world is woxen daily worse.

11 Henry Gibbons Lotspeich, *Classical Mythology in the Poetry of Edmund Spenser* (Princeton, 1932), pp. 85-6; Samuel C. Chew, 'Time and Fortune', *ELH*, 6 (1939), 83-113 (pp. 88-9, 96-8).

12 For Nature as God's vice-regent see Alan of Lille, *The Complaint of Nature*, translated by Douglas M. Moffat, Yale Studies in English, 36 (New York, 1908), p. 24. Hereafter Alan of Lille.

Mutability's ascent through 'the region of the ayre,/ And of the fire' (7) is in keeping with the Neoplatonic view of the universe which consigned time and change to the sublunary world. Problems arise, however, the moment she reaches 'the Circle of the Moone . . . Where *Cynthia* raignes in euerlasting glory'. Theoretically she should find herself unable to pass.[13] Entering at the 'silver gates' by which 'there sate an hory/ Old aged Sire, with hower-glasse in hand,/ Hight *Tyme*' (8), Mutability confounds the distinction between the sublunar and translunar worlds, passing from the proper realm of time, as man understands it, into the realm of changeless forms. Her progress is made virtually inevitable by the opinions expressed in the proem to book five, and is not without philosophic justification. 'The perfect number of time', Plato asserts, 'fulfills the perfect year when all the eight revolutions, having their relative degrees of swiftness, are accomplished together and attain their completion at the same time'.[14] In this respect, if in no other, all of the planets 'make time'.

The position of Cynthia was particularly problematic. The lunar year, one of the most ancient calendars of human time, and one to which Spenser alludes in stanza nine, depends upon the regular cycles of the moon as it waxes and wanes. It is this element of temporal change that makes the moon an obvious first target for Mutability who 'with bold presumption doth aspire/ To thrust faire *Phoebe* from her siluer bed' (21). Paradoxically, however, Cynthia's constancy was frequently deduced from the regularity of the lunar cycle, a factor Mutability entirely overlooks. Such, for example, is the argument of Lyly's Endimion when he defends the planetary deity against charges of fickleness.[15] But as in Lyly, Cynthia is also Eliza upon whose aging countenance the ravages of change were all too evident in the fifteen- nineties. Spenser's earthly pantheon is in peril.

The effect of the challenge upon cosmic order is instantaneous. As with the eclipse of the sun at the moment of Christ's death, the darkening of the world betokens a disruption of the natural order, a return to primeval chaos. Indeed the horror of the 'heavenly crew' corresponds to that of the 'earthly crew' who witnessed the famous nova of 1572.[16] Jove's first thought is that

13 Erwin Panofsky, *Studies in Iconology* (New York, 1962 — first pub. 1939), p. 134.

14 *Timaeus* (39d), translated by Benjamin Jowett in *Plato: The Collected Dialogues*, edited by Edith Hamilton and Huntington Cairns (Princeton, 1961), p. 1168; For the classic statement of the theory of the great year see Macrobius, *Commentary on the Dream of Scipio*, translated by William Harris Stahl (New York, 1952), pp. 220-2.

15 *Works*, edited by R.W. Bond, 3 vols (Oxford, 1902), III, 22.

16 On the psychological effect of novas see Lynn Thorndike, *A History of Magic and Experimental Science*, 8 vols (London, 1923-58), VI (1941), 67-98; George Williamson, 'Mutability, Decay, and Seventeenth-Century Melancholy', *ELH*, 2 (1935), 121-50 (pp. 122-6). For Spenser's response to contemporary astronomy see Russell J. Meyer, ' "Fixt in heauens hight": Spenser, Astronomy, and the Date of the *Cantos of Mutabilitie*' in

Typhaon, the most powerful of his ancient antagonists is 'againe vprear'd' (15) as in a manner of speaking he is since 'the haughty Titanesse', traces her ancestry back to Saturn's elder brother, Titan. By all the laws of primogeniture governing succession to European thrones, Mutability has an arguable right to reign since Saturn was an usurper, but the order of the heavens is contrary to that of the earth as the order of providential history frequently runs counter to human conceptions of justice.[17] Just as in the Temple of Venus hate is elder brother to love without any suggestion that hate is superior to love, Titan is senior to Saturn although the latter, who inaugurated the Golden Age, is obviously superior. So in Genesis Chaos remains inferior to the creation it precedes. Mutability argues both for a rightful order of succession, and a return to that first confusion. She represents the interests of those powers from which she is descended, Chaos and Titan: in *A Theatre for Voluptuous Worldlings* the latter is identified with Antichrist.[18] Hence the validity of Jove's argument that Titan was defeated 'by eternall doome of Fates decree' (33).

'Fatall' usurpation marks the establishment of both the Tudor and the cosmic hierarchies. Such is the paradox of the 'Tudor Myth' expounded as 'secular scripture' in the *Homilies* if less reverentially elsewhere. The question posed on Arlo Hill is one of power — 'to whether side should fall the soueraigne place' (57) — and in defending himself and 'Cynthia' Jupiter defends the Elizabethan 'state'. Predictably the outcome finds him 'confirm'd in his imperiall see' (59). This is, therefore, the most intensely political part of Spenser's poem because it probes deepest into the nature of things in pursuit of solutions to the many dilemmas that harass Spenser's 'vision'. In the 'divine right' of order to impose itself upon Chaos it finds the ultimate, and perhaps only, justification for Tudor 'pollicie' since 'powre is the right hand of Iustice truely hight' (V. 4. 1). Such an approach is essentially prudential — the cynical might call it Machiavellian — anticipating Pascal's endorsement of potentially redemptive doctrine's for the sake of that very potential. The Tudor Myth justifies itself in the stability of the Tudor State while the State justifies itself through the Myth. Yet to understand such complexity is automatically to deprive oneself of half its emotional consolation. Like Orwell's Winston Smith, Spenser is too deeply involved in the business of propaganda to worship the gods he has helped create. In the

Spenser Studies IV, edited by Patrick Cullen and Thomas P. Roche (New York, 1984), pp. 115-29.

17 For the critical argument in favour of Mutability's claims see Ricardo J. Quinones, *The Renaissance Discovery of Time*, Harvard Studies in Comparative Literature, 31 (Cambridge, Mass., 1972), pp. 283-4. See also Mary K. Woodworth, 'The Mutabilitie Cantos and the Succession', *PMLA*, 59 (1944), 985-1002.

18 *A Theatre*, fol. 42v.

fifteen-nineties Pascal's prudential universe was still too unfamiliar to endorse although already too insistent to ignore. *The Faerie Queene* stands hesitantly at the crossroads uncertain whether to accommodate faith to experience or experience to faith. All Spenser can do is identify mutable agents with universal causes in the hope that, as Sidney argued, certain fictions prove truer than fact, that the creative imagination promotes insight rather than self-delusion.

According to *The City of God* (V. 8), Jupiter was himself commonly identified with Fate, the force upon which he relies, and in rejecting his arguments Mutability may be said to appeal from Fate to Providence — as she has every right to do. However, because Spenser's Fate serves merely as the instrument of Providence, the appeal is, in this instance, ill-advised. Thus even while emphasising his opponent's mortality, Jove also proffers the possibility of regaining 'that place from which by folly Titan fell' (34) through 'grace and goodnesse' — an unmistakable gesture towards the Christian allegorization of the myth.[19] But Mutability represents that aspect of human folly which seeks to gain its objectives through embracing the worst consequences of the fall rather than through self-reformation. The proper alternative to her blasphemous aspirations is presented in diametrically opposed terms in *The Teares of the Muses* where even mutable men may ascend '*in contemplation* of things heauenlie wrought' from the realm of nature to the attributes of God:

> Through knowledge we behold the worlds creation,
> How in his cradle first he fostred was;
> And iudge of Natures cunning operation,
> How things she formed of a formelesse mas:
> By knowledge wee do learne our selues to knowe,
> And what to man, and what to God wee owe.

Regarded from this perspective, Mutability's appeal to the God of Nature, together with her daring ascent through the skies, emerge as travesties of the meditative life, symbols of self-ignorance and aberrant will:

> From hence wee mount aloft vnto the skie,
> And looke into the Christall firmament:
> There we behold the heauens great *Hierarchie*,
> The Starres pure light, the Spheres swift mouement,
> The Spirites and Intelligences fayre,
> And Angels waighting on th'Almighties chayre.

19 For the development of this theme in the Faunus and Molanna incident see Richard N. Ringler, 'The Faunus Episode', *MP*, 63 (1965), 12-9.

And there with humble minde and high insight,
Th'eternall Makers maiestie wee viewe,
His loue, his truth, his glorie, and his might,
And mercie more than mortall men can vew. (499-514).

The *Mutabilitie Cantos* may be said to present the material for such contemplation and if the overall effect is ultimately that of *contemptus mundi* this too forms part of the desired pattern: 'so loathing earth, I looke vp to the sky,/ And being driuen hence I thether fly' (527- 8).[20] This, in effect, is the hope of grace which Jove proffers to the Giantess.

The hermaphroditic character of Spenser's goddess Nature associates her with the Lucretian Venus as the universal principle of biological generation while at the same time recalling the Idol of Venus in book four and the image of passionate embrace with which the third book originally concluded. But Neoplatonists assigned the symbol a yet deeper significance representing not merely the totality of the generative process but also the primordial unity from which creation emanates and to which it must ultimately return. Thus Plato's account of the androgynous nature of early man was even used to explain the sudden shift from singular to plural in Genesis 1:27.[21] According to Spenser's version of the legend in *Colin Clovts Come Home Againe*, it was an androgynous Venus that gave birth to Cupid in the Gardens of Adonis (794-806). In the *Mutabilitie Cantos* the more profound implications of Nature's composition are suggested by the elaborate comparison between her appearance and that of the transfigured Christ, 'glorious . . . in strange disguise' (7). The mysterious veiling of her face alludes to the tradition that it is forbidden to see God and live. Nature may be viewed 'but like an image in a glass' and such a glass is Spenser's poem. The aesthetic image of Nature strives towards her Platonic 'idea'. Regarded in this way she displays, or reflects, many divine attributes yet remains distinct from the deity. According to the received Elizabethan view Nature was 'nothing but the very finger of God working in his creatures'.[22] In *De Planctu Naturae*, the work Spenser acknowledges as the supreme source for the depiction of the figure, Alan of Lille has the goddess assess her own status in the following terms carefully balancing her active and contemplative components:

But lest I should seem, in this my prerogative and power, to be detracting

20 Spenser's attitude towards contemplation is discussed in detail in Joseph Burns Collins, *Christian Mysticism in the Elizabethan Age* (Baltimore, Md., 1940), pp. 192-231.

21 Wind, pp. 212-4.

22 Thomas Cooper, *Certaine Sermons* (London, 1580), pp. 163-5 (p. 163). See also Richard Hooker, *Works*, edited by John Keble, seventh edition, 3 vols (Oxford, 1888), I, 209-10: 'Who [is] the guide of nature, but only the God of nature? *In him we live, move, and are* . . . Nature therefore is nothing else but God's instrument'.

> arrogantly from God, I profess most emphatically that I am the lowly disciple of the Supreme Ruler. For I, as I work, am not able to press my step in the footprints of God as He works, but I contemplate Him in His activity from a long way off, as it were with longing. His operation is simple, mine is multiform; His work is faultless, mine is defective; His is marvellous, mine is transient.[23]

Attempts have been made to identify Nature in Neoplatonic terms with the 'universal soul' which has two phases: 'turned in the direction of pure thought . . . as it contemplates the Ideas of the Mind of God Plotinus called it the world soul; but . . . turned in the direction of the world, it acts as the creative force and is called Nature'.[24] The problems inherent in such a view have been exhaustively demonstrated by Robert Ellrodt who points to a fundamental distinction amongst Renaissance Neoplatonists between Nature and the Cosmic Soul. This distinction, however, is far from clear-cut, and the footnotes to Ellrodt's discussion indicate an area of complexity undeveloped in the main argument.[25] Though undeniably the lowest in the hierarchy of spiritual existences, Nature, as Plotinus defines it, is nonetheless the active faculty of the World-Soul, 'born of *contemplation*' and contemplative itself. Hence the moment of intense meditation preceding her judgement on Arlo Hill.

Despite Ellrodt's arguments, the contemplative cast of Nature, argued at great length by Plotinus, is central to the Neoplatonic outlook. In the third *Ennead* Nature, the 'rational forming principle', is identified as the 'primary mover' operating in the cosmos, at rest itself while moving others, or, as Spenser puts it, 'still moouing, yet vnmoued from her sted' (13). Its 'stillness' is used to explain its attainment of contemplation:

> If it stays unmoved as it makes, and stays in itself, and is a forming principle, it must itself be contemplation. For action must take place according to a rational principle, and is obviously different from the principle; but the principle itself which accompanies and supervises the action, cannot be action. If, then, it is not action but rational principle, it is contemplation.[26]

23 Alan of Lille, p. 29: For the controversy concerning Spenser's knowledge of Alan see Edwin Greenlaw, 'Some Old Religious Cults in Spenser', *SP*, 20 (1923), 216-43 (pp. 219-31); Helen Andrews Kahin, 'Spenser and the School of Alanus', *ELH*, 8 (1941), 257-72.

24 Josephine Waters Bennett, 'Spenser's Venus and the Goddess Nature of the *Cantos of Mutabilitie*', *SP*, 30 (1933), 160-92 (pp. 162-3).

25 Ellrodt, *Neoplatonism in the Poetry of Spenser* (Geneva, 1960), pp. 63-4 (See especially p. 64, fn. 32).

26 *Plotinus*, translated by A. H. Armstrong, Loeb Classical Library, 6 vols (London, 1965-), III (1967), 367.

Coming closer to Arlo-Hill, Nature is then requested to explain its relationship to the world of mutable matter — an episode which may well have suggested the idea of the debate to Spenser. 'What comes into being', it replies, 'is what I see in my silence, an object of contemplation which comes to be naturally . . . and my act of contemplation makes what it contemplates, as the geometers draw their figures while they contemplate'.[27] As in Spenser the answer is brief as Nature prefers silence. Plotinus deduces that 'what is called nature is a soul . . . that it quietly holds contemplation in itself, not directed upwards or even downwards, but at rest in what it is, in its own repose and a kind of self-perception'.[28] The implications for the world of man seem to bear strongly upon the significance of the Spenserian quest particularly in their acknowledgement of circularity: 'Action, then, is for the sake of contemplation and vision, so that for men of action, too, contemplation is the goal, and what they cannot get by going straight to it, so to speak, they seek to obtain by going round about'.[29]

It would seem, therefore, that Spenser has gone to such lengths to fuse the two complementary aspects of Nature's character in the person of his goddess, that to pull them asunder is to do violence to the fable. Indeed this twofold image of Nature is as crucial to her function as is her ambivalent sexuality. In certain circumstances experience breeds distrust of providence, but the voice of Nature is the voice of ultimate experience, of experience consciously and rationally assessing its own value in the light of the fullest knowledge possible to any created being. As a result, in stark contrast to Alan of Lille, Nature in Spenser is not the complainant but the judge. In attaining the state of active contemplation (as the Latin verb *contemplor* is passive in form but active in meaning), she achieves the synthesis of apparently contradictory life-styles demanded of the questing knights. Since the concept of providence emerges through the conflict of opposing philosophies, her mentality is ruthlessly dialectical. All physical combat is merely the material expression of this perpetual internal debate. Eternity is both the end of contemplation and the medium of its resolution.

The great paradox of the present debate is that the cure is found in the disease since Mutability is discovered to constitute a vital part of the natural order. The more evidence she adduces, the more obvious this becomes. Correctly employed, experience prompts contemplation: thus, at the conclusion, Spenser can 'thinke on that which Nature sayd' in the light of his own personal aspirations. Nature, the sum total of all action and experience perpetually reflecting upon its relation to its creator, is the cosmic equivalent

27 *Ibid.*, p. 369.

28 *Ibid.*, p. 371.

29 *Ibid.*, p. 377. On this aspect of Plotinian thought see William Ralph Inge, *The Philosophy of Plotinus*, 2 vols (London, 1918), I, 155-63.

of the hermit of book six whose 'sage counsell' emerges 'through the long experience of his dayes' (VI. 6. 3). She resembles Sapience who, in the last of the *Fowre Hymnes*, 'rules the house of God on hy,/ And menageth the euer-mouing sky,/ And in the same these lower creatures all/ Subiected to her power imperiall' (IV. 193-6). Having heard the evidence the goddess acknowledges creation's antipathy to 'stedfastnes' but immediately qualifies this concession in the light of her own profound self-awareness. The Titaness overlooks the 'still' or contemplative aspect of her make-up. In fact, the case is lost from the moment *Order* marshals the witnesses at Nature's bidding (27), since order is the principle at stake both in cosmos and state.[30] Mutability either ignores or fails to recognise this aspect of the pageant, embracing attitudes which easily foster despair. Indeed her final argument is that time itself is merely a facet of change. As we have seen, Jove is indebted to Plato's *Timaeus* for his reply arguing, predictably, that since all of the planets unite in 'making' time they transcend it.[31] Plato attributed man's ignorance of this truth to his habit of resting content with appearances and, true to form, Mutability remains sceptical for precisely the same reason:

> The things
> Which we see not how they are mov'd and swayd,
> Ye may attribute to your selues as Kings,
> And say they by your secret powre are made:
> But what we see not, who shall vs perswade? (49)

The sharp distinction between 'we' and 'ye' separates the narrow from the expansive mind thereby putting Mutability on the wrong side of the Platonic argument amongst the unenlightened. She is one of Plato's cave dwellers. According to Calvin, 'it is an insufferable wickedness to think that we, who can hardly crawl on the earth, should take nothing as true except what submits itself to investigation by our eyes'.[32]

The weakest link in Mutability's argument is the suggestion that since

30 Boethius (Book 3, Poem 2) calls attention to how 'mighty Nature guides the reins of all things; how she providently governs the immense world by her laws; how she controls all things, binding them with unbreakable bonds'. *The Consolation of Philosophy*, translated by Richard Green (Indianapolis, 1962), p. 45.

31 Jove, of course, is merely an instrument of God — a common theme of late Medieval and Renaissance art. See Jean Seznec, *The Survival of the Pagan Gods*, translated by Barbara F. Sessions (New York, 1953), p. 81. See pp. 161-3 for the status of the planet Jove or Jupiter. In relation to human destiny or fate, Jupiter was commonly regarded as the 'maior Fortuna' hence his own 'fortunate successe' here.

32 *Concerning the Eternal Predestination of God*, translated by J.K.S. Reid (Cambridge, 1961), p. 169. Calvin is remembering St Paul, II Corinthians 4:18. See *A Theatre*, fol. 9r.

creation exists in a state of motion, a species of change, motion is 'loved' purely for its own sake.[33] The implications of such a view are developed in one of Harvey's letters to Spenser:

> There is a veriable course and revolution of all thinges. Summer gettith the upperhande of wynter, and wynter agayne of summer. Nature herselfe is changeable, and most of all delightid with vanitye; and arte, after a sorte her ape, conformith herselfe to the like mutabilitye. The moone waxith and wanithe; the sea ebbith and flowith; and as flowers so ceremonyes, lawes, faishions, customs, trades of livinge, sciences, devises, and all thinges else in a manner floorishe there tyme and then fade to nothinge. Nothing to speake of ether so restorative and comfortable for delighte or beneficiall and profitable for use, but beinge longe togither enioyed and continued at laste ingenderith a certayne satietye, and then it soone becumeth odious and lothsum. So it standith with mens opinions and iudgmentes in matters of doctrine and religion.[34]

Taken seriously — and the piece is *not* so intended — the philosophy of constant change for the sake of change leads to a completely relativistic approach to human values and finally to the chaos from which Mutability traces her descent. Harvey's joke is Mutability's creed and she expounds it methodically recapitulating all of the poem's primary cyclical patterns. Thus her argument proceeds from the four elements, the material base of the world, through the temporal dimension in which matter exists and on towards the supposedly eternal spheres.

Stanza fifty-seven introduces a tense, dramatic pause as creation 'hangs' in 'long suspence' — an incisive pun since no less is threatened than the dissolution of the chain of being — awaiting Nature's reply. In effect, she interprets the allegory of which she herself is part. The pause is of the essence of a poem written in predominantly end-stopped stanzas, a form which, to a far greater extent than blank verse, facilitates the reader's reflection upon each individual segment of the narrative continuum. In this case, the meditator's silent gestures reflect the nature of the problem as she first looks downwards with 'firme eyes affixt' upon the mutable earth and then joyously upwards 'with chearefull view'. Like her more perceptive children, she sees beyond Mutability's arguments discovering intimations of eternity within the recurrent cycles of generation, decay and death.[35] The dramatic tension is

33 On the various ironies in Mutability's outlook see Alastair Fowler, *Triumphal Forms: Structural Patterns in Elizabethan Poetry* (Cambridge, 1970), p. 60.

34 *Works*, edited by A.B. Grosart, 3 vols (London, 1884-5), I, 148-9.

35 Calvin contended that the unalterable order of the natural cycles demonstrated the providence of God at work in worldly affairs. *Eternal Predestination*, pp. 162-3.

heightened, however, as her first words seem to endorse the complainant's point of view:

> I well consider all that ye haue sayd,
> And find that all things stedfastnes doe hate
> And changed be . . .

There is no denying the truth of this. Change is a fundamental principle of the universe as Mutability has argued. Alan of Lille has Nature herself expound the divine intention that 'by the round of mutual relation of birth and death there should to perishable things be given stability through instability, infinity through impermanence, eternity through transientness'.[36] It is the final clause that Mutability has overlooked and to this factor Nature now returns, changing the direction of her remarks with the key word 'yet':

> yet being rightly wayd
> They are not changed from their first estate;
> But by their change their being doe dilate:
> And turning to themselues at length againe,
> Doe worke their owne perfection so by fate:
> Then ouer them Change doth not rule and raigne;
> But they raigne ouer change, and doe their states maintaine. (58)

By thus returning upon itself, Nature's answer becomes a paradigm of the situation it describes. In effect, since Mutability constitutes part of nature, the debate represents a *psychomachia* within the consciousness of the goddess herself. The use of the verb 'weigh' is particularly pointed in the light of Mutability's initial request: 'Then weigh, O soueraigne goddesse, by what right/ These gods do claime the worlds whole souerainty' (16). Associated as she is with images of the fall, there is something intensely sinister about the Titan's request and her words recall those of Despair: 'Thou wretched man, of death hast greatest need,/ If in true ballance thou wilt weigh thy state' (I. 9. 45). That is the 'weighing' Mutability desires and it entails no less than Nature's 'suicide'. Our first glimpse of the Giant of Book Five is of a figure perched upon a rock amid a crowd of fools, 'holding forth on hie/ An huge great paire of ballance in his hand,/ With which he boasted in his surquedrie,/ That all the world he would weigh equallie' (V. 2. 30). Later smashed in a mood of petulance, the Giant's scales travesty those provided by Astraea 'to weigh both right and wrong/ In equall ballance with due recompence' (V. 1.

36 Alan of Lille, p. 44.

11). By 'weighing' the evidence in the scales of Cosmic justice, Nature endorses the doctrine of 'due recompense' thereby making of mutability not the end but the tool of creation.

It now appears that for the cosmos, as for the individual, existence takes the form of a circular quest for lost perfection. Thus all things are fated to end as they began, 'turning to themselues at length againe'. As Ficino put it, man 'will return to his own Idea through which he was created. . . . True man and the idea of man are one and the same; therefore each of us separated from God on earth is not a true man since he is separated from the Form and Idea of himself. To this Idea divine love and piety will lead us, although we are here divided and mutilated'.[37] The term 'dilate' frequently seems to have been used in the context of achieving perfection through form, but Spenser's own favourite usage has the sense of relating or unfolding the successive episodes of a story.[38] Both are clearly appropriate here since the legends of each protagonist illustrate the development — and eventual 'dilation' — of his spiritual being through the medium of mutable contingency. Spenser's characters 'dilate' accounts of their own adventures, the allegorical significance of which constitute the stages of their moral progress.[39]

Perhaps the most important aspect of Nature's reply is her prophecy of a timeless, changeless state beyond the apparently endless cycles of recurrence. This brings to a Christian conclusion a canto which could so easily have endorsed the eternal return of the Stoics' great year. Their philosophy of honourable suicide fits well with such a world-view since history would then repeat itself interminably: Arthurian vision would become Arthurian nightmare.[40] Nature foresees an escape from such relentless repetitions into a state of permanence related to the *nunc-stans* of the Christian God, what the *Fowre Hymnes*, identify as 'th'Idee of his pure glorie *present still*' (III. 284). In effect, she perceives the 'pillars of eternity' upon which rest the vast, mutable structures of the temporal world. Despite the sinister connotations of 'motion' within Mutability's philosophy, the phenomenon was traditionally regarded as indicative of the existence of a motionless Prime Mover.[41]

37 *Marsilio Ficino's Commentary on Plato's Symposium*, edited and translated by Sears R. Jayne, University of Missouri Studies, 19, no 1 (Columbia, 1944), p. 215.

38 John Erskine Hankins, *Source and Meaning in Spenser's Allegory* (Oxford, 1971), p. 291; Brents Stirling, 'The Concluding Stanzas of *Mutabilitie*', *SP*, 30 (1933), 193-204.

39 See II. 5. 37; III. 3. 62; V. 6. 17; VI. 10. 21.

40 'Repetition emptied of its religious content necessarily leads to a pessimistic vision of existence . . . when it is desacralized, cyclic time becomes terrifying; it is seen as a circle forever turning on itself, repeating itself to infinity.' Mircea Eliade, *The Sacred and the Profane*, translated by Willard R. Trask (New York, 1959), p. 107. See also, Lewis J. Owen, 'Mutable in Eternity: Spenser's despair and the multiple forms of Mutabilitie', *Journal of Medieval and Renaissance Studies*, 2 (1972), 49-68.

41 F.C. Copleston, *Aquinas* (Harmondsworth, 1955), pp. 114-5, 121-2.

According to received medieval belief, the deity 'moved' the Primum Mobile as an object of desire moves those who desire it, the resulting motion taking circular form in direct imitation of the loved one's perfection.[42] As Ficino maintained, 'motion itself cannot be its own end, since it flows perpetually from one point to another and on again. . . . Hence creation's supreme and final end . . . will not be motion, but rest. Rest is more perfect than motion . . . and it is in that state of supreme consummation that the body of the universe will be transfigured.'[43] For man, this ultimate state will coincide with the resurrection of the body, at which point the course of the heavens will have ceased.[44] Since such stability is the peculiar property of the eternal, he will finally have transcended time.[45]

Spenser's personal meditation upon the conclusion of the debate passes from the 'speech . . . of mutability' (1) to 'that which Nature sayd' (2) in a manner designed to demonstrate the complementary nature of their moral effect. The 'pillours of Eternity', allegorical prefigurements of which feature in the Temples of Venus (IV. 10. 37) and Isis (V. 7. 5), offer a sense of security which eludes even the 'thousand Crystall pillours of huge hight' upholding Cynthia's palace (VII. 6. 10).[46] In a poem prolific in architectural images of transience they guarantee the ultimate permanence anticipated by Ficino when he termed love 'the perpetual knot (nodus) and bond (copula) of the world, the immobile prop (immobile sustentaculum) of its parts, and firm foundation of the entire structure'.[47] To contemplate (or *contemple*) is to enter the sacred mental 'space' where time gives way to eternity. The insistence upon the world's '*short* time', which here affords no 'endlesse moniments', gains added significance from the designation of its creator as 'the God of Sabbaoth' a name associated by St Paul with the speed of divine retribution: 'for he will finish the work, and cut it short in righteousness: because a short

42 C.S. Lewis, *The Discarded Image* (Cambridge, 1964), pp. 113-4.

43 'Motum ipsum ideo finem revera esse non posse, quoniam semper ab alio fluit in aliud. Hoc ipsum vero scilicet in aliud tendere . . . Itaque summum ultimumque universi finem . . . motum non fore, sed statum. Statum enim motu perfectiorem esse . . . mundi corpus in eo statu, utpote consummatissimo, fore pulcherrimum.' *De Immortalitate Animorum* (XVIII. 9) in *Opera*, 2 vols (Basle, 1576), I, 416.

44 'Expleto tandem coeli cursu . . . singula hominum corpora, quorum gratia prius generabantur omnia, e terra, iubente Deo, resurrectionem primum auctoritate divina confirmant'. *Ibid.*, in *Opera*, I, 416.

45 'Status autem aeternitatis est proprius'. *Ficino's Symposium*, edited by Jayne, pp. 99, 210.

46 The pillars form part of 'a cosmological image that has been very widely disseminated — the cosmic pillars that support heaven and at the same time open the road to the world of the gods.' Eliade, *Sacred and Profane*, p. 34. In Job 26:11 the 'pillars of heaven' tremble at God's reproof.

47 *Ficino's Symposium*, edited by Jayne, p. 56. The translation is my own.

work will the Lord make upon the earth' (Romans 9:28).[48] Time is God's 'consuming sickle'. Likewise in Saint James the cries of the exploited enter the ears of the 'Lord of Sabaoth' whose coming rapidly 'draws nigh' (5:4-8). But the Lord of Sabaoth is also Lord of the Sabbath (of the seven days of creation, the seven ages of the world, and of time itself since seven is its 'number') and the resulting wordplay in the concluding couplet of the second stanza, suggested by the reference to eternal rest in the previous line, lends depth to the invocation: the day which witnesses the completion of creation must witness the accomplishment of its redemption.[49] The time 'when no more Change shall be' would then be identical with the 'time of refreshing' spoken of in the Acts of the Apostles, the time 'of restitution of all things which God hath spoken by the mouth of all his holy prophets since the world began' (3:21).

II. *Reflexive Images: A Pattern for the Poem*

A famous paradox of Zeno asserts that owing to the infinite divisibility of continuous space, no journey can ever be completed since this would necessitate the completion of an infinite number of subsidiary journeys.[50] The falsity of this claim has been the subject of innumerable refutations, ancient and modern, but Spenser's heroes — and Spenser's readers — might well be forgiven an instinctive sympathy for so apt a metaphor for the manifold frustrations and disappointments of human endeavour. The six extant books of *The Faerie Queene* constitute merely half of a promised twelve, and these twelve merely half of a projected twenty-four. Within the existing books one looks in vain for finality. No journey ever ends in any absolute sense, nor is any purpose entirely accomplished. As episode follows episode in apparently endless and inconclusive succession, Britomart speaks for all her fellow protagonists when she compares the rhythm of events to the perpetual motion of a tempestuous sea (III. 4. 8). Periods of physical 'haven' are also periods of emotional or moral anxiety, of nervously anticipating new developments. George leaves Una at the close of book one abandoning 'rest' for six further years of active life; after the defeat of Acrasia Guyon and the Palmer hasten

48 A. Kent Hieatt suggests that 'short time' makes a specific reference to planetary time and links the phrase with the last two lines of the *Epithalamion*: 'Be vnto her a goodly ornament,/ And for short time an endlesse moniment'. *Short Time's Endless Monument: The Symbolism of Numbers in Edmund Spenser's 'Epithalamion'* (Port Washington, New York, 1960), pp. 56-9.

49 On seven as the number of time see Pierre de la Primaudaye, *The French Academie*, translated by T.B. (1586), pp. 563-4. For a synopsis of the controversy concerning these lines see Don Cameron Allen, 'On the Closing Lines of *The Faerie Queene*', *MLN*, 64 (1949), 93-4.

50 See Aristotle's *Physics*, VI. 9 (239b).

to catch the tide of events which hurries them back to the turbulent world of book three; having 'long in drede/Awayted . . . *Britomarts* returne' Scudamour deserts his station in despair thereby deferring his own happiness; the marriage of Florimell and Marinell is postponed until book five where the celebrations surrounding it end in some disarray; Artegall's reformation of Irena's homeland proves abortive although he has sacrificed immediate union with Britomart to attempt it; the Blatant Beast escapes from the world of romance narrative into the world of Eliza's court. The questing knights are doomed to search for self-identity in a poem which has not found its own. Seen in this context, there is something inevitable about the running title to the last two verses of the *Mutabilitie Cantos*, 'the VIII. Canto, vnperfite'. It is ironic that these stanzas should so often be regarded as the 'end' of *The Faerie Queene* since the poem is, in fact, continuing. One must observe the textual distinction between what might have been stanzas sixty and sixty-one of canto seven and what are actually the first and second stanzas of canto eight serving not merely as an epilogue to the Mutability episode but also as a prelude to something new.[51]

As far as Spenser's narrative is concerned one detects a studied refusal to conclude. Yet running contrary to this inconclusiveness is a persistent emphasis upon achievement and success. It would appear, therefore, that what really matters is not temporal finality but moral significance. Although the war may continue, battles are constantly being won. The reader detects clear signs of spiritual development in all of the poem's major protagonists as also in many of the minor figures who benefit from their assistance. There is a sense in which many of the questing knights — notably George, Britomart, Artegall, and Calidore — are at once more self-assured and self-aware at the conclusion of their adventures than at the outset. In effect, to use a paradox Spenser loved, they are more 'themselves'. A primary goal of each quest is the 'dilation' of the quester's moral integrity just as the primary goal of

51 It is clear that Matthew Lownes, the publisher of the 1609 folio edition of *The Faerie Queene*, had no exact information concerning the relationship between the *Mutabilitie Cantos* and the rest of the poem. He labelled them 'The seuenth booke' only for convenience. His considered opinion was that the cantos 'both for Forme and Matter, appeare to be parcell of *some following Booke*' of the poem. Since Lownes would have had no reason for arbitrarily dividing the verses into cantos, it is probably safe to assume that such divisions as we now possess are Spenser's own. Even had Lownes thought of imposing such divisions he would have had no reason for labelling the resulting cantos 'VI', 'VII' and '*The* VIII. *Canto, vnperfite*'. Indeed the eighth canto poses a particular problem since it alone has no epigraph — the only such omission in the poem. Had Lownes been manufacturing the canto divisions himself, he would surely have joined the two lone stanzas of canto eight to the fifty-nine of canto seven. The fact that these two stanzas stand as the opening verses of a new canto, despite its lack of an epigraph, strongly suggests that Lownes was merely reproducing what he found in his source.

Nature's quest is the recovery, through the media of trial and change, of creation's original innocence. Both macrocosm and microcosm seek union with their respective Ideas. The heroes of the poem, no less than the heavenly bodies, are in the process of 'returning to themselues at length againe' in order to regain their 'first estate'. But to 'work' one'e 'perfection' as fate has decreed is necessarily to operate within time even though the ultimate attainment of that perfection lies in another dimension. Thus time and eternity intersect. It is in this sense that the term 'eternal' may justly be applied to human endeavour. So 'union', 'happiness', 'fame', and 'glory' attract the adjective as do 'treason', 'woe', 'despair', and 'torment'.[52] Thus do the products of flux crystallize in eternity. The function of the various visions, dreams, and prophecies is to lend their recipients an eternal perspective upon the temporal world, to place the four familiar dimensions in the context of a fifth. For this reason they are often associated with periods of educational or contemplative retreat and their effect is invariably inspirational.

During the course of her argument, Mutability asserts that the four elements 'are chang'd . . . into themselues', by which she means into one another, and 'lose their natiue mights'. By adopting Mutability's own terminology in her reply — 'turning to themselues at length againe' — Nature exposes the latent irony of the remark, converting the complaint into one of the poem's most successfully 'reflexive' images. The Platonism of her outlook completely reverses the Aristotelian emphasis of the challenge through its insistence upon the symbiotic relationship of time, mutability, and decay. According to the *Physics*, for example,

> all change is in its nature a 'passing away'. And it is 'in time' that everything begins and ceases to be; so some have called it the wisest of things, because it brings all knowledge, but the Pythagorean Paron said it was the most ignorant, because it is in time too that everything is forgotten, and he was nearer the mark. Indeed, it is evident that the mere passage of time itself is destructive rather than generative . . . because change is primarily a 'passing away'.[53]

Nature espouses the contrary Platonic view, developed by Ficino and his circle, that the divided and mutilated creatures of the material world ('discerpti . . . et mutilati') seek to become whole men ('integri homines') by recovering or embracing their true selves ('nos ipsos . . . amplectamur') through the assistance of grace. This results in the glorious reintegration of

52 See I. 4. 46; I. 9. 54; II. 8. 45; II. 10. 66; III. 3. 49; IV. 3. 43; IV. 9. 2; VI. 9. 2.

53 *The Physics*, translated by Philip H. Wicksteed and Francis M. Cornford, Loeb Classical Library, 2 vols (London, 1929-34), I, 415.

an identity shattered at the Fall.[54] It is the goal of all moral aspiration. Not suprisingly, the movement of *The Faerie Queene* is irresistibly towards the court of Gloriana. Presumably even Britomart must go there since it serves both as her lover's point of origin and his last known destination. Thus even the most apparently linear narratives tend to curve almost imperceptibly — there are no straight lines on a spherical world.

The return of elect soul to risen body constitutes the Christian answer to the pagan theory of reincarnation. St Augustine drew the parallel himself in *The City of God* (XXII. 28) arguing that belief in the reconstitution of the body in relation to the return of particular individuals radically undermined attacks upon the Christian doctrine of resurrection.[55] Thus even the much admired 'prowess' of the body, no less than its spiritual counterpart, are destined for ultimate fulfilment. In the final analysis, the pervasively mystical outlook of Christian Platonism expands to embrace corporeal satisfaction — perhaps the most astonishing paradox of a system so wary of sensual gratification. Thus Spenser cultivates images of resurrection from the triple 'rising' of St George, through the conflicts with Malegar and Triamond to the description of undeniably corporeal life *after* death in Mutability's central pageant.[56]

Throughout the poem, also, characters, places, and objects are found to 'become' or be 'restored to' themselves (or alternatively 'robbed' from themselves) in a variety of ways. These patterns stretch from purely localized effects of imagery to the structure of whole books. Indicative of this process is the frequent strengthening of the verb 'return' with the apparently tautological addition of the words 'back', 'again', or 'former'. Sometimes three or four combine in the one line as in 'thence backe returning to the former land', where the effect is further emphasised by the initial 'thence' (III. 7. 61). Spenser revels in the notion of returning not once but repeatedly. Not merely are his protagonists returning to their point of origin, but they spend must of their time retracing their steps through labyrinthine woods and deserts, 'amazed' in every sense in fairyland. Towards the close of book one, a formal close undercut by narrative continuity, George twice declares his intention, 'backe to returne to that great Faerie Queene' but after that to 'hither backe returne againe' finally abandoning the fairy court for Una. In coming

54 *Ficino's Symposium*, edited by Jayne, pp. 103, 215. Nature's pattern is worked out in miniature, through Arthur's assistance, in the case of Poeana (IV. 9. 16). See also the episode of Matilda's child (V. 4. 31)

55 Richard Sorabji, *Time, Creation and the Continuum* (London, 1983), p. 189.

56 By way of conclusion come '*Life*, and lastly *Death*' but this sombre finale is reversed by the structure of the stanza in which it occurs (VII. 7. 46). Death is entirely negative, 'vnbodied, vnsoul'd, vnheard, vnseene' but the passage ends with Life, 'a faire young lusty boy . . . Deckt all with flowres, and wings of gold fit to employ'.

to 'Eden' in the first place he has already 'returned' to the origins of human history and the land quickly renews its 'incorrupted' antique nature (I. 11. 47). It too is restored to itself thereby confirming the expected pattern.

Similar instances pervade the poem. Towards the end of book two Guyon requests that Acrasia's victims 'returned be vnto their former state' (II. 12. 85), but finds himself resisted by the sensual Grill. Cycles of generative and social recurrence dominate books three and four, while books five and six see their heroes temporarily lose and then regain their true identities — as Timias loses his a little earlier (IV. 7. 40). The 'Legend of Covrtesie' supplies one of the work's most effective reflexive images in its presentation of Elizabeth-Gloriana as the source and end of the relevant virtue: 'so from the Ocean all riuers spring,/ And tribute backe repay as to their King' (Proem, 7). This theme of courteous reciprocation is further developed in the self-enclosing dance of the Graces upon Mt Acidale. In all such cases return is not a matter of repetition so much as development. One of the factors that serves to distinguish the 'Sonnes of Day' from their evil counterparts is the entrapment of the latter within degenerative cycles of recurrence — such as the annual penance of Duessa, the perpetual suicides of despair, the ceaselessly repetitive Masque of Busirane, the endless renewal of Malbecco's fears — which debase and debilitate the moral character.

Elsewhere in Spenser's poetry even the verb 'dilate' which, as we have seen, plays so prominent a part in Nature's response to Mutability is closely associated with the phenomenon of outward motion and circular return:

> for now your light doth more it selfe dilate,
>   and in my darknesse greater doth appeare.
> Yet since your light hath once enlumind me,
>   with my reflex yours shall encreased be. (*Amoretti*, 66)

Much of the imagery of reflected lights and colours which enriches the poetic texture of *The Faerie Queene* partakes of this idea of complementary reciprocation. In particular, love is the medium through which such fulfilment occurs. So we learn in the *Hymne in Honovr of Beavtie* that,

>   gentle Loue, that loiall is and trew,
> Will more illumine your resplendent ray,
> And add more brightnesse to your goodly hew,
> From light of his pure fire, which by like way
> Kindled of yours, your likenesse doth display,
> Like as two mirrours by opposd reflexion,
> Doe both expresse the faces first impression. (176-82)

Thus double reflection restores the original image. In reading the poem Elizabeth is invited to see herself, and her realms, reflected 'in mirrours more than one' (3 Proem, 5) and, presumably, interpret what she sees by 'reflecting' upon its 'veiled' intention (2 Proem, 4-5). Within the romance narrative the crystalline Cleopolis reflects the glory of the New Jerusalem and finds its own reflection in the hearts of those who serve it (I. 10. 58). The fundamentally Platonic pattern of emanation, prismatic fragmentation, and eventual return to unity is thereby upheld.[57]

The essential function of all such imagery is to illustrate the theme of self-development through progressive stages of moral and physical education upon which, as Madeleine Cosman has demonstrated, Arthurian romance had long insisted.[58] Spenser underscores this motif not merely by constant emphasis upon the youth of his protagonists but even more pointedly by persistently drawing the reader's attention to their ignorance of self-identity. His narrative is full of characters whose knowledge of their true 'lignage' is seriously defective. Amongst the more prominent are George, Arthur, Artegall, Pastorella, Matilda's foundling, and Serena's savage man. In some cases the truth is hidden from the reader as well. It seems clear, therefore, that Spenser is using this well-worn topos, so familiar from Greek and Celtic romance, as an effective narrative analogy for deeper, spiritual levels of self-deception. Thus, for example, in accepting Duessa's false notions of personal honour George stumbles from the House of Pride to the Dungeon of Ignorance losing his integrity to such an extent that Una can ask 'what euill starre/ On you hath fround, and pourd his influence bad,/ That of your selfe ye thus berobbed arre' (I. 8. 42). Spenser's stars may influence or incline but not compel. Understandably, Una is reluctant to pursue her 'forward course . . . till he recouered had his former hew' (I. 9. 20) — one notes the recurrence of vocabulary familiar from the *Hymnes*. Her worst fears are confirmed some stanza's later when 'her *chosen* knight' — a sly Calvinist pun — attempts to commit suicide. Indicative of the subtle relationship between ignorance of

57 C.S. Lewis, *Studies in Medieval and Renaissance Literature*, collected by Walter Hooper (Cambridge, 1966), pp. 149-63.

58 Madeleine Pelner Cosman, *The Education of the Hero in Arthurian Romance* (Chapel Hill, 1965), p. 180. 'Enfances' of the type which interest Cosman are provided for (amongst others) Arthur (I. 9. 3-5) and Artegall (V. I. 5-12). Spenser does not concern himself in a methodical way with the seven — or six — 'ages' of man, although examples of such categories are plentiful throughout the poem. Rather his interest centres upon the rites of passage from adolescence to adulthood and the eventual transformation of knight into hermit (or sage) as the active life yields to the contemplative. Because of the complexity of Spenser's vision of experience, the characteristics of no age group may be taken for granted. As the contrasting figures of Ignorance (I. 8. 32-4) and Tristram (VI. 2. 5-37) illustrate, wisdom is not necessarily the prerogative of age, nor folly the fault of youth.

identity and spiritual ignorance are the contrasting modes of address employed by Despair and Heavenly Contemplation. The former appeals to the 'faeries sonne' George imagines himself to be, the latter to the 'faire ymp, sprong out from English race,/ How euer now accompted Elfins sonne' (I. 10. 60). Since the House of Holiness works to reconstitute George's shattered self-esteem by deepening his experience of the virtue he patronises, Spenser has no further use for the device which had served him so well up to this point. As a result he now underlines George's spiritual progress by allowing him to learn his personal, national, and ecclesiastical identity at one and the same moment thereby intimating the intricate unity of providential design.

As George and Arthur are so closely associated in book one, the former's illumination, victory, and marriage were doubtless intended to herald similar stages in the latter's development. Arthur has twelve books in which to accomplish the necessary self-fulfilment as George has twelve cantos. In both cases the ideal would seem to involve, as so often in earlier Arthurian romance, a fusion of courage ('fortitudo') and wisdom ('sapientia').[59] Both Merlin and Gloriana insist upon the need for time to resolve the twin problems of concealed ancestry and dream vision. Presumably there was intended for the Prince a moment of illumination equivalent to that experienced upon the Mount of Contemplation, and presumably too, in the absence of any real suitors for the aging Elizabeth's hand, any encounter with Gloriana would prove as mystical an affair as the 'marriage' of George and Una, or the ecstatic vision of Sapience which concludes the *Fowre Hymnes*.

To the Renaissance mind the ideal of self-knowledge embraces more than a modern reader might expect. For example, Sir John Davies's *Nosce Teipsum*, which takes as its title the celebrated watchword of the Delphic oracle, involves not merely an awareness of one's personal make-up but of man's spiritual and intellectual stance in relation to the most profound philosophical problems. Similarly, Pico della Mirandola endorsed the same precept on the grounds that it 'arouses us and urges us towards the knowledge of all nature, of which man's nature is the medium and, as it were, the union. For he who knows himself knows all things in himself as . . . Plato wrote in the *Alcibiades*'.[60] According to Lodowick Bryskett's *Discourse of Ciuill Life* (largely translated from Giraldi Cinthio's *Hecatommithi* with the insertion of personal allusions) the doctrine is 'of such importance, as without it no man

59 Cosman, pp. 167-9.

60 *On the Dignity of Man, On Being and the One, Heptaplus*, translated by Charles Glenn Wallis, Paul J.W. Miller, Douglas Carmichael, The Library of Liberal Arts (Indianapolis, 1965), pp. 14-5. Hereafter Pico della Mirandola. For the pseudo-Platonic discussion of 'nosce teipsum' see *Alcibiades* I, 128-35. See also Jonathan Goldberg, *Endless Worke: Spenser and the Structures of Discourse* (Baltimore, Md., 1981), pp. 73-121.

may be happie' (p. 112).[61] Prudence, one of its key elements, is the product not merely of education but of experience, for which reason, 'humane felicitie cannot be attained in yong yeares, since by the definition thereof it is a perfect operation according to vertue in a perfect life: which perfection of life is not to be allowed but to many yeers'. Hence the moral value of time. 'Knowledge of vniuersalities', we learn, 'springeth from singularities' (p. 162). Philosophy is designated a 'singular helpe' in the gaining of such knowledge. At this point, however, 'Spenser' raises an objection to the effect that Oriental philosophers are reputed to demand a level of self-knowledge prior to further instruction. This quality is identified as an assessment of natural aptitude or 'disposition' for 'all men are not apt for all things' and 'there must be a custome of wel-doing in them that wil learne to be vertuous, which may frame in them an aptnesse to learne, by making them loue what is honest and commendable' (p. 164). The attribution of the objection to Spenser is particularly interesting for precisely such a 'disposition' motivates his protagonists at the outset of their adventures, however defective or insufficient their moral characters may later prove. Even those who falsely believe themselves to be fairys' sons, profit from the error in terms of their resulting devotion to Gloriana. Within such a scheme there can arise no contradiction in having a knight naturally disposed towards holiness or temperance instructed, at a relatively late stage of his career, in the 'house' of his virtue.

The deeper self-knowledge which arises from the fostering of one's initial disposition forms the basis of all private and public endeavour (p. 166). As man is of a composite nature, 'compounded of seuerall qualities' he must understand the proper ends of his vegetative, sensitive, and intellectual powers or otherwise risk degeneration to the level of plants and animals: 'the consideration hereof perhaps caused some of the auncient Poets to faine, that men were turned into brute beasts, and into trees . . . hauing made the most excellent part of man, which is the mind and reasonable soule, subiect to the basest and sensual parts and pleasures of the bodie' (p. 189).[62] One thinks of the various transformations throughout *The Faerie Queene*: of Fraudubio and Fraelissa into plants, of Grill into a hog, of Adicia into a tiger and so forth. By contrast there are those who learn to know themselves so well that they become 'diuine creatures' living 'according to reason': 'And such haue

61 *Literary Works*, edited by J.H.P. Pafford (Germany, 1972). All references supplied in the text are to this edition.

62 The same point is made by Pico della Mirandola: 'if you see a man given over to his belly and crawling upon the ground, it is a bush not a man that you see. If you see anyone blinded by the illusions of his empty and Calypso-like imagination . . . delivered over to the senses, it is a brute not a man that you see' (p. 6). Sir John Davies reinforces the idea with specific reference to the three 'powers' of the soul in *Nosce Teipsum* (1245-1252).

aunciently bin called *Heroes*, because they approched in their actions neerer to God then others that liued not so' (p. 207). Spenser alludes directly to such beliefs by interpreting the legends of Bacchus, Hercules, and Isis euhemeristically.[63] According to Bryskett, 'two speciall offices appertaine to the vse of reason . . . the one contemplation, and the other action'. The former pertains to the ultimate spiritual happiness of the individual, the latter to his civic life, 'because he knoweth that he is not borne to himselfe alone, but to ciuill societie and conuersation' (p. 208). As the title of the *Discourse* suggests, Bryskett is primarily concerned with civic felicity, his declared purpose being 'to discourse vpon the morall vertues, yet not omitting the intellectuall, to the end to frame a gentleman fit for ciuill conuersation' (p. 5). The parallels with Spenser's 'Letter to Raleigh' are obvious, and the two enterprises certainly share a direct interest in self-knowledge through experience and instruction. But Spenser's is the deeper vision because his leanings towards mysticism lead him to explore more fully the primarily contemplative basis of the active life. Thus so many of the quests are delineated within the internal landscapes of psychomachia.[64]

The centrality of the search for self-knowledge to the aims of *The Faerie Queene* is clarified in book two in the encounter between Guyon and an Acrasian figure masquerading as Genius:

> Not that celestiall powre, to whom the care
> Of life, and generation of all
> That liues, pertaines in charge particulare . . .
> That is our Selfe, whom though we do not see,
> Yet each doth in him selfe it well perceiue to bee. (II. 12. 47)

The role of the true Genius in promoting constructive 'foresight' has been discussed in chapter one, but now it is time to notice his similarity to the goddess Nature, 'vnseene of any, yet of all beheld'. Like her, Genius is an elemental power — witness his appearance both in the Gardens of Adonis and the more personalized *Epithalamion* — promoting the generative forces within each individual, 'therefore a God him sage Antiquity/ Did wisely make, and good *Agdistes* call' (48). To this power the Acrasian imposter is 'quite contrary': 'the foe of life, that good enuyes to all,/ That secretly doth vs procure to fall,/ Through guilefull semblaunts which he makes vs see'. As the 'governor' of the 'Gardin' — a false Eden or Fools' Paradise — he emerges as the antithesis of the Genius operating in book three. His 'guilefull semblaunts' associate him rather with Archimago than Merlin or the priests

63 See V. 1. 1-2; V. 7. 2-3. See also Seznec, pp. 11, 21-2, 30.
64 Hankins, pp. 21-33, 119-25, 128-34.

of Isis, while his 'mighty Mazer bowle of wine' has strong allegorical affinities with the 'cup of Bacchus' notorious for inducing self-forgetfulness. 'Mazer' subtly suggests the moral effect of the libation and if, as seems likely, it bears a specific reference to maple wood, one may be intended to recall the characterization of that tree in the Wood of Error as 'seeldom inward sound' (I. 1. 9).[65] To drink from the bowl is to lose self-knowledge, to be governed by one's false genius and become, according to Natalis Comes, lascivious, cruel, and avaritious.[66] So do the true and false Agdistes battle against each other within each individual.

The episode proves even more crucial to Spenser's philosophy once it is remembered that, according to the best classical sources including Strabo and Pausanias, Agdistes is also the title of Cybele or Magna Mater, a figure easily identifiable with the goddess Nature herself.[67] Agdistes was originally hermaphroditic and Comes duly reports the legend that he was born 'ambiguo sexu'.[68] The true Agdistes shares the wholeness of experience characteristic of Spenser's goddess Nature or the Venus of book four, reintegrating the shattered components of the human soul in accordance with Plato's fable of early androgynous man in *The Symposium* — the passage which inspired Ficino to develop his theory of man's desire for reunion with his Idea.[69] As Spenser portrays him, the Acrasian 'genius' is not a true hermaphrodite but merely an effeminate man dressed as a woman: 'his looser garment to the ground did fall,/ And flew about his heeles in wanton wize,/ Not fit for speedy pace, or manly exercize' (46). His 'semblaunce pleasing *more than naturall*' is, in effect, unnatural. This contrast between the true and false Agdistes was probably inspired by the iconography of Cebes's *Table*, a primary source for the figure of Genius. There he stands by the gates of birth instructing the newly-born 'what method to observe in the course of their Life . . . what they must follow, upon peril of their utter destruction'. Close by, however, stands a throne and 'a Woman sitting thereon, with a Vizor on her face, and a Cup in her hand'. Her name is Imposture 'that seduceth all the World' and the drink she offers 'error and Ignorance'. To partake is to fall prey to 'Opinions, Desires and Pleasures' in the expectation of 'all dainties and delights; of perpetual Safety and perfect Happiness'.[70] As in the Bower of Bliss, not

65 *The Faerie Queene*, edited by A.C. Hamilton (London, 1977), p. 290.

66 *Mythologiae* (Venice, 1567), fol. 92v.

67 Strabo, *Geographica*, X. 3. 12-13; Pausanias, *Description of Greece*, VII. 17. 9-12. See also Lotspeich, p. 62; Douglas Brooks Davies, *Spenser's 'Faerie Queene': A Critical Commentary on Books I and II* (Manchester, 1977), p. 189.

68 Comes, fol. 92v.

69 *Ficino's Symposium*, edited by Jayne, pp. 58, 103, 155-6, 215.

70 *The Tablet of Cebes the Theban Philosopher or A True Emblem of Human Life*, translated by Robert Warren (Cambridge, 1699), pp. 7-10. For Genius's antagonism to Fortune see p. 46.

spiritual development but self-oblivion is the end result. By saving Verdant Guyon overcomes his own 'false genius' and saves himself. The pseudo-Platonic *Alcibiades* specifically relates the attainment of temperance to the development of self-knowledge.[71]

The bisexuality of the false Agdistes travesties that of the providential relationship between soul (form) and body (matter) within each individual 'self': 'The one imperfect, mortall, foeminine;/Th'other immortall, perfect, masculine' (II. 9. 22).[72] By contrast, the true hermaphroditism of Venus and the goddess Nature is essential to a world-view in which the supreme quest is towards the mysterious 'justice' of divine providence. In this respect Artegall, patron of justice and ancestor of the Tudors, is 'equall' to Arthur as his name implies. Hence the instinctive 'intire affection' which marks their meeting even though their kinship remains unrevealed (V. 8. 12). It is the 'law' of nature that Mutability would infringe (VII. 6. 6) and the 'law' of mortality that rules the Gardens of Adonis (III. 6. 40). Justice constitutes the chief argument of Despair (I. 9. 37-8), the obsession of Amavia (II. 1. 36) and Scudamour (III. 11. 9-10), the goal of history (III. 3. 44), the principle of generation (III. 6. 34), the supreme attribute of God (5 Proem, 10-11), the quality of time (V. 7. 4), the defence of Mercilla (V. 9. 36), the pretence of tyranny (V. 12. 14), and the basis of reciprocal love and friendship (VI. 8. 23). But according to Ficinian Neoplatonism, 'Justice is called Bi-Sexual; feminine inasmuch as because of its inherent innocence it does no one any wrong, but masculine inasmuch as it allows no harm to be brought to others and with more severe censure frowns upon unjust men.' Courage he designates as 'masculine', and temperance (including what Spenser terms 'chastity') as feminine. The three, led by Prudence, correspond to Sun (Courage), Moon (Justice), and Earth (Temperance).[73]

Britomart, a courageous paragon of chastity, rides forth in male disguise to find her lover Artegall in the 'vnmanly maske' of 'womanishe attire' (V. 7. 37). Succumbing to Radigund, as his mythical prototype succumbed to Omphale, he abuses his true 'self' to fall into the 'unnatural' state of the false Agdistes, 'robde . . . of . . . manly hew' (40). In purely human terms Britomart's revulsion is understandable although her lover's appearance is no more nor less incongruous than her own. Allegorically speaking, however, bisexuality is a necessity of providential justice since Sun, Moon, and Earth

71 Harry Berger argues that in Verdant Guyon sees 'a ruined apparition of himself'. *The Allegorical Temper: Vision and Reality in Book II of Spenser's 'Faerie Queene'* (New Haven, 1957), p. 217. On Agdistes, pp. 211-3. See *Alcibiades* I, 128-35.

72 For Sir Kenelm Digby's famous commentary on this stanza see *Variorum Edition*, Book Two, pp. 472-8. See also J.B. Bamborough, *The Little World of Man* (London, 1952), p. 31; Alastair Fowler, *Spenser and the Numbers of Time* (London, 1964), pp. 260-88.

73 *Ficino's Symposium*, edited by Jayne, p. 160. (See also, p. 156).

are also identified on a more exalted level as aspects of divine 'Prudence'. Artegall's appearance is equivalent to the androgynous portrait of Francis II designed to illustrate his transcendence of fallen nature through the cultivation of the 'male' and 'female' virtues appropriate to Minerva, Mars, Diana, Amour, and Mercury.[74] From a strictly moral viewpoint Artegall's transvestism illustrates the danger of allowing the feminine aspect of justice to usurp the rightful place of its masculine counterpart. On a higher level it enacts by way of 'maske' the blending of equity and justice envisaged in the Temple of Isis and stands as a parodic prefigurement of the final union with Britomart when both become 'one flesh' as equity and justice fuse in the 'imperium' thereby created. In the 1596 edition of the poem Britomart is denied the vision of Amoret and Scudamour's hermaphroditic embrace but learns instead of the dual nature of Venus in book four ('She syre and mother is her selfe alone', IV. 10. 41) and elevates her lover from 'bisexual' bondage to 'bisexual' love by defeating her dark *alter-ego*, Radigund.

At its most profound, the figure of the hermaphrodite symbolises the reintegration of male and female components of the soul divided at the fall. Thus Pierre de la Primaudaye divides justice into seven 'parts' of which the last and most personal is 'integritie of life'.[75] In the domain of sense, sexual union either partakes of this hermaphroditic integration or degenerates into what Iago terms 'the beast with two backs'. According to Pico della Mirandola the creation of the two sexes shadows one of the great 'mysteries' of the celestial world: 'it is the prerogative of the heavenly souls to perform simultaneously both the function of contemplation and that of governing their own bodies . . . it was commonly the practice of the ancients, as we observe in the Orphic hymns, to designate by the terms male and female these two powers in the same substance'.[76] Sanctified sexuality both partakes in and symbolises the fulfilment of experience foreseen by the goddess Nature. Union with others constitutes a 'return' to the totality of the 'self' thereby defeating the potentially selfish and self-destroying isolation of individual spirits within individual bodies. The hermaphrodite is the supreme image of Spenser's poem as justice is its supreme virtue.

For the poem's evil characters existence is a matter of perpetual recurrence, and the process of return a spiritual solipsism. The 'false genius' promotes stagnation and decline. By contrast the questing characters develop perceptibly: the strange melancholy which besets George is dispelled by the heavenly music of canto twelve (38) and he can properly assess his own past history in the light of a new spiritual illumination (31-2); Britomart, who begins her adventure as an immature, ignorant young girl, can assert her trust

74 Wind, pp. 213-4.

75 *The French Academie*, p. 746.

76 Pico della Mirandola, p. 104.

in divine providence by canto eleven (14) and fulfil Scudamour's quest shortly after. As the chains fall from Amoret's body an imaginative grammatical ambiguity allows them to fall from the heroine also (12. 37-8); Cambel and Triamond discover that one may perfect one's own identity by sacrificing personal glory to the demands of friendship (4. 27-33) while Marinell recovers his own humanity in love (12. 12-3); Artegall puts off the 'quyent disguise' of 'Saluagesse sans finesse' to join with Britomart in tempering justice with equity and further the Arthurian race. A mark of his development is his refusal to release Talus against his personal enemies at the close of book five (12. 43); Calidore, who is described as having 'lost himselfe' in his pastoral retreat to the apparent detriment of his quest (9. 26), recovers after the vision of the Graces to win Pastorella, restore her to her true parents and true identity, and ensnare the Blatant Beast. Thus by using and 'redeeming' time the questers escape the fate of Shakespeare's Richard II who feels he has become a mere 'Jack o' the clock', a soulless automaton 'wasted' by the time he is fated to record. The many visions and prophecies they enjoy afford them a providential perspective upon the structure of temporal existence. That the ultimate fulfilment lies beyond the present life is only to be expected since the sainthood awaiting George represents the perfection of identity: 'thou Saint *George* shalt called bee,/ Saint *George* of mery England, the signe of victoree'. As it is for the chosen man, so for the chosen race. Activity tends towards rest and beneath all desire for happiness lurks the desire for death, a paradox beautifully expressed by Leonardo da Vinci in what might well stand as an epigraph to *The Faerie Queene*:

> Now you see that the hope and the desire of returning home and to one's former state is like the moth to the light, and that the man who with constant longing awaits with joy each new spring time, each new summer, each new month and new year — deeming that the things he longs for are ever too late in coming — does not perceive that he is longing for his own destruction. But this desire is the very quintessence, the spirit of the elements, which finding itself imprisoned with the soul is ever longing to return from the human body to the giver. And you must know that this same longing is that quintessence, inseparable from nature, and that man is the image of the world.[77]

The Faerie Queene is also an image of the world, all the more exact for being incomplete. Both exercise the fearful fascination of self-perpetuating

77 *The Literary Works of Leonardo da Vinci*, edited and translated by J.P. Richter, 2 vols (London, 1883), II, 291.

narratives. Poetic allegory emulates divine allegory in complexity. Every recorded act invites exposition, yet no single interpretation, or mode of interpretation, does justice to the intricacy of the overall design. How could it when the design itself eludes identification? During the sixteenth century both human and divine will were compared to labyrinths and Spenser duly reflects the enigma of maze within maze intersecting interminably. Thus the critical pursuit of meaning becomes analogous to the spiritual pursuit of enlightenment. Because the denouement was never reached, the poet's 'providence' challenges that of his reader. His creation frequently anticipates but never quite achieves, its own fulfilment, never 'dilates' into itself. In one sense it fell victim to its own theme: its time simply ran out. Yet in another it attained its own peculiar perpetuity. Allegory involves its readers in the creative processes which produce it, inviting them to undertake perpetual quests for arcane meaning amongst wandering woods and floating islands. As Merlin before him, Spenser left his daemons, not frozen in historic time, but frenetically active and, like Britomart, we enter their enchanted cave in pursuit of the magus only to discover ourselves. No theory of allegory proves adequate to the experience of reading the poem just as no theory of time proves adequate to the experience of its passage. This is inevitable since such theories have been abstracted from particular — and often limited — facets of the phenomena they seek to encompass. The same is true of providence. Strictly speaking, it pertains solely to *being*, while its would-be interpreters remain trapped in the process of *becoming*. The symbols through which it may be apprehended intuitively are irreducible to discursive prose. Thus repetition is of the essence of *The Faerie Queene* while all its major characters desire deliverance from repetition.

Romance provides Spenser with the means of fashioning images of a universe beyond comprehension, allegory with a tool for exploring it in the light of his own contradictory attitudes and aspirations. The poetry works best when, as in the *Mutabilitie Cantos*, omniscient author is also ignorant protagonist. If the first book of Spenser's epic mirrors the ideal order of providential history albeit tentatively, the remaining books reflect the familiar experience of a world where poetic justice is repeatedly relegated to the realm of fantasy. Ironically, the further one proceeds into fairyland the more recognisably human it becomes. Humanity, not doctrine, inspires Spenser's greatest verse but integral to that humanity is an imaginative, enquiring spirit. The integrity of the quest is paramount.

APPENDIX A

Providence, Predestination, and Free Will in Lodowick Bryskett's *Discourse of Ciuill Life*

The issues of providence, predestination, and free will are discussed in some detail in Lodowick Bryskett's *Discourse of Ciuill Life*, a philosophical dialogue closely based upon (and to a large extent translated from) the second part of Giraldi Cinthio's *Hecatommithi* (1565).[1] In Bryskett's version Spenser himself is one of the speakers, and the numerous parallels between the *Discourse* and *The Faerie Queene* strongly suggest that the work provides a unique insight into the intellectual nature of Spenser's Irish circle. Of particular interest to the present study is the vocabulary Bryskett employs when attempting to distinguish between Christian and pagan notions of fate and providence. For the purpose of such illustration, it matters little whether the treatise was composed before or after the poem.[2] The important thing is the nature of the distinctions being made.

The third book of the *Discourse* begins with a discussion of self-knowledge, but this is interrupted at an early stage when Captain Carleil raises an objection concerning the relationship between destiny and free will.[3] If man's actions are predetermined, he argues, self-knowledge is useless. Bryskett replies that the classical doctrine of fate or destiny is entirely unacceptable since it limits man's stature and destroys the basis of moral philosophy: 'What difference were there betweene the wise men and the foole, the carefull and the rechlesse, the diligent and the negligent? . . . For euery thing being done by the order of fatall disposition, and not by election, no man could either deserue praise, or incurre blame' (pp. 168-9). This concept of 'fatall disposition', associated throughout the discussion with the

1 Lodowick Bryskett, *Literary Works*, edited by J.H.P. Pafford (Germany, 1972). All quotations and citations in the text are from this edition. For the original see Giraldi Cinthio, *Hecatommithi*, Parte Seconda, 'Della Vita Civile' (Venice, 1608), pp. 74-85 (Dialogo Terzo).

2 On the date of composition see Henry R. Plomer and Tom Peete Cross *The Life and Correspondence of Lodowick Bryskett* (Chicago, 1927), pp. 77-84; Janet Spens, *Spenser's 'Faerie Queene': An Interpretation* (London, 1934), pp. 139-44.

3 For Carleil see Plomer and Cross, pp. 81-2.

Stoics, renders the will redundant, 'for to say that our mind or will concurred, by willing or not willing whatsoeuer destinie drew vs vnto, was nought else but a taking away of free choice from our vnderstanding or will' (p. 169). Were this to be true, men would be little better than 'bond-slaues' and Glauce's view of history (III. 3. 25) would indeed be upheld: 'nature should in vaine haue giuen vs the vse of reason, to discourse or to consult, or the abilitie to will or chuse any thing; for whatsoeuer were appointed by destinie, should of necessitie come to passe; and if of necessitie, then neither prudence, counsell, nor election can haue any place' (p. 169). As in Merlin's reply to Glauce, Bryskett finds the solution to this problem in the conscious accommodation of human will to the divine, asserting that 'though God (as an vniuersal cause) concurred to accomplish our deliberations; yet we were to endeuour our selues, and to sharpen our wits to consult on the best meanes to compasse our good purposes, if we desire to haue his fauour, and not to sit idle, expecting what will fall out' (p. 187).[4] In the world of the *Discourse* no less than the world of the poem, the quest is all important.

In approaching the problem of astrology, Bryskett freely admits that the heavens 'haue power ouer vs to incline or dispose vs more to one thing then to another' (p. 171), but this power is exercised over bodies rather than minds 'which are diuine, simple, and spirituall substances . . . wholy free from their influences' (p. 172). Accordingly, there is no question of moral determinism since 'all those things that haue the beginning of their working in themselues, do worke freely and voluntarily' (pp. 171-2). This principle is supported from scripture where God is said to have created man 'and left him in the power of his owne counsell' (p. 173). Man is therefore to be considered free unless he chooses to enslave himself, and life is to be regarded as an unceasing combat against the forces of evil:

> And therefore do the best of the *Platonikes* say very wel, that man must oppose himselfe against his destinie, fighting to ouercome the same with golden armes and weapons, to wit, vertues, which is (as *Plato* saith) the gold of the mind. For he that behaueth himselfe well, that is to say, ruleth his mind or soule, which is the true man indeed . . . shall neuer be abandoned to destinie or fortune: against which two powers mans

4 Bryskett acknowledges a classical variation on the concept of destiny regarding the prevalence of fortune or contingency. Some philosophers 'supposed the beginnings and the endings of things to be of necessitie, but the meanes and circumstances they yeelded to be subiect to the changes and alterations of fortune' (p. 170). This is applied to Aeneas whose departure from Troy and arrival in Italy are guided by 'fatall disposition' but whose progress is nevertheless subject to the vicissitudes of fortune. This view is mentioned more for completeness than anything else and the passage concludes on an entirely divergent note.

> counsell and wisdome resisteth in such sort, if he set himself resolutely thereunto, as it may wel appeere that he is Lord and master ouer his owne actions.[5] (p. 172)

Up to this point, despite an occasional allusion to scripture, the discussion has proceeded in the realm of 'morall philosophy', but now Archbishop Long, speaking as a Christian, introduces the issue of predestination. 'Is it not necessary', he enquires, 'that whatsoeuer God hath determined of vs from the beginning in his fore-knowledge (being the most certaine and true knower of all things) shall come to passe?' (p. 173). In keeping with the tone of the question, Bryskett now shifts his terminology from fate and destiny to 'heauenly prouidence' (p. 174), reflecting a similar move on the part of Cinthio.[6] It is providence, for example, that ensures the perpetuation of the species despite the 'mortal and perishable' nature of its individual members. As in Spenser's Gardens of Adonis, they 'are made perpetual . . . through generation' (p. 174).

As one might expect, grace and free will become the key factors in the ensuing attempt to establish the exact relationship between predestination and autonomy of action. The former is defined as, 'an ordinance or disposition of things in the mind of God from the beginning, of what shal be done by vs in this life through grace' (p. 174). As in the *Institutes*, grace would appear to be the controlling power, yet the will somehow remains free since 'they go both together . . . our well doing is acceptable and pleasing to God, and our euil deeds displeasing'. The explanation is less than satisfactory and an acute element of unease begins to pervade the whole discussion. Cinthio was a Roman Catholic and Bryskett is more interested in his philosophy than his theology. At this point, therefore, he wisely retreats behind his author's profession of inadequacy: 'the further discussing whereof appertaining rather to Diuines then Morall Philosophers, he thinketh fit to referre vnto them, and to beleeue that this is one of those secrets which God hath layed vp in the treasury of his mind, whereunto no mortall eye or vnderstanding can reach or penetrate, humbling our selues to his holy will, without searching into that which we cannot approch vnto' (p. 174). For this reason those who adopt an overly dogmatic stance are to be 'misdoubted' (p. 175). Essential to a correct attitude is confidence in the boundless goodness and charity of God, and a determination to lead a good life even 'were a man certaine to be damned'. But Bryskett will not allow of Calvinist reprobation, favouring the view that 'al they, that are signed with the character of Christ in baptisme, may

5 The 'best of the Platonikes' were those who, like Plotinus, disagreed with the Stoic doctrines of fate and necessity (p. 170).

6 'Della Vita Civile', pp. 79, 84.

stedfastly beleeue that they are predestinated and chosen to saluation' (p. 175). 'Chosen' is the word Spenser uses in the same context (I. 9. 53), and Bryskett proceeds to clarify its relationship to human choice. From this it would appear that God has chosen those who have chosen him: 'Not that our predestination giueth vs a necessitie of well doing, but because we hauing the grace of God to assist vs, dispose our selues by the same grace to keep his commandements for our saluation, and for the honor and glory of his maiestie: whereas by doing otherwise it is our owne wickednesse that excludeth vs from that blisse' (p. 175). Again, although 'necessitie' is expressly discounted, the influence of grace remains rather problematic and the discussion is abruptly terminated with another authorial disclaimer: 'And further mine author saith not' (p. 175).

The matter, however, is too important to rest here. Like Hooker, Sir Robert Dillon invokes 'common experience' to boulster the doctrine of 'free election', observing that, contrary to the workings of Stoic 'destinie', providence leaves man free and ennobled, 'imposing no necessitie of doing good or euill vpon vs'. Unfortunately, the clarity of this summary is greatly undermined by the immediate addition of the following qualification: 'And if any [necessitie] it did impose, it should be onely to good, and neuer to euill' (p. 176). This is to argue on both sides of the question at once. From the Calvinist viewpoint, the qualification is crucial and its impact is reinforced by a provocative analogy between the providence of God and the providence (or 'foresight') of prudent men who seek only the 'perfection' of whatever lies 'vnder their gouernement'. How exactly God may 'perfect' the workings of human will without diminishing its freedom, Sir Robert makes no attempt to explain. Even in the *Discourse*, therefore, the possibility of a benignly irresistible grace cannot be discounted completely. Sir Robert is more concerned with attacking the 'seruitude' of reprobation (p. 176) than the notion of election to life. If his arguments are designed to counter those of Calvin, they do so through gross misrepresentation. For the third time, the issue ends in irresolution: 'the particular consideration and debating of this matter being fitter for Diuines then for vs [the presence of the Archbishop is presumably overlooked], let vs leaue the scanning of it to them, and be content like men seeking by the rules of Morall Philosophie to find the ready way to humane felicitie in this life, to referre our selues in that point to the mercifull goodnesse of Almightie God' (p. 177).

There can be little doubt that Bryskett tends towards the moderate side of the great debate, but he does so uneasily speaking more as a moral philosopher than a divine — precisely the criticism Calvin levelled against his opponents. Concerning Spenser's attitudes towards such issues, one can draw no conclusions from the *Discourse*. His fictional *alter-ego* plays no part in the discussion and the work remains primarily important for its illustration of the complexity of the debate from which his personal convictions must have been born. The issue of predestination, raised by Archbishop Long, is an embarrassment to a discussion during the course of which divinity must be 'put . . . to silence' (p. 168).

In Bryskett's tolerant and moderate view, baptism opens up the way to salvation for all who genuinely desire it, and those who make such a choice are fortified by grace. Throughout the treatise the word 'election' is used, as Sir Thomas Elyot had used it, in the sense of human choice.[7] It is defined as, 'a voluntary deliberation following a mature and aduised counsel' (p. 185). Time is of the essence of the matter since 'election is the office of prudence' (p. 187), and prudence considers both the 'end' and the 'meanes'. 'Hast' is the arch-enemy of moral deliberation. Again the conclusion is a Spenserian commonplace. As with Guyon and his prudent Palmer, 'God set before man life and death, good and euill, that he might take whether he list to chuse' (p. 177).

In order to explain the closely related problem of evil choice Bryskett turns to the Aristotelian notion that all men desire the good though many mistake its true nature. This tendency towards error is described in allegorical terms reminiscent of Spenser's wandering knights since 'ill doing is an infinite thing, and . . . by a thousand wayes men are led to wickednes and vicious actions, all easie to be taken: but to vertue there is but one onely way, and the same so enuironed and crossed with the bypaths that guide men to vice, as it must needs be hard to keepe it without entring into some of the by-wayes leading to vice and errour' (p. 178-9). It is not to be concluded, however, that ignorance excuses sin. Two sorts of ignorance are clearly distinguished. Drunkards, for example, are morally culpable for their actions since they know in advance what the consequences of over-indulgence are likely to be. On the other hand, a man who infringes a law without knowing he is doing so may not be held responsible. Nevertheless, as regards the basic moral law, the latter situation can never arise, 'for all men ought to know those things that generally are to be knowne, touching honest and ciuil conversation; and if they do not know them when they do il, it is because they chuse not to know that which is necessary for them to know' (p. 180). Such people are wicked by 'free wil and election' since all reasonable men have the capacity to understand 'what is fit and honest for vertuous life'. Similarly in *A View of the Present State of Ireland* Spenser declares that the 'ignoraunce of the Priestes shall not excuse the people nor the auctoritye of the greate Pastor Peters successours shall not excuse the priestes'. Hence, in any attempt to

7 Elyot, *The Book Named the Governor*, edited by S.E. Lehmberg, second edition (London, 1962), pp. 85-6.

reform the country spiritually, men must be led 'firste to vnderstande and afterwardes to imbrace the doctrine of theire salvacion'.[8]

Bryskett's *Discourse* endorses a providential view of human life as an 'earthly pilgrimage' during the course of which 'vertue and vice are in our power, vertue growing in vs by the right vse of our free choice, and vice by the abuse of the same' (p. 185). Providence is, therefore, entirely distinct from Stoic 'destinie' in that it imposes no necessity of action upon its subjects and is, moreover, wholly benign in its general intention. Consequently life is to be regarded as a period of spiritual trial the calamities and frustrations of which must be endured as contributing to the ultimate good of those who suffer them. Despite the opinion of the Stoic philosophers, despair and suicide have no place in the proper scheme of things (pp. 182-4). Man is entirely responsible for his own wayward actions since choice or 'election' is free, and everyone is endowed with the innate capacity of knowing right from wrong. The difficulties encountered in following the right path may be overcome through the assistance of divine grace the precise relationship of which to human will remains mysterious.

8 *Prose*, pp. 138, 221.

APPENDIX B

Spenser and Bruno

Advancing a humorous defence of Fairyland in the proem to book two, Spenser asks,

> Why then should witlesse man so much misweene
> That nothing is, but that which he hath seene?
> What if within the Moones faire shining spheare?
> What if in euery other starre vnseene
> Of other worldes he happily should heare?
> He wonder would much more: yet such to some appeare. (3)

Who are the 'some' that Spenser has in mind? The passage has been identified as one of the earliest English references to Bruno's theory of the multiplicity of worlds, as propounded in *De l'infinito universo et mondi* published in London (despite bearing 'in Venetia' on the titlepage) in 1584.[1] As the first two lines quoted are certainly characteristic of Spenser's attitude to dogmatism, the question arises as to his probable attitude towards Giordano Bruno who similarly identifies unwarranted trust in the senses as the cause of human ignorance.[2]

The proem to book five bespeaks Spenser's disillusionment with the Ptolemaic universe and, as we have seen, many of his notions concerning perpetuity and decline anticipate radical arguments of the seventeenth century. Regarding the proem in this light one is led to re-examine the exact intention of the line 'And all this world with them amisse *doe moue*' (6). This need imply no allusion to Copernican cosmology if the 'motion' is merely metaphorical but the context suggests otherwise. The other planets have wandered 'out of their proper places farre away' and the earth goes with them. A contemporary reader would, at the very least, be reminded of the Copernican controversy and left in some doubt as to Spenser's precise meaning. On the surface he seems to be saying that 'learned *Ptolomaee*' was

1 Paul H. Kocher, *Science and Religion in Elizabethan England* (San Marino, 1953), p. 86. The stanza may be influenced by Ariosto (*Orlando Furioso*, VII. 1) but the reference to multiple worlds is original to Spenser.

2 Dorothea Singer, *Giordano Bruno, His Life and Thought with Annotated Translation of his Work 'On the Infinite Universe and Worlds'* (New York, 1968 — first pub. 1950), pp. 250, 302. All quotations and references supplied in the text are to this edition.

right initially, but that the universe has since declined and is now close to dissolution. Beneath the surface, however, we may detect something of Pascal's instinctive terror in confronting a vast, alien universe guided by no apparent plan. Infinity of space — and Spenser's planets and constellations seem to wander unconfined — implies infinity of time and Spenser could have found both ideas in Lucretius and Nicholas of Cusa, Bruno's own sources.[3] Both would doubtless be amongst the 'some' who might favour the possibility of a multiplicity of worlds, but Bruno himself was the one who had most deeply considered its implications.

The fifth dialogue of *De l'infinito universo et mondi* comprises a discussion between Elpino, a spokesman for Bruno's viewpoint, and Albertino, 'a learned person . . . educated in the contrary doctrine' but open-minded and willing to be convinced of his errors (p. 242). Albertino advances the arguments of Aristotelian physics, as traditionally interpreted, to support the Ptolemaic model, concluding that 'the world or universe is unique, and should be perfect' (p. 360). Elpino responds by exploiting the complex cruxes of the received system to enhance the attractions of the alternative outlook:

> For instead of these numerous heavens, these many swift and stubborn mobile bodies, straight and oblique, to the east and to the west, on the axis of the world, on the axis of the zodiac, in so far and so much, in greater or lesser declination, we have but one single heaven, a single space through which our own star in which we reside, and all other stars perform each their own circuits and courses; these are the infinite worlds, the innumerable stars; this is the infinite space, the heaven comprehending all, traversed by all. Banished is the fantasy that the whole revolveth around ourselves as centre; for we are now well aware that it is our earth which revolveth; and that she, spinning around her own centre, hasteneth during each twenty-four hours to the successive view of the surrounding luminaries. (pp. 370-1)

Spenser's Mutability argues for 'infinite' changes in the material universe (VII. 7. 23) and he himself speaks of the 'infinite shapes of creatures' bred in the Gardens of Adonis (III. 6. 35). He also attributes infinity both to Phantastes or imagination (II. 9. 50) and Eumnestes or the collective memory (II. 9. 56). However, Mutability cannot be held to speak for her creator, and careful consideration of Spenser's use of the term 'infinite' reveals that it is often employed not in any technical sense but as a poetic synonym for vast or enormous. Thus the 'infinite shapes of creatures' produced in the Gardens

3 *De Rerum Natura*, I. 951-1117; II. 1040-1076. For Nicholas of Cusa see Ernst Cassirer, *The Individual and the Cosmos in Renaissance Philosophy*, translated by Mario Domandi (Oxford, 1963), pp. 7-72.

of Adonis may be compared with the 'infinite shapes of creatures' born after '*Nilus* invndation' earlier in the same canto (III. 6. 8). Similarly the term is also used for conscious hyperbole: 'infinite' lords and ladies attend the marriage celebrations of Florimell and Marinell (V. 3. 2). On the one occasion when Spenser does seem to use the word technically in a cosmological context in *An Hymne of Heavenly Beavtie*, it is to contrast the empyrean heavens with their material counterparts:

> For farre aboue these heauens which here we see,
> Be others farre exceeding these in light,
> Not bounded, not corrupt, as these same bee,
> But infinite in largenesse and in hight,
> Vnmouing, vncorrupt, and spotlesse bright,
> That need no Sunne t'illuminate their spheres,
> But their owne natiue light farre passing theirs. (64-70)

The numerous heavens dismissed by Bruno are here endorsed by Spenser. Bruno's theories tend to make nonsense of such distinctions and the logical conclusion to his arguments (at least in the treatise before us) is clearly a form of pantheism quite alien to the author of *The Faerie Queene*. What one misses in *De l'infinito universo et mondi* is any sense of man's personal involvement in the system there envisaged. There is rapture certainly but of a most intellectual kind, the rapture of the scientist as he cries 'eureka'. Bruno intellectualizes the passions while Spenser emotionalizes the intellect. Such personal consolation as Bruno offers is abstract and remote:

> Here . . . is the reason of the constant change of all things, so that there existeth no evil beyond escape, nor good which is unattainable, since throughout infinite space and throughout endless change all substance remaineth one and the same. From these reflections if we apply ourselves attentively, we shall see that no strange happening can be dismissed by grief or by fear, and that no good fortune can be advanced by pleasure or hope. Whereby we find the true path to true morality; we will be high-minded . . . for we shall attain to true contemplation of the story of nature which is inscribed within ourselves, and we shall follow the divine laws which are engraved upon our hearts. (pp. 243-4)

Bruno is contemplating the advancement of man as a species led to 'salvation' by the light of reason: 'thus by means of this science we shall certainly attain to that good which by other sciences is sought in vain' (p. 244). His portrait of a universe of flux resembles that of the Gardens of Adonis or the *Mutabilitie Cantos*, but Spenser ends both on a note of rest. Rest is precisely what is lacking in *De l'infinito universo et mondi*. Not the 'pillars of eternity' but eternal, restless energy excited Bruno's imagination. Spenser ends speaking of himself, 'graunt *me* that Sabaoths sight', but Bruno submerges the self in the destiny of the race.

That Spenser knew of Bruno's theories I have little doubt; that he exploited their more imaginative aspects to envigorate his physical allegory seems likely; that he deduced the same spiritual conclusions is untenable.[4] His interest lay not in abstract theory but in practical religious experience. To his way of thinking, the more vast and wayward the universe, the more precious the consolation of a personal God: Copernicus lent urgency to Spenser's faith. Belief in a multiplicity, even an infinity, of worlds need not compromise traditional dogma, but it does tend to blur the distinction between creator and creation. Indeed, this was one of Bruno's central tenets: an infinite universe more properly reflects its maker's nature than a finite one:

> Thus is the excellence of God magnified and the greatness of his kingdom made manifest; he is glorified not in one, but in countless suns; not in a single earth, a single world, but in a thousand thousand, I say in an infinity of worlds. (p. 246)

More characteristic of Spenser's thought is the staggering discrepancy between the deity and his creatures, between their finitude and his infinite being. The doctrine of the fall, central to Spenser's philosophy, seems to have impinged but little upon Bruno's imagination. Rather, he attributes to an infinite, but material, universe the sort of wondrous awe Spenser reserves for the most mystical episodes of his narrative. In Bruno the mystical and the material converge in a manner Spenser was not prepared to contemplate, at any rate not before the resurrection of the body. That there may be a multiplicity of worlds he allows, albeit tongue-in-cheek, on the precedent of recent geographical discoveries, but he has no great interest in them. They merely serve to strengthen a rhetorical point made in passing. His basic argument is that fairyland mirrors the real world, the world upon which his concern centres. Its 'infinity' lies in its potential for achieving eternal joy or eternal damnation.

Despite Spenser's gestures towards the 'new philosophy' a stubborn conservatism underlies his attitude. In the Gardens of Adonis, for example, he contemplates the ceaseless reproduction of the species, a process both predictable and independent of human interference. In the *New Atlantis* his contemporary, Lord Bacon, was to suggest that man would enter Spenser's

4 See also, Ronald B. Levinson, 'Spenser and Bruno', *PMLA*, 43 (1928), 675-81; Angelo M. Pellegrini, 'Bruno, Sidney, and Spenser', *SP*, 40 (1943), 128-44.

garden to 'plant' creatures of his own, deliberately altering the genetic process to produce — or is it 'create'? — new species of plants and animals, species themselves capable of reproduction and not barren as more pious theorists would have insisted.[5] In the works of Bruno and Bacon man looks set to become master of nature; in the work of Spenser, even at the peak of civil and moral development, he is still very much its slave.

5 Bacon, III, 158-9.

Bibliography

The following bibliographies are intended primarily as aids to the reader of the present volume, supplemental to the footnotes. They are in no sense exhaustive. For a full bibliography of Spenser scholarship see Waldo F. McNeir and Foster Provost, *Edmund Spenser, An Annotated Bibliography 1937-1972* (New Jersey, 1975). Details of more recent publications may be found in the tri-annual issues of the *Spenser Newsletter*.

SELECT PRIMARY BIBLIOGRAPHY

Alan of Lille, *The Complaint of Nature*, translated by Douglas M. Moffat, Yale Studies in English 36 (New York, 1908).

Aquinas, *The Summa Theologica*, literally translated by Fathers of the English Dominican Province, revised edition (London, 1912-36).

Aristotle, *The Physics*, translated by Philip H. Wicksteed and Francis M. Cornford, Loeb Classical Library, 2 vols (London, 1929-34).

Augustine, *The City of God*, translated by George E. McCracken, Loeb Classical Library, 7 volumes (London, 1957-72).

___ *Confessions*, translated by R.S. Pine-Coffin (Harmondsworth, 1961).

Bacon, Francis, *Works*, edited by J. Spedding, R.L. Ellis and D.D. Heath, 14 vols (London, 1857-74).

Bale, John, *The first two partes of the Actes, or unchast examples of the Englysh votaryes* (London, 1551).

___ *King Johan* in *Four Morality Plays*, edited by Peter Happé (Harmondsworth, 1979).

Boccaccio, Giovanni, *Genealogie Deorum Gentilium Libri*, edited by Vincenzo Romano, 2 vols (Bari, 1951).

Boethius, *The Consolation of Philosophy*, translated by Richard Green (Indianapolis, 1962).

Bourchier, John, Lord Berners, trans., *The Boke of Huon of Burdeux*, edited by S.L. Lee, Early English Text Society, Extra Series, 40, 41, 43, 50, 2 vols (New York, 1973 — first pub. 1882-7).

Bryskett, Lodowick, *Literary Works*, ed. J.H.P. Pafford (Germany, 1972).

___ *The Life and Correspondence*, edited by Henry R. Plomer and Tom Peete Cross (Chicago, 1927).

Calcidius, *Timaeus a Calcidio Translatus Commentarioque Instructus* edited by J.H. Waszink (London, 1962).

Calvin, John, *Institutes of the Christian Religion*, ed. John T. McNeill, translated by Ford Lewis Battles, The Library of Christian Classics, 2 vols (Philadelphia, 1960).

___ *Concerning the Eternal Predestination of God*, translated by J.K.S. Reid (Cambridge, 1961).

Camden, William, *The History of Princess Elizabeth* (London, 1675).
Cebes, *The Tablet of Cebes the Theban Philosopher or A True Emblem of Human Life*, translated by Robert Warren (Cambridge, 1699).
Comes, Natalis, *Mythologiae* (Venice, 1567 — first pub. 1551).
___ *Mythologiae* (Frankfurt, 1584).
Cooper, Thomas, *Certaine Sermons* (London, 1580).
Dante, Alighieri, *La Divina Commedia*, edited by C.H. Grandgent (London, 1914).
___ *The Divine Comedy*, translated by Dorothy L. Sayers and Barbara Reynolds, 3 vols (Harmondsworth, 1949-62).
Donne, John, *Complete Sermons*, edited by G.R. Potter and E.M. Simpson, 10 vols (Berkeley, 1953-62).
Elyot, Thomas, *The Book Named The Governor*, edited by S.E. Lehmberg, second edition (London, 1962).
Ficino, Marsilio, *Commentary on Plato's Symposium*, edited and translated by Sears R. Jayne, University of Missouri Studies, 19, no. I, (Columbia, 1944).
___ *The Letters*, translated by Members of the Language Department of the School of Economic Science, London (1975-).
___ *Opera Omnia*, 2 vols (Basle, 1576)
___ *The 'Philebus' Commentary*, edited and translated by Michael J.B. Allen (Berkeley, 1975).
Foxe, John, *Actes and Monuments* (1583).
___ *The Acts and Monuments of the Church*, edited by M. Hobart Seymour (London, 1838).
Fulgentius The Mythographer, translated by Leslie George Whitbread (Ohio, 1971).
Geoffrey of Monmouth, *Historia Regum Britanniae*, edited by A. Griscom (New York, 1929).
___ *The History of the Kings of Britain*, translated by Lewis Thorpe (Harmondsworth, 1966).
Giraldi Cinthio, *Hecatommithi*, 2 pts (Venice, 1608).
Goodman, Godfrey, *The Fall of Man, or the Corruption of Nature, proved by the Light of our Naturall Reason* (1616).
Hakewill, George, *An Apologie or Declaration of the Power and Providence of God in the Government of the World* (Oxford, 1630).
Harrington, James, *The Political Works*, edited by J.G.A. Pocock (Cambridge, 1977).
Harvey, Richard, *Philadelphus, or A Defence of Brutes, and the Brutans History* (London, 1593).
Hawes, Stephen, *The Pastime of Pleasure*, edited by William Edward Mead, *Early English Text Society*, OS 173 (London, 1928).
Holinshed, Raphael, *Chronicles of England, Scotland and Ireland*, 6 vols (London 1806-8).
Hooker, Richard, *Works*, ed. John Keble, seventh edition (Oxford, 1888).
Knox, John, *Works*, edited by D. Laing, 6 vols (Edinburgh, 1846-64).
Leland, John, *The Assertion of King Arthure*, translated by Richard Robinson with the Latin Original in Christopher Middleton, *The Famous Historie of Chinon of England*, edited by William Edward Mead, Early English Text Society, Original Series, 165 (London, 1925).
Leonardo da Vinci, *The Literary Works*, edited and translated by J.P. Richter, 2 vols (London, 1883).
Lipsius, Justus, *Two Bookes of Constancie . . . Englished by Sir John Stradling* ed. Rudolf Kirk (New Brunswick, N.J., 1939).
Malory, Thomas, *Works*, edited by Eugene Vinaver, second edition (Oxford, 1977).
Martianus Capella, *The Marriage of Philology and Mercury*, translated by William Harris Stahl, Richard Johnson, and E.L. Burge in *Martianus Capella and the Seven Liberal*

Arts, 2 vols (New York, 1971-7).

Petrarch, *The Triumphs*, translated by Ernest Hatch Wilkins (Chicago, 1962).

Pico della Mirandola, Giovanni, *On the Dignity of Man, On Being and the One, Heptaplus*, translated by Charles Glenn Wallis, Paul J.W. Miller, Douglas Carmichael (Indianapolis, 1965).

___ *Opera* (1557-73), ed. Cesare Vasoli, 2 vols (Hildesheim, 1969).

Plato, *The Collected Dialogues*, edited by Edith Hamilton and Huntington Cairns (Princeton, 1961).

Plotinus, *Enneads*, edited and translated by A.H. Armstrong, Loeb Classical Library, 6 vols (London, 1965-).

Raleigh, Sir Walter, *History of the World* (London, 1614).

___ *The History of the World*, edited by C.A. Patrides (London, 1971).

Starkey, Thomas, *A Dialogue between Reginald Pole and Thomas Lupset*, edited by Kathleen Burton (London, 1948).

Tasso, Torquato, *Discourses on the Heroic Poem*, translated by Mariella Cavalchini and Irene Samuel (Oxford, 1973).

Van der Noodt, John, *A Theatre for Voluptuous Worldlings* (1569), i.e. *A Theatre wherein be represented as wel the miseries and calamities that follow the voluptuous Worldlings, As also the greate ioyes and plesures which the faithful do enioy.*

SELECT SECONDARY BIBLIOGRAPHY

Unless otherwise stated, place of publication is London.

Albright, Evelyn May, 'Spenser's Cosmic Philosophy and his Religion', *PMLA*, 44 (1929).

Allen, Don Cameron, 'The Degeneration of Man and Renaissance Pessimism, *SP*, 35 (1938).

___ 'On the Closing Lines of *The Faerie Queene*', *MLN*, 64 (1949).

Aptekar, Jane, *Icons of Justice: Iconography and Thematic Imagery in Book V of 'The Faerie Queene'* (New York, 1969).

Arestad, Sverre, 'Spenser's *Faery* and *Fairy*', *MLQ*, 8 (1947).

Arthos, John, *On the Poetry of Spenser and the Form of Romances* (1956).

Auerbach, Erich, *Scenes from the Drama of European Literature*, translated by Ralph Manheim (Gloucester, Mass., 1973).

Axton, Marie, *The Queen's Two Bodies* (1977).

Baker, Herschel, *The Race of Time* (Toronto, 1967).

___ *The Wars of Truth: Studies in the Decay of Christian Humanism in the Earlier Seventeenth Century* (Gloucester, Mass., 1952).

Battenhouse, Roy W., *A Companion to the Study of St. Augustine* (New York, 1955).

Benbow, R. Mark, 'The Providential Theory of Historical Causation in *Holinshed's Chronicles*: 1577 and 1587', *TSLL*, 1 (1959-60).

Bennett, Josephine Waters, *The Evolution of 'The Faerie Queene'* (Chicago, 1942).

Benjamin, Edwin B., 'Fame, Poetry and the Order of History in the Literature of the English Renaissance', *SR*, 6 (1959).

Berger, Harry Jr., *The Allegorical Temper: Vision and Reality in Book II of Spenser's 'Faerie Queene'* (New Haven, 1957).

Bicknell, E.J., *A Theological Introduction to the Thirty-Nine Articles of the Church of England* (1933).

Blatt, Thora Balslev, *The Plays of John Bale: A Study of Ideas, Technique and Style* (Copenhagen, 1968).

Bondanella, Julia Conaway, *Petrarch's Visions and their Renaissance Analogues* (Madrid, 1978).

Brabant, Frank Herbert, *Time and Eternity in Christian Thought* (1937).

Brandon, S.G.F., *History, Time and Deity: A Historical and Comparative Study of the Conception of Time in Religious Thought and Practice* (Manchester, 1965).

Broek, R. Van den, *The Myth of the Phoenix* (Leiden, 1972).

Brooks-Davies, Douglas, *Spenser's 'Faerie Queene': A Critical Commentary on Books I and II* (Manchester, 1977).

Cain, Thomas H., *Praise in 'The Faerie Queene'*, (1978).

Carpenter, Frederick Ives, *A Reference Guide to Edmund Spenser* (Chicago, 1923).

Cheney, Donald S., *Spenser's Image of Nature: Wild Man and Shepherd in 'The Faerie Queene'* (New Haven, 1966).

Chew, Samuel C., *The Pilgrimage of Life* (Port Washington, New York, 1973 — first pub. 1962)

___ 'Time and Fortune', *ELH*, 6 (1939).

Cohn, Norman, *The Pursuit of the Millennium* (London, 1970 — first pub. 1957).

Copleston, F.C., *Aquinas* (Harmondsworth, 1955).

Cosman, Madeleine Pelner, *The Education of the Hero in Arthurian Romance* (Chapel Hill, 1965).

Craig, Hardin, *The Enchanted Glass: The Elizabethan Mind in Literature* (Oxford, 1950 — first pub. 1936).

Cullen, Patrick, *Infernal Triad: The Flesh, The World and the Devil* in *Spenser and Milton* (Princeton, 1974).

Curtius, Ernst R., *European Literature and the Latin Middle Ages*, translated by Willard R. Trask (New York, 1953).

Dunseath, Thomas K., *Spenser's Allegory of Justice in Book Five of 'The Faerie Queene'* (Princeton, 1968).

Durr, Robert Allen, 'Spenser's Calendar of Christian Time', *ELH*, 24 (1957).

Eccles, Audrey, *Obstetrics and Gynaecology in Tudor and Stuart England* (1982).

Eliade, Mircea, *The Myth of the Eternal Return or, Cosmos and History*, translated by Willard R. Trask (Princeton, 1954).

___ *The Quest: History and Meaning in Religion* (Chicago, 1969).

___ *The Sacred and the Profane: The Nature of Religion*, translated by Willard R. Trask (New York, 1959 — first pub. 1957).

Ellrodt, Robert, *Neoplatonism in the Poetry of Spenser* (Geneva, 1960).

Fairfield, Leslie P., *John Bale, Mythmaker for the English Reformation* (West Lafayette, Indiana, 1976).

Ferguson, Arthur B., *Clio Unbound: Perception of the Social and Cultural Past in Renaissance England* (Durham, Nt. Carolina, 1979).

___ *The Indian Summer of English Chivalry* (Durham, Nt. Carolina, 1960).

Firth, Katharine R., *The Apocalyptic Tradition in Reformation Britain 1530-1645* (Oxford, 1979).

Fletcher, Angus, *The Prophetic Moment: An Essay on Spenser* (Chicago, 1971).

___ *Allegory: The Theory of A Symbolic Mode* (New York, 1964).

Fowler, Alastair, *Spenser and the Numbers of Time* (1964).

___ *Triumphal Forms: Structural Patterns in Elizabethan Poetry* (Cambridge, 1970).

___ 'Oxford and London Marginalia to *The Faerie Queene*', *NQ*, 206 (1961).

Frushell, Richard C. and Bernard J. Vondersmith, ed., *Contemporary Thought on Edmund Spenser* (Carbondale, 1975).

Frye, Northrop, *Anatomy of Criticism* (Princeton, 1957).

___ *The Great Code: The Bible and Literature* (1982).
___ *The Secular Scripture: A Study of the Structure of Romance* (Cambridge, Mass., 1976).
Fujii, Haruhiko, *Time, Landscape and the Ideal Life: Studies in the Pastoral Poetry of Spenser and Milton* (Kyoto, 1974).
Giamatti, A. Bartlett, *The Earthly Paradise and the Renaissance Epic* (Princeton, 1966).
Goldberg, Jonathan, *Endlesse Worke: Spenser and the Structures of Discourse* (Baltimore, Md., 1981).
Gottfried, Rudolf B., 'Spenser's *View* and Essex', *PMLA*, 52 (1937).
Graziani, Rene, 'Elizabeth at Isis Church', *PMLA*, 79 (1964).
Greenlaw, Edwin, *Studies in Spenser's Historical Allegory* (Baltimore, Md., 1932).
Hankins, John Erskine, *Source and Meaning in Spenser's Allegory* (Oxford, 1971).
Hanning, R.W., *The Vision of History in Early Britain from Gildas to Geoffrey of Monmouth* (New York, 1966).
Harris, Victor, *All Coherence Gone: A Study of the Seventeenth Century Controversy over Disorder and Decay in the Universe* (1966).
Harper, Carrie Anna, *The Sources of the British Chronicle History in Spenser's 'Faerie Queene'* (Philadelphia, 1910).
Hawkins, Sherman, 'Mutabilitie and the Cycle of the Months' in *Form and Convention in the Poetry of Edmund Spenser*, ed. William Nelson (New York, 1961).
Heller, Agnes, *Renaissance Man*, translated by Richard E. Allen (1978).
Heninger, S.K. Jr., *The Cosmographical Glass: Renaissance Diagrams of the Universe* (San Marino, 1977).
___ *A Handbook of Renaissance Meteorology, with Particular Reference to Elizabethan and Jacobean Literature* (Durham, N. Carolina, 1960).
___ 'The Tudor Myth of Troy-novant', *The South Atlantic Quarterly*, 61 (1962).
Henley, Pauline, *Spenser in Ireland* (Dublin, 1928).
Hieatt, A. Kent, 'The Daughters of Horus: Order in the Stanzas of *Epithalamion*' in *Form and Convention in the Poetry of Edmund Spenser*, ed. William Nelson (New York, 1961).
___ *Short Time's Endless Monument: The Symbolism of Numbers in Edmund Spenser's 'Epithalamion'* (New York, 1960).
Holland, Joanne Field, 'The Cantos of *Mutabilitie* and the Form of *The Faerie Queene*', *ELH*, 35 (1968).
Hoopes, Robert, '"God guide thee, Guyon": Nature and Grace Reconciled in *The Faerie Queene* Book II', *RES*, 5 (1954).
Hume Anthea, *Edmund Spenser: Protestant Poet* (Cambridge, 1984).
Inge, William Ralph, *The Philosophy of Plotinus*, 2 vols (1918).
Jayne, Sears R., 'Ficino and the Platonism of the English Renaissance', *CL*, 4 (1952).
Jenkins, Raymond, 'Spenser and Ireland', *ELH*, 19 (1952).
Judson, A.C., *The Life of Spenser* (Baltimore, Md., 1945).
Kantorowicz, Ernst H., *The King's Two Bodies: A Study in Medieval Political Theology* (Princeton, 1957).
Kastan, David Scott, *Shakespeare and the Shapes of Time* (London, 1982).
Kelly, Henry Ansgar, *Divine Providence in the England of Shakespeare's Histories* (Cambridge, Mas., 1970).
Kennedy, Judith M. and James A. Reither, *A Theatre for Spenserians* (Manchester, 1973).
Kermode, Frank, *Renaissance Essays: Shakespeare, Spenser, Donne* (1971).
___ *The Sense of an Ending: Studies in the Theory of Fiction* (Oxford, 1966).
Kocher, Paul H., *Science and Religion in Elizabethan England* (San Marino, 1953).
Koller, Kathrine, 'Two Elizabethan Expressions of the Idea of Mutability', *SP*, 35 (1938).

Kouwenhoven, Jan Karel, *Apparent Narrative as Thematic Metaphor: the Organization of 'The Faerie Queene'* (Oxford, 1983).
Kristeller, Paul Oskar, *Eight Philosophers of the Italian Renaissance* (1965).
___ *The Philosophy of Marsilio Ficino*, translated by Virginia Conant (Gloucester, Mass., 1964).
Latham, Minor White, *The Elizabethan Fairies* (New York, 1930)
Leslie, Michael, *Spenser's 'Fierce Warres and Faithfull Loves'* (Cambridge, 1983).
Levin, Michael, *The Myth of the Golden Age in the Renaissance* (New York, 1969).
Lewis, C.S., *The Allegory of Love: A Study in Medieval Tradition* (Oxford, 1936).
___ *The Discarded Image, An Introduction to Medieval and Renaissance Literature* (Cambridge, 1964).
___ *Spenser's Images of Life*, ed. Alastair Fowler (Cambridge, 1967).
___ *Studies in Medieval and Renaissance Literature* (Cambridge, 1966).
Loomis, Roger Sherman, *Arthurian Literature in the Middle Ages* (Oxford, 1959).
Lotspeich, Henry G., *Classical Mythology in the Poetry of Edmund Spenser* (Princeton, 1932).
Lovejoy, Arthur O., *The Great Chain of Being* (Cambridge, Mass., 1936).
McCabe, Richard A., 'The Masks of Duessa: Spenser, Mary Queen of Scots, and James VI', *ELR*, 17 (1987).
MacCaffrey, Isabel G., *Spenser's Allegory: The Anatomy of Imagination* (Princeton, 1976).
McGinn, Bernard, *Visions of the End: Apocalyptic Traditions in the Middle Ages* (New York, 1979).
Marcus, G. J., *Saint George for England* (1929).
Marshall, William H., 'Calvin, Spenser, and the Major Sacraments', *MLN*, 74 (1959).
___ 'Spenser and General Election', *NQ*, 203 (1958).
Martz, Louis, *The Poetry of Meditation*, revised edition (New Haven, 1962).
Meyer, Russell J., '"Fixt in heauens hight": Spenser, Astronomy, and the Date of the *Cantos of Mutabilitie*' in *Spenser Studies IV*, edited by Patrick Cullen and Thomas P. Roche (New York, 1984).
Millican, Charles Bowie, *Spenser and the Table Round: A Study of the Contemporaneous Background for Spenser's use of the Arthurian Legend* (Cambridge, Mass., 1932).
Mills, Jerry Leath, 'Spenser and the Numbers of History: A note on the British and Elfin Chronicles in *The Faerie Queene*', *PQ*, 55 (1967).
Morris, Christopher, *The Tudors*, revised edition (1976).
Neale, J.E., 'Elizabeth and the Netherlands, 1586-1587', *EHR*, 45 (1930).
___ *Queen Elizabeth I* (1934).
Needham, Joseph, *A History of Embryology*, second edition, revised by Arthur Hughes (Cambridge, 1959).
Neuse, Richard, 'The Triumph over Hasty Accidents: A note on the Symbolic Mode of the *Epithalamion*' in *Essential Articles for the Study of Edmund Spenser*, ed. A.C. Hamilton (Hamden, Conn., 1972).
Neill, J. Kerby, '*The Faerie Queene* and the Mary Stuart Controversy', *ELH*, 2 (1935).
Nohrnberg, James, *The Analogy of 'The Faerie Queene'* (Princeton, 1976).
Northrop, Douglas A., 'Spenser's Defence of Elizabeth', *UTQ*, 38 (1969).
O'Connell, Michael, *Mirror and Veil: The Historical Dimension of Spenser's 'Faerie Queene'* (Chapel Hill, 1977).
Owen, Lewis J., 'Mutable in eternity: Spenser's despair and the multiple forms of Mutabilitie', *Journal of Medieval and Renaissance Studies*, 2 (1972).
Parker, M. Pauline, *The Allegory of 'The Faerie Queene'* (Oxford, 1960)
Panofsky, Erwin, *Idea: A Conception in Art Theory*, translated by Joseph J.S. Peake, revised

edition (New York, 1968 — first pub. 1924).

___ *Studies in Iconology: Humanistic Themes in the Art of the Renaissance* (New York, 1962 — first pub. 1939).

Patch, Howard R., *The Goddess Fortuna in Medieval Literature* (Cambridge, Mass., 1927).

Paton, Lucy Allen, *Studies in the Fairy Mythology of Arthurian Romance*, revised edition (New York, 1960).

Patrides, C. A., *The Grand Design of God* (1972).

Pearce, Roy Harvey, 'Primitivistic Ideas in *The Faerie Queene*', *JEGP*, 44 (1945).

Phillips, James Emerson, *Images of a Queen: Mary Stuart in Sixteenth-Century Literature* (Berkeley, 1964).

Pocock, J.G.A., *The Machiavellian Moment: Florentine Political Thought and the Atlantic Republican Tradition* (Princeton, 1975).

Quinones, Ricardo J., *The Renaissance Discovery of Time* (Cambridge, Mass., 1972).

Raggio, Olga, 'The Myth of Prometheus: Its Survival and Metamorphoses up to the Eighteenth Century', *JWCI*, 21 (1958).

Rathborne, Isabel E., *The Meaning of Spenser's Fairyland* (New York, 1937).

Reeves, Marjorie, *Joachim of Fiore and the Prophetic Future* (1976).

Roche, Thomas P., *The Kindly Flame: A Study of the Third and Fourth Books of Spenser's 'Faerie Queene'* (Princeton, 1964).

Rodgers, Catherine, *Time in the Narrative of 'The Faerie Queene'* (Salzburg, 1973).

Satterthwaite, Alfred W., *Spenser, Ronsard, and Du Bellay: A Renaissance Comparison* (Princeton, 1960).

Saxl, Fritz, 'Veritas Filia Temporis' in *Philosophy and History, Essays Presented to Ernst Cassirer* (Oxford, 1936).

Seronsy, Cecil C., 'The Doctrine of Cyclical Recurrence and Some Related Ideas in the *Works* of Samuel Daniel', *SP*, 54 (1957).

Seznec, Jean, *The Survival of the Pagan Gods: The Mythological Tradition and its Place in Renaissance Humanism and Art*, translated by Barbara F. Sessions (Princeton, 1972 — first pub. 1953).

Skinner, Quentin, *The Foundations of Modern Political Thought*, 2 vols (Cambridge, 1978).

Snyder, Susan, 'The Left Hand of God: Despair in Medieval and Renaissance Tradition', *SR*, 12 (1965).

Sorabji, Richard, *Necessity, Cause and Blame: Perspectives on Aristotle's Theory* (London, 1980)

___ *Time, Creation and the Continuum* (London, 1983).

Stewart, Stanley, *The Enclosed Garden: The Tradition and the Image in Seventeenth-Century Poetry* (1966).

Strong, Sir Roy C., 'The Popular Celebration of the Accession Day of Queen Elizabeth I', *JWCI*, 21 (1958).

___ *Portraits of Queen Elizabeth I* (Oxford, 1963).

Stafford, Helen Georgia, *James VI of Scotland and the Throne of England* (New York, 1940).

Sypher, F. Wylie, *The Ethic of Time* (New York, 1976).

Thomas, Keith, *Religion and the Decline of Magic* (Harmondsworth, 1973 — first pub. 1971).

Tolman, Albert H., 'The Relation of Spenser and Harvey to Puritanism', *Modern Philology*, 15 (1917-18).

Tonkin, Humphrey, *Spenser's Courteous Pastoral: Book Six of the 'Faerie Queene'* (Oxford, 1972).

Toulmin, Stephen and June Goodfield, *The Discovery of Time* (1965).

___ *The Fabric of the Heavens* (1961).

Tuve, Rosemund, *Allegorical Imagery: Some Medieval Books and their Posterity* (Princeton, 1966).

Waller, G.F., *The Strong Necessity of Time* (The Hague, 1976).

___ 'Transition in Renaissance Ideas of Time and the Place of Giordano Bruno', *Neophilologus*, 55 (1971).

Weiss, Rudolf, *Humanism in England during the Fifteenth Century* (Oxford, 1967).

Wells, Robin Headham, *Spenser's 'Faerie Queene' and the Cult of Elizabeth* (London, 1983).

Wells, William, ed., *Spenser Allusions in the Sixteenth and Seventeenth Centuries*, 2 Pts (Chapel Hill, 1971-2).

Whitaker, Virgil K., *The Religious Basis of Spenser's Thought*, Stanford University Publications, 7 (Stanford, 1950).

Wilson, Robert Rawdon, 'The Deformation of Narrative Time in *The Faerie Queene*', *UTQ*, 41 (1971).

Williams, Arnold, 'Typology and the Cycle Plays: Some Criteria, *Speculum*, 43 (1968).

Williamson, George, 'Mutability, Decay and Seventeenth-Century Melancholy', *ELH*, 2 (1935).

Wind, Edgar, *Pagan Mysteries in the Renaissance*, revised edition (1967).

Woodhouse, A.S.P., 'Nature and Grace in *The Faerie Queene*', *ELH*, 16 (1939).

Woodworth, Mary K., 'The Mutabilitie Cantos and the Succession', *PMLA*, 59 (1944).

Yates, Frances A., *Astraea: The Imperial Theme in the Sixteenth Century* (Harmondsworth 1977 — first pub. 1975).

Index